"[A] spicy and saucy hybrid of memoir and novel . . . Feminists and fans of Nin's work will enjoy this unique insider's portrait of a complex, pivotal figure in women's liberation."

—*Kirkus*

"Rainer blends memoir and imagination in this engaging examination of her relationship with author Anaïs Nin . . . a fascinating personal journey."

—*Publishers Weekly*

"Mysterious, glamorous, intellectual . . . with vivid language and lush scenes, this memoir makes for an exciting read."

—*Bust* magazine

"There are fateful decisions which mark one for life. Young Tristine Rainer's first encounter with charismatic, enigmatic Anaïs Nin unfolds into a decades-long apprenticeship suspenseful as a thriller. The advantages and perils of a mentor/apprentice relationship with such a seductive, brilliant and dangerous mentor is absolutely spellbinding. Revelations, especially toward the end of the book, changed my understanding of the Nin story"

—Janet Fitch, *New York Times*
bestselling author of *White Oleander*

"This stunning, achingly honest memoir confirms that the erotic is neither obscene nor ordinary, and that the heart's desire is both dangerous and innocent."

—Mark Sundeen, author of *The Unsettlers*

"This is one of those delicious memoirs one can't stop reading . . . Tristine Rainer takes us into the hot pulsing heart of Nin's world . . . an alluring as well as compulsively readable story."

—Jay Parini, author of
*Empire of Self: A Life of Gore Vidal*

"The action-packed adventures of the larger-than-life Anaïs Nin and her young friend Tristine are vivid and glorious, but what broke my heart wide open were the haunting meditations on passion and devotion and the secrets that bond and bind us. A brave and beautiful work."

—Kathleen Adams, author of *Journal to the Self*

"Stunning, intoxicating, original. Apprenticed to Venus is nothing short of phenomenal, and we owe Tristine as much for her craftsmanship as we do Anaïs for flipping infidelity on its chauvinist head!"

—Chip Jacobs, author of *Strange As It Seems:
The Impossible Life of Gordon Zahler*

"A fascinating introduction to an extraordinary woman who raised lying to an art form, but whose essential honesty transcends the falsehoods. A book that will challenge and enthrall."

—Joanna Hodgkin, author of *Amateurs in Eden:
The Story of a Bohemian Marriage: Nancy and Lawrence Durrell*

"An unforgettable, intimate narrative that brilliantly captures one of the most fascinating personalities of the twentieth century."

—Crystal King, author of *Feast of Sorrow*

"An inherently fascinating read from cover to cover, *Apprenticed to Venus: My Years with Anais Nin* is a 'must' for the legions of Anaïs Nin fans. An extraordinarily well written, deeply personal, impressively candid memoir."

— *Midwest Book Review*

# *Apprenticed to*

# VENUS

Also by Tristine Rainer

*The New Diary*
*How to Use a Journal for Self-Guidance and Expanded Creativity*

*Your Life as Story*
*Discovering the New Autobiography and Writing Memoir as Literature*

# *Apprenticed to*
# VENUS

## *my years with*
## ANAÏS NIN

# TRISTINE RAINER

ARCADE PUBLISHING · NEW YORK

First Paperback Edition 2019

Arcade Publishing books may be purchased in bulk at special discounts for sales promotion, corporate gifts, fund-raising, or educational purposes. Special editions can also be created to specifications. For details, contact the Special Sales Department, Arcade Publishing, 307 West 36th Street, 11th Floor, New York, NY 10018 or arcade@skyhorsepublishing.com.

Arcade Publishing® is a registered trademark of Skyhorse Publishing, Inc.®, a Delaware corporation.

Visit our website at www.arcadepub.com.

10 9 8 7 6 5 4 3 2 1

Library of Congress Cataloging-in-Publication Data

Names: Rainer, Tristine, author.
Title: Apprenticed to Venus : my secret life with Anaïs Nin / Trinstine Rainer.
Description: First edition. | New York : Arcade Publishing, [2017]
Identifiers: LCCN 2017032162 (print) | LCCN 2017032305 (ebook) | ISBN 9781628727791 (ebook) | ISBN 9781948924191 (paperback) | ISBN 9781628727784 (hardcover) |
    Subjects: Nin, Anaïs, 1903–1977. | Rainer, Tristine. | Nin, Anaïs, 1903–1977—Friends and associates. | Authors, American—20th century—Biography. | Biography & Autobiography / Literary. | Literary Collections / Essays.
Classification: LCC PS3527.I865 Z84 2017 (print) | DDC 818/.5209 B
LC record available at https://lccn.loc.gov/2017032162

Cover design by Erin Seaward-Hiatt

Printed in the United States of America.

I dedicate this work to Marcia Daniels, MD. Anaïs said that the happiness she achieved in maturity would never have been possible without her psychoanalyst Dr. Inge Bogner. This book would not have been written nor the happiness that I have today possible without my years of psychotherapy with the rare and gifted Dr. Daniels.

"We have the right to re-create our lives!"
                    —Anaïs Nin to Tristine Rainer, Los Angeles, 1974

# Author's Note

I call this book a *novoir*—a memoir with true characters and actual dialogue, but with the structure and stylistic elements of a novel. It is my story and that of my mentor Anaïs Nin, intertwined as we were, based on her diaries, published and unpublished, and on mine. I have taken liberties with chronology, point of view, and dramatization of events, disguised a few identities, and used novelistic devices to quicken the narrative—but the emotional arc of my complex and intimate relationship with Anaïs is true, as is the story of her life.

# Preface

I don't know how the *Los Angeles Times* journalist got my phone number at the remote Hawaii house I co-owned. She interrupted my prep for a filmmaking class I was teaching that summer for the university in Hilo.

"I'm calling you because Anaïs Nin's husband, Rupert Pole, died. I understand that you were Nin's friend and protégée. You and she wrote *The New Diary*."

"No, that's a mistake on Amazon. I wrote that book. She just wrote the preface."

"Whatever, you worked together. You were also friends with Rupert, so I was hoping you'd comment . . ."

I was dumbstruck. Not by news of Rupert's death (he'd had several strokes) but because it meant—after forty-two years—I was finally free from my pledge to Anaïs that I would hide her secrets involving him.

"No one can keep a secret forever." She'd given me a canny smile. "You need only keep silent until Rupert dies."

Now, some thirty years after her death, Rupert had died. This journalist was phoning now that I was the age Anaïs had been when I'd made my vow—long after her dirt had been unearthed by biographers who'd never met her. Could this young reporter think there was still something worth digging for? I threw her a bone, quickly hung up, and sat in a muddle, watching the surf snake along the shore.

In the following months, as I drove to University of Hawaii at Hilo's small campus to teach, snippets from my years as Anaïs' accomplice buzzed and nipped at me, giving me an itch to look inside my own diaries written between 1962 and 1976, when Anaïs was my mentor in the realm of the senses.

When I got back to my home in Los Angeles, I climbed a stepladder to reach the high shelf where my diaries from the sixties and seventies moldered. I had written those diaries for my older self to read, and now I was my older self. With maturity, though, I'd developed a prudishness that disowned the young woman who had scribbled those journals. As I hoisted down a hippyish handmade volume with wooden-covers, I dreaded what I'd find. Only a quarter of the way through that fervent diary I put it aside, nauseated.

I was embarrassed by my exaggerated language and preoccupation in those diaries with getting and losing guys.

What I'd thought was independence and sexual freedom then, I now saw as a tragic waste of a young woman's heart and mind. I was ashamed of my impressionability and the erotic adventures inspired by Anaïs which did nothing to prepare me for a loving, committed relationship.

As I relived the risks I'd taken, I became fearful that my daughter and granddaughter would throw themselves away in hunger for acceptance.

Yet as the first decade of the twenty-first century slid in its downward arc, I realized that I again needed my younger self's passion and daring, needed to remember a time when material things mattered not at all, needed the inspiration that comes with exalting a mentor, deserved or not. Entangled as I had been with Anaïs, I would finally have to sort out her influence on my life. For me that meant setting down our intertwined stories, now that I could: her divine seductiveness, her madcap ruses and countless deceptions, my too eager complicity, and our shared injury of having been abandoned by our fathers which forged our bond as co-conspirators and seductresses.

So it was that I followed the fuzzy twine of memory, rather than the diary's sharp shards, back into Anaïs' silken web. In reveries, I felt again the touch of her cool fingers and heard the chime of her laughter as we walked in late afternoon, our figures, so similar, casting before us as long, Giacometti shadows. Once more, the angled sun in that century past caught the scar along her delicate ear and polished her silvery lids as she whispered confidences to me, delivered like a kiss.

# CHAPTER 1

# Greenwich Village, New York, 1962

WHEN I PRESSED THE BUZZER beneath a card that read *Nin-Guiler*, it sounded my fate—whether for good or ill, I will here try to resolve. I was pretty much a virgin in every way then, including never having seen saturated gold leaves like those skittering on the sidewalk. Before staying with my godmother for the summer, now almost over, I'd spent my entire seventeen years and eleven months in the boring San Fernando Valley.

As I waited under the awning of Anaïs Nin's brownstone, I imagined the scalloped leaves at my feet as precious, exotic fans. Forgetting that at eighteen now I was too grown-up to collect leaves from a dirty sidewalk, I scooped up an armful as though grabbing real gold.

"*Ahloo? Ahloo?*" A high French voice arrested me.

I dropped a handful of leaves to press the intercom. "Are you *Anna-ees* Nin?" I pronounced her name the way my godmother had instructed when sending me on this errand.

"*Oui?*"

"Lenore Tawney sent me to get the books you promised her."

"Who-oo?" Anaïs's birdsong raised a note at the end.

"Lenore Tawney, the fiber artist? You took a small weaving of hers in exchange for your books and . . ." Never brought the books, my godmother had groused. Lenore loathed to part with her work except to a few museums. She didn't trust anyone to care for it as she would.

With a pleasant hum the entry door unlocked, and the elevator opened by itself. As the lift delivered me to the fourth floor, my stomach fluttered with excitement; I was going to meet the "underground novelist" Anaïs Nin. Until the previous day I'd never heard of Anaïs Nin, but my godmother had said that in the 1930s, Nin had hung out with Henry Miller and Lawrence Durrell in Paris. I hadn't read them either—because they were on a list of banned authors the nuns at Immaculate Heart High had handed out—but I intended to.

The elevator slid open, revealing Anaïs posed at her apartment door like a movie star, a raised arm resting on the mahogany doorframe, one hand on her hip.

"And you are?" She gave me a Cheshire grin, nothing like a movie star's. Her teeth were slightly bucked, like a little girl's, yet long, and their color hinted she was older than she otherwise appeared. (She was then sixty.) The effect was that she seemed all ages at once. When she composed her face, it was hauntingly familiar: beautiful and mysterious like a geisha's with kohl-rimmed eyes and high-peaked, penciled lips. Her fitted sheath dress showed off a figure as girlish as mine.

"I'm Lenore Tawney's goddaughter," I said. "I'm staying at her loft. She went to Monhegan for the weekend . . ."

"What is your name?" Anaïs's turquoise eyes flashed like sunlight on water.

I told her and she repeated it, rolling the "r" in the back of her throat and chiming the "teenne" on her palette: *Trchrriss-teennne.* I thrilled to the sound of my name in her mouth. She grinned again, revealing pink upper gums. "Are those beautiful Maidenhair leaves for me?"

Suddenly I was aware I was still clutching the pile of leaves to my chest. I glanced back at a trail of them on the hall's oriental runner. "Oh, I'm sorry. I . . . Would you like them?" I thrust the leaves forward, more falling.

"Follow me," she said, her smile so encouraging I would have followed her anywhere.

We entered a softly lit hallway through which I saw straight ahead to a living room, where people in evening clothes sipped martinis. Anaïs ducked left into a small kitchen, and I followed.

A dark-skinned, slender woman, whom I later learned was Haitian, rose from her reading chair smoothing her cotton skirt, printed with dancing salamanders.

"Millie Fredericks, this is Tristine . . ." Anaïs looked at me, stricken. "I am so sorry, I don't have your surname."

She made me spell it and then cried, "Like my friend, the actress Luise Rainer!" Only Anaïs pronounced it, "*Rriiiner.*" She lowered her voice as if sharing a confidence. "Luise was an intimate friend of mine when she was married to Clifford Odets. I put them in my diary. Are you related to her?" She lifted my chin gently with her manicured fingers. "You have the same beautiful, almond-shaped eyes."

Unused to compliments, I blurted, "I'm not related to anyone important." Anaïs looked so disappointed, I jumped to add, "Except my godmother, I guess, though we're not blood related."

"Certainly, your godmother! Tawney is a genuine artist. So pure!"

There was an involuntary quiver in my voice when I said, "My godmother told me that you write a diary."

"Do you keep a diary?" Anaïs gave me her extraordinary smile of approval.

I nodded. I felt transparent, but also, as never before, completely accepted, completely safe. Growing up, I'd been a misfit in Southern California, neither blond nor cheerful, constantly accused of having my head in a book or in the clouds, and usually dressed in ill-fitting hand-me-downs since my father split. But Anaïs's smile said: *I understand you as you always hoped to be understood; I see your great specialness as you have always dreamt of being seen.*

"One afternoon we will have a long talk about our diaries!" She beamed.

I nodded so vigorously that more leaves fell to the floor. Anaïs laughed gaily, speaking in French with Millie, but seeing my incomprehension, changed back to English. "We're looking for a *crrrystal* bowl."

Millie produced one from a cabinet and told me, "Hon, why don't you dump those leaves in the sink?"

I did so and saw they had soiled the front of my pink shirtwaist dress, which I had bought for starting college in the fall with my waitressing tips. Without a word, Millie took a cloth and dabbed at the spots. Then she dusted each leaf before handing it to Anaïs. We *oohed* and *ahhed* as Millie presented each gold-specked fan and Anaïs arranged them in the bowl.

Waving one flirtatiously, Anaïs said, "Do you think it's a coincidence we call these leaves maidenhair, while the Chinese, who call it gingko, consider it an aphrodisiac?"

She must have noticed my blush for she gave me another gummy smile as she picked up the artistically filled bowl and instructed me to follow her into the living room. She carried the bowl high over her head like a temple priestess.

"I want you all to meet my new friend, Tristine Rainer." Anaïs set the bowl of leaves on a table inlaid with Moroccan tiles. "She has brought us poetry from the street!"

The four people in the living room exclaimed and clapped. I felt as exalted as when I'd been applauded as the lead in my high school plays.

A jowled, sixtyish woman with lacquered bouffant hair intoned in a deep voice, "Street poetry is my kind of poetry."

"This is Caresse Crosby." Anaïs smiled at me. "She is the founder of Black Sun Press. Caresse, and her deceased husband Harry, published D. H. Lawrence, James Joyce, Hemingway, and Henry Miller before anyone else would take a chance on them."

I had to keep myself from curtsying. "I'm so honored to meet you!"

I followed Anaïs as she glided over to the older and taller of the two men in the room. "And this handsome man is my husband, Hugo Guiler." She put her arm around his trim waist as he gave her shoulders a squeeze.

I said, "But your last name is Nin."

Her laughter tinkled. "Nin is my professional name. My *nom de plume.*"

"Of course." I flushed over my naiveté.

With the soulful mien and aristocratic bearing of a greyhound, Hugo lowered his narrow, angular head and asked if I'd like a martini, even though I was a teenager and looked like one.

Then, with a kiss to Anaïs's forehead, he strode into the kitchen.

Anaïs took me by the hand and introduced me to Jean-Jacques, a short, wiry man in his thirties, expensively dressed. Though I later noticed that his French accent was heavier than hers, he used slang Americanisms with no accent at all. "How ya doin?"

He reached for my hand as if to shake it but instead kissed the top, lingering so that I felt the air from his Gallic nose tickle my skin. He and Anaïs joked in French while he held onto my hand, and I cursed myself for having elected Spanish in high school.

Hugo returned with Millie, who had put on a white, scalloped pinafore over her colorful dress. She carried a tray balancing a martini glass filled to the brim. Everyone watched as I lifted the glass it by its narrow stem, trying not to spill it. Successfully! Almost.

Hugo rescued me from my embarrassment. "Caresse was telling us about her efforts to start a women's world peace organization."

"Her greatest invention since the bra!" Anaïs exclaimed. "And both inventions are custom-fitted for women."

I didn't know what she was talking about then but later learned that Caresse Crosby, as a socialite in her early twenties, had invented and patented the first brassiere.

Caresse lifted her large head from the mauve settee. "My organization, Women of the World Against War, denounces war as mass murder."

"Say the point I like about individualism," Anaïs prompted.

"We will guard our individualism and feminine qualities and use them for good!"

With his heavy accent, Jean-Jacques volunteered, "*Aahving* no feminine qualities, I will just *aahve* to be bad."

"So that's your excuse." Anaïs's laugh jingled.

Anaïs, Hugo, Caresse, and Jean-Jacques continued their good-humored banter, looping from experimental music and off-Broadway theater to Bette Davis's performance in *All About Eve,* to Marilyn Monroe's death the previous week. As I was thinking how inconceivable Marilyn's suicide was, given she was famous and had everything I wanted, they segued to Hemingway's suicide the year before. Anaïs said that the way Hemingway had written—by denying all feeling—had predicted his end.

I sat spellbound by Anaïs and Hugo and their guests, whose speech and gestures seemed to be from the black-and-white movies I'd watched on TV over long summer afternoons. Anaïs especially, with her delicate skin, bowed lips, and arched brows, had the glamour of a 1930s ingénue. Her every movement flowed as if there were a camera always on her. I'd studied the mannerisms of those beautiful people, who lived in mansions with balustraded stairways, chandeliered drawing rooms, and carts with ice and crystal liquor bottles from which to prepare cocktails. They were always going to or giving parties, falling in or out of love, and confiding their indiscretions to a doting maid. To a latchkey kid in front of her TV, it looked like an idyllic life.

Now I felt as if I had walked onto the set of one of those old films, which was thrilling but also terrifying, because—as in one of my recurring nightmares where I'd been cast in a play but never learned my lines—I was afraid of saying the wrong thing and ruining the show.

For the moment, though, I wasn't called upon to deliver any lines. Everyone's attention was on Anaïs. She was talking about Henry Miller's novels.

"Henry's genital obsession is part of American realism. I'm more interested in the atmosphere of love in my novels, in sensuality, which for me is everywhere; a shrub can be erotic at twilight, the lines of an Eames chair, the moan of a sax from a curtainless window, the hiss of sprinklers in the morning, the way my husband refolds his *Wall Street Journal*." She glanced affectionately at Hugo.

I had never heard a woman speak that way, precisely and boldly, but also musically, and I agreed with her. I didn't even want to go all the way with the boys I dated. I was happy just making out with them for hours. And I, like she, found sensuality everywhere, especially here in her apartment with its rosy, flattering lamplight and her carpets and furniture that seemed out of *The Arabian Nights*.

"It's time to get going," Hugo announced.

Millie reappeared, having removed her pinafore and now wearing dangling, seed pearl earrings.

Hugo looked down at me from his height. "We're going dancing in Harlem. You should come."

"Oh, I couldn't crash your party," I replied.

"Nonsense, come along," Hugo said. "We'll look after you. I've ordered a car."

"There won't be room," I answered, not knowing then that by car, Hugo meant limo. "And I'm not dressed." I'd thought my sleeveless pink shirtwaist was smart when I'd arrived, but not anymore.

"You shouldn't miss new experiences." Anaïs fixed me with her gemstone eyes, imparting the first of many lessons I would eagerly heed. "Have you ever been to Harlem?"

"No."

"Do you like jazz?"

"I love jazz!"

"Well, you don't know when you'll be invited again," she said.

And that was that.

∞

Once we were settled in the limo I kept my eyes on Anaïs, who was gazing out the window, looking distant and pensive. We listened to Ella Fitzgerald singing "Autumn in New York" on the radio, as though the deejay had dedicated it especially to us. As the others hummed and sang phrases, I thought I was the dreamer with empty hands sighing for this exotic land. I squeezed my mind as I sometimes did to save the moment in my memory so I wouldn't forget, so one day I could, as in the song, live it again. I told myself to remember Millie and Jean-Jacques and Caresse swaying, Hugo holding Anaïs's hand, and Anaïs with her black-crayoned eyes, arched brows, and crimson mouth, looking like the French clown Pierrot we'd learned about in my high school drama class.

Anaïs became aware of me watching her and gave me a soft smile, then retrieved from her purse a gold and black box. As though the move had been choreographed, Jean-Jacques pulled out his lighter and flicked it while she brought a gold-tipped Balkan-Sobranie to her lips. Jean-Jacques then offered around his Gitanes before lighting his own.

"All the other clubs in Harlem have closed," Hugo was saying.

Exhaling smoke, Anaïs addressed me. "We used to go to a place called the Jitterbug. It was owned by the prize fighter and actor Canada Lee."

Caresse nudged me. "Do you know who he is?"

I was excited. I knew the answer. I remembered the Hitchcock movie *Lifeboat* I'd seen on TV and the Negro actor in it who'd recited the 23rd Psalm for a dead child they had thrown overboard. I'd wept alone in the living room hearing the compassion in that man's deep, reverberating voice.

"He was in *Lifeboat*!"

Anaïs beamed at me approvingly.

"He was also blacklisted," Caresse added. "They hounded that beautiful man into an early grave."

Anaïs said, "Canada Lee was Caresse's lover."

"Oh." I looked at fleshy Caresse with her collapsed face in a new light.

Anaïs whispered in Hugo's ear. He lowered his head, smiling, and brought his wife's watermelon-polished fingertips to his lips. They leaned into each other as she kissed him on his neck. Watching them, a void ached in my chest. I'd never seen married people be affectionate and romantic; my parents had fought until they divorced and my aunt and uncle never touched. I imagined Anaïs and Hugo's love, their marriage, as what I yearned for but never expected to find.

Jean-Jacques tapped my hand. I looked down. He was passing me a burning hand-rolled cigarette. I'd noticed an odor, distinct from the Gitanes and Sobranies, and when Jean-Jacques said, "Kif," under his breath, I guessed what it was. No one I'd ever known had tried pot, but that didn't stop me from putting the rolled cigarette to my lips and inhaling as I would a Kent.

"*Oold* it in," Jean-Jacques said in my ear.

Coughing, I tried to hand it back, but Jean-Jacques murmured, "To Caresse." It went around the circle of passengers without comment, each hand covering it as the next received it, though I didn't notice who smoked and who didn't. I was too absorbed in the sudden inten-sification of sound, the beauty of streetlights streaming through the inky night, and my release from self-consciousness. The limo, Ella on the radio, their animated faces, Anaïs snuggling with Hugo, the bursts of laughter—everything blended and flowed.

Until my feet hit the ground. The pavement lurched under my heels, and Hugo chivalrously stabilized me. Languidly, arm in arm, Anaïs, Millie, and Caresse were walking toward the art deco facade of the Lenox Lounge. It seemed to be taking them a long time.

From above my head, someone growled, "Look at that white and pink flower." I looked up past the club's neon sign to a narrow metal balcony where a sinewy man, so dark he gleamed purple, was lean-ing forward in a folding chair looking down at me. "Pretty enough to pick."

I wanted to be where Anaïs, Millie, and Caresse were, but my legs seemed to pull like taffy, getting nowhere. Then I felt Hugo's hands on my waist from behind while Jean-Jacques stepped in front of me, and we all filed, like a Chinese dragon with twelve legs, through the entrance of the narrow bar into the back room.

Sconces glowed like hot embers against the orange walls. A table had been reserved for us, the only white people there, it seemed. When Anaïs selected her chair, I willed myself beside her.

A waitress with large hoop earrings asked for our drink orders. She didn't even give me a second look when I ordered a bourbon and ginger ale, a drink my aunt once let me try.

The room quieted when a man in tight pants and a ruffled shirt took his place at the conga drums in the corner. As if sharing a secret, Anaïs leaned in to me, "I know this *conguero* from Havana. Mongo Santamaria."

Mongo had a V-shaped grin that wrinkled the skin over his wide nostrils like soft black leather. Suddenly his hands were a flock of birds taking off. A trumpeter and tenor sax joined in and people started to fill the floor, hips swinging, shoulders pumping to the Afro-Cuban beat.

Hugo and Anaïs rose and danced flirtatiously, apart and together. Later I learned that they had both studied flamenco dancing. That night what I saw was a couple joyfully seducing each other, sharing a secret in their movements.

My feet moved under the table, and I could feel a smile on my face.

Caresse, who was seated between me and Jean-Jacques, nudged us both. "See that mixed couple?" I saw a blond woman I hadn't noticed before clasped to the chest of a black man. "That's how Canada Lee and I were together. Sweet as hot fudge on vanilla ice cream." My giggle caught in my throat when she hissed, "Anaïs had an affair with Canada, too. She doesn't know that I know."

Jean-Jacques lifted a groomed eyebrow. I didn't believe Caresse. I assumed she was jealous of Anaïs because Anaïs had Hugo who adored her, while Caresse's husband Harry, I'd gathered, had killed himself.

Caresse donned a glamorous smile when Millie, Anaïs, and Hugo returned to the table out of breath. Saying goodbye, Millie left for home, and Hugo, after pulling out Anaïs's chair, excused himself for the *toilette*.

Dropping her smile, Caresse leaned toward Anaïs. "While Hugo's gone, there's something I have to say to you."

I was afraid she was going accuse Anaïs of being with Canada Lee, but instead Caresse said, "You know that you and Hugo are always welcome at Rocca Sinibalda, but please do not bring *the other one*."

Anaïs paled. I wondered what Caresse meant.

"I understand," Anaïs said to Caresse and abruptly turned to me and Jean-Jacques. "Rocca Sinibalda is a castle outside Rome that Caresse purchased as a home for Women of the World Against War."

"Is that where I should write to join?" I asked Caresse.

She ignored me and continued speaking to Anaïs. "Hugo isn't passive like you think. When you're in Los Angeles he pesters me with questions." Anaïs came to Los Angeles, where I lived? I wanted to ask when, but Caresse kept on, "I love Hugo and can't bear to see him hurt. You'd better watch out or somebody like me who appreciates him will grab him while you're dallying on the other coast."

Anaïs cried, "You think I don't appreciate Hugo? You think I don't love him?"

"You should mind your own business!" I heard the words shoot out of my mouth at Caresse.

There was stunned silence. The others looked at me with a mixture of pity and concern, like arguing parents who become aware of an upset child in the room. My nightmare had come to life. I had stopped the drama by saying the wrong thing—as if I were still a kid coming to my mother's defense.

Anaïs broke the paralysis of the moment. "Out of the mouth of babes." As if offering me a reward, she wrapped a lock of my hair around her index finger. "Your hair is so silky. It's the shade mine was at your age. I never appreciated it."

"Because brown hair is so boring," I said.

"Not at all. It has gold and amber highlights. Brown is the color of polished wood and mink coats, of brandy and cellos." She must really have wanted to make me feel good, because years later I learned that she hated the color brown.

Jean-Jacques jumped up. "Mambo *avec* Mongo, Anaïs?" He took her hand and she rose to join him, but then we all saw Hugo returning to the table. Anaïs brushed right past Jean-Jacques and coquettishly entered Hugo's arms, calling back to us, "I promised this dance to my husband."

Jean-Jacques turned to me. "You're it." He took my hand to lift me out of my chair.

"I can't dance to this," I objected. I only knew rock and roll and the formless slow dancing we did at St. Cyril's parish mixers.

"Don't dance. Just move to the rhythm." Jean-Jacques revealed small, even teeth in a seductive smile. Though he wasn't tall, he gave that impression because of his erect posture. His posture changed as he danced, hunched like a hipster, slender legs in his finely tailored pants loose and easy. I tried to mirror him.

Anaïs sped by with Hugo. "That's it, Tristine!"

Jean-Jacques took me in his arms. "Allow me to move you."

I followed his instructions, amazed that my body twisted and whirled under the guidance of his hands and that my feet kept the rhythm without tripping. He pulled me close so I was aware of my breasts pressed against his chest and of his leg pushing between my thighs. The thumping congas, the blasting trumpet, the squealing sax, our hearts drumming violently, harder, faster, built to a crescendo.

When the music stopped, people stood apart, panting, but Jean-Jacques squeezed his body against mine so that our pounding pulses slowed together. I looked around the spinning room to find Anaïs. She and Hugo were speaking in Spanish with Mongo.

From what I could pick up, they were asking for a *son* they'd danced to in Cuba. When it began, without separating our clasped torsos, Jean-Jacques and I began to move in a slow dance. When I pulled back to look into his face, his mouth was closed in an ironic smile, though his dark eyes were kind. I had assumed that Jean-Jacques's age and sophistication put him out of my league. The creases in his cheeks and the hardness of his mouth had frightened me, but now I was flowing with the feelings in my body. I was scared and excited, yet my muscles were relaxed and melded to his.

He put his mouth to my ear and blew softly, giving me a shiver. He whispered, "I can tell how firm your breasts are under that schoolgirl dress." I knew he was being fresh, but liquid pleasure coursed through me.

We danced to Mongo's Afro-Cuban rhythms and boogaloo riffs until the club closed. At one point, everyone started dancing with everyone, changing partners, then gyrating in a circle. I danced with Hugo, with Anaïs, with the men and women from Harlem, whirling, the floor vibrating under our feet. Caresse couldn't dance because she had a bad leg, but she clapped and danced with her hands, and whatever tension may have remained between her and Anaïs, or me, dissolved.

Though I had missed dinner and drunk too many bourbon and ginger ales, the music held me up. When it stopped, I would have fallen like a puppet from cut strings were it not for Jean-Jacques's supportive arms. Without knowing how I'd gotten there, I found myself nuzzled next to him in the limo, my head on his shoulder, drifting out of a stupor only when the chattering between Anaïs and Caresse rose to laughter.

When we arrived back at the Guilers' brownstone, I roused myself. I heard Hugo say to Jean-Jacques, "Why don't you take the car and see her home." I mumbled my godmother's address and fell back into oblivion.

∞

The next thing I knew, Jean-Jacques was pulling gently on my arm to encourage me to leave the limo.

"I don't feel good," I complained as he helped me out onto the street. "I'm dizzy."

"Keys," he said.

Not getting a response from me, he took my purse from over my shoulder and found Lenore's key ring while supporting me against his trim frame.

"Walk. Just to the door."

"I can't."

"I won't let you fall." He skillfully negotiated the keys. We made it into the freight elevator, and he held the cage doors as we stumbled out into Lenore's foyer. We removed our shoes, and he unlocked the door to my godmother's huge work space, which had once been a sail-maker's loft.

"Wow!" He took in the 10,000 square feet of open space punctuated by painted columns, wooden looms, and long worktables. Lenore's towering woven sculptures hung from the high cathedral ceilings: one a ten-by-ten black cross made entirely of tight little knots, another a circle filled with open airy threads enclosed by a solid, dense weave. The tallest weavings, twenty feet high, were narrow, woven totems that swung slightly to and fro, great sacred beings that seemed to breathe and watch us.

As if we were in church, Jean-Jacques whispered, "Where do you sleep?"

I pointed to a muslin screen that partially concealed my rollaway bed. Once I'd collapsed on it, I realized I couldn't get up again. The loft was rising over my head, circling under the bed, and coming up repeatedly from the metal frame at my feet. My hands grabbed the mattress and held on.

"The room," I murmured.

"Stay there," Jean-Jacques said. Where would I go?

He rifled around in Lenore's bathroom and brought back two aspirin with a glass of water. He supported my spine as I swallowed the pills. "These will help in the morning."

I sank back down on the feather pillow, and though I worried that I'd never be able to get up to pee, I did feel better from his care. It made me think of my mother's tenderness when she used to bring me baby aspirin and a rubber hot-water bottle. Maybe that's why it seemed the most natural thing in the world for him to be unbuttoning the front of my dress as if I were a sleepy child.

"Let's get you some air," he said. He tried to pull my slip over my head.

"No," I said weakly. He stopped and, sitting on the edge of the cot, leaned down to kiss me. I responded, lost in his musk of exertion, Gitanes, and French cologne. His fingers traced my arms and his lips softly brushed mine. I'd expected, because he was French, that he would put his tongue in my mouth, which I didn't like when the boys my age tried it. But Jean-Jacques just kept touching his lips to mine tenderly, and I responded with the same light touch. When, after a long, dreamy time his tongue entered my mouth, it wasn't slobbery or pushy at all.

Unwrapping himself from me gently, he stood up, looked at me, bent to place a finger to my lips, then quickly removed his slacks. He was wearing gray satin shorts, sort of like a prizefighter's, but smaller, and in the dim light I saw a horizontal tent protruding in the front of them. Only then did I realize his intentions.

"I'm a virgin," I said, my voice so faint I wondered if he'd heard.

He must have, for after a moment's pause, he said, "I respect that. Don't worry."

He carefully folded his slacks and laid them on one of Lenore's worktables. He unbuttoned his shirt so it fell open but he did not remove it. He stood over me, shorts still on, and lowered himself so he was sitting next to me on the rollaway bed. He attempted to raise my slip again, and this time I helped him by lifting my weightless arms, inhaling my own bouquet of sweat and deodorant. He deftly unfastened and removed my bra, watching me in the light of the streetlamp shining through the high loft windows. He touched my breasts with a kind of reverence, then kissed them. I was floating, enjoying, without the fear I'd always felt when boys I made out with wanted to go farther. The nuns had indoctrinated me so well that I was terrified of sex, yet that night I could not find my fear and didn't want to.

I still had on the light girdle with garters that held up the nylons I'd ruined by dancing holes in the feet.

"Why do you wear a girdle?" Jean-Jacques asked. "You have no need."

I couldn't answer because I didn't know why; my mother was fat and wore a girdle, and I thought that's what all women did. I allowed him to unfasten the nylons and skillfully roll them down. Then he pulled down the girdle, expertly, as if he'd done it many times. I felt so much better with it off, and I was still safe because I still had on my panties, and he did not try to touch them, as he covered my body with his.

The totem gods hanging above us swayed, nodding in approval as he pushed his pelvis against mine. I had never experienced a man moving his body on mine like that before, and it seemed so natural, so right.

He raised himself with one arm and ran his fingertips from my nipples down my abdomen, sending shivers of pleasure through me. Then he lowered his frame over mine again on the cot. I could feel the satin of his shorts protruding against the nylon of my crotch. I looked down and caught sight of his penis coming through the opening in his shorts. I had the impulse to touch it, because a girlfriend had told me that touching a penis felt like petting a horse's nose, and I loved the soft nose of a horse. I slipped one hand between us as he rose up and let my fingers brush against it. I was surprised by its heat and pulled my hand away.

The great totems were watching from above, saying *yes, touch it, feel it, do it; it is right, it is nature.* I closed my hand over it. He stopped moving then. "What do you want?"

"I don't know," I said and pulled my hand away again. What I wanted was to stay unknowing, just moving. I thrust my pelvis upward and he pushed against me, his rhythm my rhythm, the rhythm of the totems, again and again, as I looked up at the swaying gods, watching us, pulling us through a spinning siphon of pleasure into their world.

The next thing I knew, Jean-Jacques was standing above me with a washcloth and a towel. I was confused.

"Did I throw up?" I said.

"No," he laughed. He must have seen my alarm. "Nothing happened," he assured me. His voice was comforting, and the washcloth with which he wiped my stomach was wet and warm. I let my hand go to my tummy. To my relief I was still wearing my panties, but where the elastic top met my bare skin, I felt something sticky. He wiped my fingers then with the towel and softly patted my tummy dry.

Later I could hear the toilet flush in the bathroom, and he came back to my bedside. I tried to slide over in the cot so he could sleep next to me, but he kissed me on the forehead. "Goodnight, little one."

My last thought before I drifted back to sleep was, *I forgot to get the books from Anaïs.*

# CHAPTER 2

# The East Village, New York, 1962

TODAY, WHAT JEAN-JACQUES DID WHILE I was intoxicated would likely be considered a form of date rape. But in 1962 there was no such concept. In fact, for me, having come of age in the 1950s, a man taking you while you were helpless was a secret fantasy. One where I could have pleasure without guilt, as when I imagined myself being bound to a factory conveyor belt and carried on it to a man like nougat centers to the chocolate dip—moving toward desire free of volition.

I did realize that I should not have let a man into my godmother's loft. Lenore had told me that she had given up men for the sake of her art, and this loft was her sanctuary. She would not be happy if she knew how Jean-Jacques had defiled it. So when I awoke after my night with Jean-Jacques, grateful not to have a hangover, I gathered up my panties and the bed sheets and carried them to the laundry closet, noticing in wonder little translucent chips flaking off the fabric. I argued to myself that nothing had really happened. Jean-Jacques hadn't taken my virginity. Although he'd been aroused, he hadn't tried to enter me, which told me he really respected and cared for me—and that, in my innocence, meant the beginning of love.

I was confused that he hadn't said anything about seeing me again but I assumed he'd written down Lenore's number from the phone dial so he could call me later. When I checked her telephone, though, there was no number on it.

Maybe Jean-Jacques would ask Anaïs for it. I should have Lenore's number written down and ready when I went to retrieve the forgotten books.

That afternoon I repeated my steps from Lenore's Bowery loft to Anaïs's Greenwich Village apartment. She buzzed me right up but seemed flustered when she opened the door.

"Did I interrupt you?" I asked.

"No, but I only have ten minutes. I have to meet Gore for lunch."

I didn't know who Gore was but thought it unusual she was leaving for lunch at three. She was wearing flared silk trousers and a chiffon blouse with one large ruffle down the front, more suitable for hostessing than going out, so I guessed Gore, whoever he was, was coming there.

"Sit down for a few minutes." Anaïs indicated the couch. In the soft light of her living room with the shades drawn against the sunlight, she looked younger and more natural, and suddenly I knew why she'd seemed familiar the first time I saw her. Though aged, she had the face of Botticelli's Venus rising from the sea on a clamshell, the same heart shape, the same arched brows, identical lips, a likeness emphasized by how she penciled the upper twin peaks.

As if Anaïs knew I was thinking about her as the goddess of love, she asked gaily, "How did it go with Jean-Jacques last night?"

Hearing her pronounce his name made my inner thighs, where he'd pushed against me, melt into butterscotch pudding, but I tried to keep my voice noncommittal. "Oh, he got me back to Lenore's." For the first time, I realized he must have told the limo driver to wait for him all the while he was upstairs with me. Had the driver told Hugo? Did Anaïs know? I was afraid she could see the flush that was now burning on my chest and cheeks.

"Jean-Jacques seemed very taken with you." She smiled.

"He's too old to be interested in me," I protested, hoping she would contradict me. There was a twinkle in her aquamarine eyes, but perhaps to spare me further embarrassment, she changed the subject.

"So, tell me, how did Lenore Tawney become your godmother?"

"She and my mother were good friends when I was born. They were both Catholic—"

"I was once Catholic, too," Anaïs said, adding, "It's a very sexually repressive religion, you know."

I nodded, feeling tongue-tied. During the night with Jean-Jacques, my Catholic repression had disappeared. I would have liked to talk with Anaïs about that, but I had no words to describe what had happened.

Anaïs waited a moment patiently, then shrugged as if recognizing that I was not going to say anything, and went back to the topic of my godmother. "You said your mother and Lenore were friends in the past tense. They aren't any more?"

"Well, they lost touch after my father left."

That statement captured her interest. She asked me questions about my father's abandonment of our family and got me to tell her how he'd absconded in the middle of the night; how my mother, in shame, withdrew from her friends and hid in the house with the blinds closed; how later I'd found a letter to Mother from Lenore, worried about her silence. When I'd asked Mother about her early friendship with Lenore, she would say nothing, though she did reveal that Lenore's husband died, leaving Lenore money to move to New York and become a successful artist. For years I hid my godmother's letter as a secret passageway out of my limited life, and during my last year in high school I wrote and reminded her that she was responsible for my spiritual growth, and she'd invited me to come stay with her.

"And has Lenore addressed your spiritual growth?" Anaïs asked.

"Not really. She isn't Catholic anymore. She's a Buddhist now, though she might become a Hindu. Her art is spiritual, don't you think?"

"Yes, I do. Very. Art is my religion now."

"And mine," I eagerly agreed.

Anaïs continued studying me, then gently asked, "How old were you when your father left?"

"Eleven."

Her sympathy penetrated me like the heavy August heat, and she said with great sadness, "I was eleven, too, when my father abandoned our family."

Startled, I stared at her lovely face, amazed that she of all people had been abandoned like me. She elaborated. "We had just come home from the hospital. I'd had a burst appendix. I thought Papa was leaving because of all the trouble and the big hospital bill I'd caused."

She felt responsible for her father leaving, as I did, though in my case it had been because I couldn't keep my mouth shut. The summer of my tenth birthday, my mother, father, and I took a vacation, and my parents argued in the car the whole drive. Mother kept opening the passenger door, threatening to jump out, and he yelled at her to go ahead, even pushed her, while I sat invisible and mute in the backseat.

When we got to the grand, fairytale Banff Hotel in Canada, I had thought it would enchant them, as it had me. We were going to put on our best clothes and go to dinner in the hotel dining room, but they began shouting earsplitting curses at each other again. I put my hands over my ears and tried to make myself disappear, but this time, some cyclone seized and threw me out of my usual frozen silence, and I heard myself scream, "Stop it! Stop it! Don't you see what you are doing to me?"

Astonished, they did stop. I saw my mother's heartbreaking recognition of my pain, and my father took me for a walk in the woods even though it was pouring rain. Years later, he told me what I'd already known—that my outburst marked the moment he'd decided to leave.

I told Anaïs, "My father left us without any money when he split and moved to Mexico. He didn't even say good-bye." I had never told anyone this, but suddenly the misfortunes of my childhood no longer seemed a disadvantage, because they were like hers.

"We, too, were very poor after my father left," Anaïs said.

"You were poor?" It was hard to believe.

She nodded and looked terribly sad. "I cried and begged Papa not to go, but he pushed me away violently and escaped out the door. A year later I started my diary as an extended letter to him to try to lure him back."

"That's not why I started my diary," I said, disappointed that this detail was not the same. "I was glad my father left."

"But that's not possible, Tristine!" she cried. "He didn't molest you, did he?"

"No! Nothing like that."

"But then you must have cried over losing him. I couldn't stop crying. I cried for two years."

"I didn't cry at all." I remembered how when I learned he'd gone, I dug my cowgirl cap pistol from a pile of discarded toys, carried it to the front door and aimed at our suburban street, straight down the cement walkway. I hollered, "*Bang! Bang!* Good riddance!"

She looked at me in disbelief. "Didn't you love your father?"

"I did when I was little."

"When did you stop loving him?" Her voice was so silvery, I had to lean in to hear the question.

I thought back to the afternoon when I was eight and Mother was sitting with a cup of coffee at the kitchen table, something she never did because she was always sweeping the floor, or making our beds, or cooking the next meal, or cleaning up the last one, or planning a party for my father's doctor and lawyer friends. I took the rare chance to sit down with her. Then I saw she'd been turning her head away from me because of a big bruise on the side of her face. She said she had tripped, but when I went into their bedroom, my father's wooden clotheshorse was broken, the base split in two, the crossbar cracked and splintered. Suddenly I made sense of the banging and shrieking I'd heard the night before.

I said to Anaïs only, "I stopped loving him a few years before he left."

"So early," Anaïs exclaimed. "I didn't stop loving my father until I was an adult, married to Hugo." I was troubled by this difference, but then she asked about something I didn't think anyone else could know. "Did you ever want to get even with your father for his abandoning your mother?"

"How did you know that?" I gasped. "I wanted to become a famous actress so I could give my mother everything my father didn't. I imagined he would come to me begging and I would shun him."

"How would you shun him?"

"Outside the stage door. The press would be there, and flashbulbs would go off for a photo of me spurning my father on the street."

Her brows knit, making two delicate lines above her narrow nose. "In a way I understand that impulse. My father came back into my life when I was almost thirty. I wanted very much for him to admire and love me." From the pain twisting her face, I gathered that hadn't happened. Then she appeared to pull herself out of the memory, her tortured face recomposing itself into its usual sweet attentiveness. "Have you had any contact with your father since he left?"

"He practiced law in Mexico City for four years until my mother agreed to his measly divorce terms and then he came back to the States and restarted his practice. My little sister and I had to see him for a weekend every other month. He'd pick us up in his Cadillac with his new, big-bosomed wife."

"Did you feel attracted to him then?"

"No!" What a weird question! What was she getting at? She must be implying that I was attracted to Jean-Jacques, who was so much older than me, as a missing father figure. "You mean like in Freud? Like the Electra complex?" I said, proud of using the sophisticated term, knowing it would impress her.

"So you know about the Electra complex." She did sound impressed. "Actually, though, Freud did not accept it."

"I don't accept it either!" She seemed startled, so I explained. "I was never attracted to my father, especially when he came back when I was fifteen. I was repelled by him."

"Really? Why?"

"He wore silk iridescent suits, and his table manners were gross. He and his new wife lived in an apartment on Sunset Strip filled with gold-embossed furniture."

Anaïs laughed a little whinny and covered her teeth with her hand. "Was your father in the entertainment business, Tristine?"

"No! He was an ambulance chaser." She looked at me uncomprehendingly. "A personal injury attorney for auto accidents?"

"Oh." That didn't interest her. "My father was a famous musician," she said reverentially. "His clothes were elegant, his manners were beautifully polished, and his home with his second wife was the ultimate in good taste."

My heart plunged over the dissimilarity of our fathers. I wanted her beginnings to be identical to mine, so that I could believe I'd grow up to be just like her.

She took both my hands. "Dear Tristine, we are meant to be friends. Both wounded by the father. We have the same Achilles heel." I did not yet understand the importance of what she said but I didn't think she seemed wounded at all. She shone, and in her bright reflection, I hoped to find myself.

"Oh my goodness!" she cried. "I'm going to be late for my lunch with Gore!" She dashed to her floor-to-ceiling built-in bookcases, and

I watched her select slim volumes from swaths of the same color on two shelves. I felt the tug of something like envy—but not envy, admiration—and a longing to be, as she, a woman who could write shelves of books.

"*A Child Born Out of the Fog, Winter of Artifice, House of Incest.*" Anaïs caressed each syllable of her titles. "*This Hunger, A Spy in the House of Love, Under a Glass Bell.*" She placed the books on the Moroccan table. "For Tristine!"

Seeing her lift a fountain pen from a holder in the shape of a kneeling Bacchus, I reminded her, "Actually the books are for Lenore."

She smiled. "To be dedicated to Lenore Tawney, but for Tristine to read."

She scribbled, *For Tawney, an imaginative and poetic artist*, and handed the book to me. On another volume she dashed off, *It's not weaving, it's magic*, and placed that book on top of the first one, and so on, until they were stacked in a pile balanced against my chest.

"Phone me so we can plan your next visit." She wrote her number on a square of violet notepaper and placed it on the top book.

This would have been the perfect opportunity for me to give her the phone number at Lenore's loft in case Jean-Jacques asked for it. I had it ready in my pocket, but with my arms around the books, I didn't have a free hand. Anaïs guided me through the hallway and out the front door to the elevator. I walked stooped, with my chin pressing down on the top book to secure her note.

Anaïs touched the elevator button. "Please tell Lenore her weaving is hanging in my bedroom. With its gay little feathers entwined in the threads, I have to keep an eye on it, or it will fly out the window!" Her delight over the rambunctious weaving was so infectious that I found myself grinning.

"You look like a gargoyle." She giggled. She must have seen my horror, for she added quickly, "Not you—you are lovely! The position I've put you in with your head jutting . . ." She stifled her laugh and ran back inside the apartment, calling behind her, "I'll get you a bag for those."

When she returned with a Bergdorf's sack, her grin was so affectionate, it banished my angst over looking like a gargoyle. The upward curve of her smile mirrored the downward arcs of her eyebrows and eyes, giving the impression of features made of smiling crescent moons. Solicitously, she arranged the books for me in the sack, then surprised me with a long hug, her slender arms holding me as she spoke into my ear. "Come back and tell me what you think of my writing. We will be friends." Her fingers turned my head to kiss me on one cheek, then guided my face the other direction to plant a delicate kiss on the other cheek. "How the French say *au revoir*," she said.

∞

I almost skipped back to Lenore's loft, swinging the Bergdorf's sack, elevated by her hug and its promise. I felt like a girl in a musical with the refrain of Anaïs's singsong voice in my head, *We will be friends*.

I had found a world I wanted to live in. A sophisticated world where people owned life and enjoyed it. A world the opposite of the depressing confines I'd grown up in. Although I would defend my mother from anyone who criticized her, I hated how her mistakes had restricted my life. She should never have left the Women's Army Corps to marry my father and have me. She should never have let herself fade into a housewife. She should never have gained 120 pounds after my father left. She shouldn't have crammed all the junk she salvaged from the alley into our garage and closets and her bedroom and bathroom and the living room so there was no place to sit. She shouldn't have gotten pregnant when she was forty-two and married a construction worker who hardly ever worked, and had another baby, and gotten poorer and poorer.

Anaïs was the antithesis of my mother: slender, cared for, sophisticated, and literate. She was the antidote to my mother's depression and fears. Now that I'd had a glimpse of Anaïs's world, now that she had promised we would be friends, now that I'd learned from her how the French kiss *au revoir*, and practiced another kind of French kiss with a real French man, I never wanted to go home to the San Fernando Valley.

To think I had stood in the kitchen with a steak knife held to my wrist when I was eight, waiting for the courage to kill myself. Thank goodness I was too afraid of the sight of blood to have done it, otherwise I would never have grown up to know what happiness felt like; I would never have met Anaïs Nin.

If only I could stay in New York and go to college at NYU, just a few blocks from her apartment. But my state scholarship only covered colleges in California. I was supposed to fly home and move into the dorm at USC in two weeks, and my godmother, not used to sharing her loft with anyone, was already impatient for me to leave. My only hope for staying in New York was if Anaïs could somehow make it happen.

When I got back to Lenore's loft, I opened the largest of the books Anaïs had given Lenore. It was nearly a foot and a half high but only had seventy-two pages and lots of blank space. I ran my fingers over the indentations the title made in the heavy, soft paper. *House of Incest*. I paged through, captivated by the engraved illustrations: thick, black lines that swirled and ended in whimsical doodles. They gave me the feeling of weightlessness and freedom, mystery and excitement that I'd felt the night in Harlem.

I noted that the engravings were credited to Ian Hugo and thought it curious that the engraver had the same last name as Anaïs's husband's first name. Could Anaïs's illustrator be the "other one" Caresse had referred to? Perhaps Ian Hugo was why Anaïs dallied on the West Coast, to work on her books with him.

The poetic prose of *House of Incest* intoxicated me, but I could not make out what it was about. I read through some of the other novels, and they were also incomprehensible. I would become entranced by a sensual description of an exotic setting but then nothing would happen there. I'd get interested in one of the characters, and she would disappear from the novel. She might show up in the next novel, but other than her name, everything about her life would be different. I recognized that the writing was like the surrealist paintings I loved, but I'd been weaned on Nancy Drew, Dickens, Jane Austen, and the Brontë sisters, and I needed a good plot. Anaïs, it appeared, either could not or would not write one.

This troubled me because I wanted to love Anaïs's writing the way I already loved her. As I crawled between my freshly laundered sheets, I decided that the fault had to be mine; I had to be missing something. I tried to think what it might be but soon my mind drifted to Jean-Jacques, my feelings in the night—skin on skin, distant stars exploding.

The next morning, right after breakfast, I returned to Anaïs's novels. I had to finish them before I could phone her. I'd saved *A Spy in the House of Love* for last because it looked so plain without any illustrations, published by British Book Centre (unlike the other books that had been published, I'd noted, by Gemor Press). It turned out to be the best read, though, sort of an inside-out detective story. I thrilled to this novel's minor key. Its spare sentences suggested something secret and forbidden. Its mood incongruously brought back the thrill I'd sought as a kid going out alone at dusk by the incinerator in our alley.

The principal character, Sabina, who had appeared sporadically in the other novels, was in this one an actress living a double life. She had a loving husband but also many lovers whom she visited out of town for weeks. She lied to her husband that she was performing in regional playhouses, and for some reason he always believed her. When Sabina returned home, she felt relieved to be in her husband's protective arms but soon itched to escape and enjoy her risky behavior again.

Much of this novel I couldn't understand any better than the others, especially the ending where Sabina literally dissolved into a puddle of tears out of guilt when a detective she'd invited to follow her confronted her with her infidelity. Her friend Djuna then "reconstituted" her by saying that although Sabina had never been true to one man, she had always been true to the essence of love.

I wondered if Anaïs was the main character Sabina, the seductress wrapped in mystery and a black cape, traveling from lover to lover. The description of Sabina's husband Alan sounded like Anaïs's husband Hugo—"above average tallness so that he must carry his head a little bent." Could it be that Anaïs had lovers in other cities, as Sabina did?

No, that was impossible. Anaïs was too pure and good to be the deceptive Sabina. I'd never seen married people so in love as she and Hugo. Anyway, everyone knew that novels were made up, not real life.

∞

When my four-foot-eleven godmother returned from her weekend carrying a doll-sized suitcase, I was scribbling in my diary, trying to imitate Anaïs's poetic prose. Lenore, excited about what she'd learned in her sensory awareness workshop, told me how they'd practiced eating a grape slowly and consciously. Her description of holding the pliant grape in her fingers made me think guiltily about touching Jean-Jacques's penis, but Lenore, running in a little trot to turn on a Ravi Shankar recording, didn't notice my flush. She went right to work patiently tying knots into a gauzy weaving spread out on one of the worktables. I knew that her weaving was one of her forms of meditation, so I tiptoed as I went into to the kitchen to phone Anaïs.

"You read my books so soon?" Anaïs trilled when I finally reached her. She invited me for tea, and I was so excited that when I hung up, I blurted to Lenore, who was covering up her work for the day, "I'm going to have tea with Anaïs Nin tomorrow!"

Lenore set her round gray eyes on me with interest. "It's good that you get to know her. Did you have a chance to talk when you went to her apartment?"

"A little." Wishing to divert our conversation from the previous evening, I asked, "How did you learn that Anaïs keeps a diary?"

"She tells everyone." Lenore shrugged. "Though I don't know anyone who's actually read it. It's part of the mythology she spins about herself. She claims she knew all the surrealists, that Antonin Artaud had a thing for her, and that she was responsible for Henry Miller getting published."

"I thought Caresse Crosby published Henry Miller."

Lenore's owl eyes expanded. "You've read Henry Miller?"

"No, but I met Caresse at Anaïs's apartment."

Lenore, who loved artists' gossip, descended effortlessly into one of the miniature chairs that surrounded her small coffee table. At fifty-three, she was limber as a child gymnast from daily yoga.

I sat on a low Japanese stool next to her and answered her questions about Caresse before finally getting in one of my own. "How did you meet Anaïs?"

"I went to a gallery show of an engraver I like, and Anaïs was there."

"Was the engraver Ian Hugo?"

"Yes, did she tell you?"

"No, I guessed because he illustrated the novels she gave you."

Lenore said, "Oh, I didn't realize that. Let me see those books."

I brought them over, and my godmother paged through the illustrations, repeating, "I like his work."

When I asked her to tell me more about Ian Hugo, Lenore said, "He's tall. Reserved. Very old world manners."

"That sounds like her husband!"

"No, no, Anaïs isn't married to Ian Hugo. Ian is just an artist. She's married to some wealthy man."

"I met her husband! He has the same name, Hugo, but it's his first name. Hugo Guiler. He said he's an international investor, and he is wealthy but he's nice."

Lenore picked up some pieces of lint and thread from the floor and rolled them into a tiny ball in her palm.

I asked her, "Does your friend Ian Hugo usually live in Los Angeles?"

"No, what would make you think that?"

"Something Caresse said about Anaïs going to Los Angeles a lot."

"As far as I know, Ian lives in New York." Lenore sounded impatient. "He's represented by a SoHo gallery, and we have mutual friends here. I think that Anaïs tries to make people think she's attached to Ian. At his opening, I invited him to come visit my loft, and she was standing next to him and just invited herself along."

Lenore smashed the ball of lint in her palm with her thumb. "That's when she saw my little weaving and begged me to let her have it."

"I'm supposed to tell you how much she loves it."

Lenore sighed. "I should have kept it."

CHAPTER 3

# Greenwich Village, New York, 1962

THE NEXT DAY, MILLIE BROUGHT a tea tray out to where I'd been seated under the shade of an umbrella on the terrace. After a few moments, Anaïs sailed out in a full-skirted Mexican sundress to join me.

She smiled mischievously. "So, has Jean-Jacques called you?"

"No." My heart jumped. "Did he ask you for my number? Do you have it?"

"I haven't spoken with him. Would you like me to give him your number? I'll be happy to give you his."

Embarrassed by my obvious eagerness, I shook my head but I felt transparent, as if she already knew what had happened with him. The fib I was about to tell burned my face. "He saw Lenore's work and wanted to know if he could buy a piece, but we forgot to exchange phone numbers."

"Oh, he saw her marvelous loft!"

"Yes, he had to help me in. I wasn't feeling too well."

"Lenore was out of town?"

I nodded and as I sat, hugging my midriff with crossed arms, she gently asked me delicately phrased questions about my night with

Jean-Jacques. Bit by bit she untangled the knot of confusion, shame, and longing I held so tightly.

"So you think you are still a virgin?" she asked after considering all I had said.

"Technically."

She laughed, and then we laughed together.

"He should finish the job!" Anaïs announced gaily. "He's French, after all. He'll know what he's doing, and you can be sure he'll be sensitive to you because he already has been."

"That's what I've been thinking. How did you know?"

"I was eighteen once, though I didn't have the good fortune to meet a Jean-Jacques. Even if I had, I would have been too shy to let him know my desires. It's not just men who enjoy sex, you know, although this Puritan American culture makes women ashamed of wanting equal pleasure."

No one had ever spoken with me this way, not my mother or Lenore, certainly not the nuns, or even my girlfriends.

Anaïs urged, "You must tell him that you want him to deflower you, otherwise he will have no way of knowing."

"I can't. I couldn't get the words out."

"Sometimes it is pleasurable to be passive," she said, "but it is not always good for you to hide behind shyness. A man cannot read your mind, and things can happen that you do not want if you are not clear."

We both became thoughtful. I became aware of the sounds of traffic and a faraway jackhammer. Anaïs poured us each a tepid cup of tea.

"That was my problem when I married Hugo." The sadness in her voice made it even more melodic. "I was twenty. He was twenty-four. And neither of us had had any experience with sex. I was much too shy to tell him how to please me, so he couldn't learn."

She must have seen the shock on my face because she quickly added, touching my hand, "This is *entre nous*. Do you know that term?"

"Between us only. Yes."

"For the first two years of our marriage, I remained a virgin, because he was so afraid of hurting me. Then we went to a doctor who talked to Hugo, and after that he was able to penetrate me. It did hurt, though, because he was too large for me."

I tried not to show my fear and repugnance, but it was no use.

"Don't be afraid. It is unusual; and even so, if he had known how to prepare a woman so that her juices made her ready, it would not have been so much a problem. But he had developed bad habits during the time that we both thought only of his pleasure."

"But that must have changed," I said shyly, "because I saw how much in love you are. I've never seen a married couple so much in love."

Her eyes shifted towards the entry hall but then returned to me. She touched my hand again, a sign that she was about to give me a piece of wisdom. "It is important that you choose the men in your life carefully so the father wound is not deepened. It's important that you choose as your first lover a man who is receptive and interested in your pleasure as well as his own, a man to whom you can tell what you want and what you don't want."

"But I don't really know if Jean-Jacques is . . ."

"I'm afraid I can't tell you how he is as a lover."

"No!" I blushed. "I wasn't going to ask that. I meant to say I don't know if he's really interested in me. I don't know anything about him, if he's married or has a girlfriend."

"He probably has one of each in France. He comes from a wealthy old Parisian family. But he's a black sheep because he's an artist of sorts. He puts on 'happenings' in Paris. Have you heard of them?"

I shook my head.

"Happenings are a kind of street theater but without a script. The actors are not actors, just people he randomly chooses. They improvise their lines and business the day he phones them and tells them a location where to meet."

She saw my smile and said, "You see? He's playful, and that's what you want in a lover."

We fell silent when Millie appeared on the balcony. She set down a sliced apple and some moldy cheese and announced that she was leaving for the day.

After we heard the front door close, Anaïs declared, "You must go to Europe, Tristine! Have an affair with Jean-Jacques, and then he can sponsor you to visit him in Paris. You will see how much more sophisticated Europeans are about marriage. Here people are not faithful and believe they must get a divorce. The family falls apart; everyone is hurt. In Europe the man and the woman each have other lovers and stay married."

"But that would hurt even more."

"They are discreet. They love each other so they protect each other."

"I don't think I could ever keep secrets from the person I marry."

The corners of her mouth curled indulgently, saying *you'll learn*, but I didn't want to. What was the point of being married, I thought, if you couldn't share everything about yourself with your husband and he with you?

Anaïs lit one of her gold-tipped Sobranies from the box sitting on the wrought iron table.

"So what will it be?" She exhaled. "Will you ask Jean-Jacques to be your lover or would you like me to ask him?"

"To be *your* lover?"

"No." She laughed. "You are naughty. I'll ask him to be your lover if you are too shy to do it yourself."

"I'm much too shy, but I don't know if I want you to—"

"Don't worry. He won't even know I've spoken with you. He'll believe it was his idea, and that I simply didn't discourage him."

"But where would we . . . ? Lenore is back at her loft, so we couldn't . . ."

"That's what hotels are for." She moved the untouched cheese to the fruit plate and used the empty saucer as an ashtray. "What will you wear? I always prepare for occasions by dressing the part."

"I don't know."

"You have to wear white. White lace like a First Communion dress but with a low neckline to show off your cleavage. We'll go shopping together! Red heels."

"I don't know if I can afford that. I'm starting college, and—"

"It will be my present. To honor your courage! The new woman!"

She was enjoying the anticipation of my deflowering more than I was, and I realized that I could not back out for fear of disappointing her.

I changed the subject. "I read your novels. They're mysterious and beautiful."

"Thank you, *Tchrristeenne*," she said, lengthening her embrace of my name.

I ventured, "I wondered if you put any of your diary in the novels."

"Yes, the diary is the hothouse from which I pick the most exotic flowers." She asked me, "Do you want to be a writer?"

"That or a famous actress. But I know I'm not pretty enough."

She stubbed out her cigarette. "My father used to tell me I was an ugly child," she said. "Is that what happened to you?"

"How did you know that?"

"I sense there are many affinities between us." She smiled on me.

I felt as adopted children must when, at last, they meet their real mother and are too full of jumbled emotions to speak.

Artfully, she refocused the conversation. "Which of the women characters in my novels did you identify with?"

The question took me by surprise. I hadn't thought about myself as any of the characters; they were all older than me. I wasn't like the adulterous adventuress Sabina, or like Djuna, her intuitive, wise friend. "Maybe I'm like Stella because she is an actress and fearful," I said. "Or maybe Lillian, because she is awkward and impetuous?"

Anaïs nodded.

I said, "I see you as Djuna because you are feminine and wise like her." She smiled. I just had to ask: "Where did the character of Sabina come from?"

Anaïs raised one arched eyebrow. "My four women characters are all parts of myself and of all women. I believe that all women have these characters in them: Sabina, the seductress; Djuna, our wisdom; Lillian, driven to action by anxiety; and Stella, the fearful, reclusive one."

"I don't have a Sabina."

"You don't have a seductress? Are you sure? I think you will realize that you do."

I thought about Sabina in *A Spy in the House of Love*, cheating on her husband. That would never be me.

Anaïs explained, "Think of Sabina as akin to the goddess Artemis, with her hounds and her bow and quiver of arrows chasing her prey. It's the love of the hunt."

Suddenly I had an inkling what Anaïs meant. When I was twelve, soon after my father left, my girlfriend and I had hunted the San Fernando Valley for guys to flirt with. For three Halloweens in a row, we dressed in the same black leotard cat costumes that revealed our pubertal curves, reveling in our power to ensnare the eyes of older boys and men as we sauntered through Encino Park at night.

We put on eye makeup and stuffed our bras and hunted for boys at movie matinees, bowling alleys, and miniature golf courses, thrilling to the game of pulling in guys like reeling in fish. It was the newness of the encounters, the rush of triumphant power, the intoxication of arousal when we made out with them, the giddiness of telling each other afterwards how the guy had tried to cop a feel.

I marveled that Anaïs had intuited I'd been a pubescent huntress, like Sabina searching for new encounters and untried caresses, when

I'd forgotten it until just then. The nuns in high school had succeeded in making me demure, but now the wild thrill of those hot summer nights and the unthinking pleasure of kissing strangers in the air-conditioned La Reina theater came back to me and mingled with the recent charge I'd experienced when I'd felt Jean-Jacques's penis. Yet I could not have articulated any of this and instead said to Anaïs, "Well, I know I don't have a Djuna."

"You'll discover your Djuna, your inner wisdom, in time too," she assured me with her calm, perceptive Djuna smile.

I stared at her in wonder. We had gone past ordinary speech to a kind of female code language she'd invented.

"Which of my novels did you like best?" she asked.

"*A Spy in the House of Love*, because I could follow Sabina's story. In the other books I couldn't follow a plot . . ."

I saw anger flash across her face. She said bitterly, "You have the American obsession with plot. You know nothing about accepting the writer's *donnée*."

"What is that?"

"*Donnée, Donnée!* The given. What the writer sets out to do in the work."

Although I am not usually good about adjusting my words to the sensitivities of others, I knew in that moment that Anaïs could not take criticism of her work, and that I could never, ever say anything negative about it. I pleaded, "I want to understand. I'm going to reread the books. The language is so beautiful, they are like poetry. You can't get it on first reading."

She seemed placated, so I asked, "What is your *donnée*?"

"I am writing about the interior life, not the surface world of events and politics. The four women are playing out a kind of emotional algebra."

"Algebra wasn't my best subject," I said still trying to smooth things over.

"No, mine neither." She shrugged. "I didn't finish high school. I'm self-educated." This surprised me; she was so polished and literate, things I associated with higher education.

She continued, "You just need to feel what corresponds inside yourself to the women in my novels. They're meant to help you read your own inner world. There are plenty of other writers who will tell you about the outside world."

"I'm going to read them again that way."

"But first you need to prepare yourself for your encounter with Jean-Jacques. You should read D. H. Lawrence. He's the only male writer who understands women's sexuality. Colette would be perfect for you, if she's translated into English."

"I will, but I only have two more weeks in New York."

"Oh. I thought you were living with Lenore."

"Only for this summer. I'm supposed to go home to Los Angeles for college."

"You aren't moving to New York for college?"

I wanted to ask her to help me stay. Seeing Paris would be nice, but it would be better if Jean-Jacques sponsored me in New York, near her. "My scholarship is only good in California, but if we could figure out a way for me to stay here . . ."

She didn't respond. Afraid I'd been too presumptuous, I backtracked. "Anyway, I can come back to visit Lenore. And I could see you when you come to Los Angeles."

She snapped, "How do you know I'll be in Los Angeles?"

I had stepped onto a minefield, but there was no way out. "When Caresse said you go to LA."

"On business, and I'm very busy when I'm there." I saw the nervous movement she'd used to describe Sabina, covering her mouth with her hand as if holding back something. Then she lowered her hand and stood up, erect, poised. "I'm sorry, I'm going to be late for a meeting with Gore." That was what she had said when she'd shooed me out the door the last time. I had no choice but to follow her to the elevator.

"Shall I call you to see if you have spoken with Jean-Jacques?"

"If there's time." Her enthusiasm for putting us together had vanished.

I could hear the supplication in my voice when I said, "I'm going to read your novels again with your *donnée*."

"That's fine." Her lips curved in a smile, but its power of eternal reassurance was gone.

She pressed the elevator button and instead of the hug for which I yearned, she air-kissed me on both cheeks. I stepped inside and watched her rush away before the elevator doors shut. The cage plunged to street level and jolted with a kick.

# CHAPTER 4

# Los Angeles, California, 1964

I NEVER HEARD FROM JEAN-JACQUES or Anaïs. Although I wrote to her from LA, she sent back only a violet card announcing the French publication of her novel *Ladders to Fire*. Her world was now as inaccessible to me as Camelot. I dutifully embraced college life at USC, supplementing my scholarship with a waitressing job and joining a sorority that pledged me for my grades. I dated frat boys, drank beer from kegs at street parties, and had my hair frosted blond. In high school, I had pursued stage acting; in college, I gave up the theater to disappear behind the role of uncomplicated coed.

Despite scoring the pill from student health, I was still a virgin at twenty, thanks to the ineptitude of the business majors, ROTC plebs, and frat boys at USC—and my own fears, which had returned as if the night with Jean-Jacques had never happened.

However, the summer before my junior year, I wrangled a scholarship to study at Cambridge, England for a month, and given the affordability of Europe then at five dollars a day, I extended my stay to a three-month European tour, on which I was determined to find, as Anaïs had recommended, a European man to deflower me.

When I saw the desk clerk who checked me in at the student hostel in Rome, I recalled Michelangelo's *David*, which I'd stared at in Florence. If that was what a naked Italian man looked like, I'd thought, I was in the right country. To my everlasting good fortune, that's what Gerardo Palmieri looked like.

An hour after he had assigned me a tiny room in the hostel, Gerardo knocked on its door. Would I like to have dinner with him when he got off work?

I was certain of my intentions and, having taken note how fast the European girls moved if they were interested in a man, I said, the words igniting sparklers in my mouth, "Yes, and I'd like you to make love to me after."

Gerardo recoiled for a moment, and instantly I regretted my bravado. But after a beat, he returned to the lyric pace of his practiced seduction. "I have a very special *ristorante* in mind. It is in the countryside."

After numerous courses and tiramisu, we lingered in the cafe's courtyard, and I began to think he'd forgotten my request. Finally, Gerardo said, "Would you like to see my friend's place in the mountains?"

The gears of his little Fiat strained as we spiraled up the dark road. Halfway up the mountain that seemed to get higher with every round, I said, "I'm a virgin." He didn't say anything, just downshifted the straining gears.

I expected after such a long drive we would reach a villa with a romantic view. So when he let us into the modest single apartment, I asked, "Where's the view?" For the first time he appeared not to understand my English. What I did not understand was how difficult it was for a young man in those years to find a place for a rendezvous. He'd had to persuade the rare friend who didn't live at home and didn't have a roommate to vacate his precious apartment for us.

It may not have had a view, but the tiny apartment was prepared for romance in every other way: a stereo, soft lighting, and a single bed in an alcove.

Later, when Gerardo saw blood on the sheets, he said he hadn't believed me when I'd claimed to be a virgin. Yet he could not have been more sensitive and gentle if he had. Even as he was kissing, touching, and preparing me, I mentally thanked Anaïs for her advice to choose a European man. Unlike the many women for whom the first time is disappointing, I triumphantly had an orgasm with Gerardo sometime before dawn.

"Now I want you to teach me everything," I told him. We began immediately, and in that glorious month, we made love at the beach with sand scratching our thighs, in his boxy Fiat, in my room in the hostel during siesta, and in courtyard apartments we had to vacate hurriedly at a specified hour.

When my plane descended home, the Los Angeles basin looked unbearably flat and suffocating. Before I unfastened my seat belt, I had decided that I was going to become a college professor so that I'd have summers off and could go back to Italy for three months every year. My European trip had changed me. I'd learned about the US involvement in Vietnam, acquired a sympathy for socialism, and developed, as Anaïs had predicted, my own seductive Sabina persona. She descended the ramp with me at LAX, ready to take advantage of the "free love" ethos wending its way down the coast from San Francisco.

My new sexual confidence and the new sexual freedom in the air worked handily with my new goal of becoming a professor. Since I would now have to spend inordinate hours cracking the books, I could no longer waste time with casual dating. If I met a guy I was attracted to, I intended to have sex with him right away to see if we were compatible, and then I could get right back to studying.

No longer able to tolerate the restrictions of sorority life, I moved off Frat Row into my own apartment. Actually I moved considerably off campus, because the further one ventured into the surrounding ghetto, the cheaper the rent.

My plans for devoted studying immediately went awry, though. I was just settling in for a full night of cramming for a morning essay test when a former sorority sister phoned to remind me that I'd agreed to a blind date she'd set up for that night. Despite my pleading, she would not let me out of it.

When Harry Browne arrived at my apartment, my heart sank. He was old, at least thirty, with too short a haircut, and wearing a boxy business suit.

He announced, "I made reservations for us at a restaurant in Malibu. The Holiday House."

Damn! It would take an hour and a half to drive to Malibu, three hours round trip. It would be midnight before we got back and I could start reading Cliff's Notes on *The Faerie Queene*. My mood lifted, though, when we pulled into the parking lot and I heard the crashing surf, saw the glassed-in restaurant that hung over the Pacific in a graceful arc, and smelled butter and garlic infusing the salt air.

When we entered, a brunette, chignoned hostess introduced herself as Renate Druks. Learning that this was our first time at Holiday House, she began her routine: "Our beautiful modernist building was designed by Richard Neutra in 1950—"

"Is your accent German?" I asked, wanting to show off my travel experience.

"Viennese," she responded haughtily.

As Renate guided Harry and me toward our window table, we passed by a glass-walled room where a private party was being held. I caught a glimpse of a woman who had Anaïs Nin's petite figure, arched brows, and heart-shaped face. I heard that high, silent ring that accompanies coincidences we sense are fate, and I determined somehow to find out if the woman really was Anaïs.

As Harry and I sat with leather menus in our hands, the October sun warmed the floor-to-ceiling windows and turned the ocean carnival hues. I noted that Harry was broad-shouldered and attractive, despite his parrot-like overbite.

He held forth about a book he'd just written: "It explains Libertarian economics in a way people can understand."

I looked past him through the glass wall to the stylishly bohemian group enjoying their private party. They were bending in laughter like willows in the wind, reveling in the unfettered life I wanted, while I was worrying about an essay test and half listening to what Harry was saying. "In the next book I'm going to apply my Libertarian philosophy to the topic of sex."

That regained my attention. I imagined a nation of self-pleasuring Libertarians who didn't believe that sex should be shared.

Harry shook the ice cubes in his second scotch and leaned in towards me. "There's this myth that couples are supposed to have simultaneous orgasms. But my research shows it almost never happens."

"What research? Just your own?" I asked.

"No, I've talked to men and women, married and single, and all these people told me that they feel like failures at sex because they don't have simultaneous orgasms. But the truth is almost nobody does."

"That hasn't been my experience," I said. "Did you talk to anyone besides Libertarians?"

Beyond the translucent wall, hors d'oeuvres were being served. A waiter held out a tray to the woman with Anaïs's elegant carriage. Something she said to the waiter made him smile broadly and stand more erect.

I excused myself from Harry for the restroom. On my way back, I stopped at the door to the private party, hearing the unmistakable jingle and cymbal song of Anaïs's accented voice: "I don't accept that your so-called objectivity is more true than my subjectivity."

I slipped inside the door and was about to approach her when the middle-aged hostess Renate stepped in front of me. "Excuse. This is a private party."

"I just want to say hello to Anaïs Nin."

"And who are you?" Renate glared at me through impossibly long eyelashes. I told her my name, and she crossed her arms. "I've never heard of you, and I am Anaïs Nin's best friend."

"We met in New York," I said as I dashed toward Anaïs.

Renate, wearing three-inch heels, got there before me and announced, "Anaïs, you have a fan who wants to say hello, Tristine Rainer."

"I met you and Hugo in New York," I reminded Anaïs.

She shot a frightened look at Renate so I added, "We all went to Harlem, and Hugo—"

"Tristine!" Anaïs broke from a young man with his arm around her. With his chiseled nose and even smile, he was handsome as a TV soap star. She quickly enclosed me in a hug, whispering in my ear, "You will keep my secret, won't you?"

"Yes," I responded, though I wasn't sure what it was.

But when she returned to the side of the young man and nuzzled into him, I guessed that the secret was that they were having an affair. He must be "the other one." I was impressed how much younger he was than Anaïs. His golden skin shone, and he had sun streaks in his brown hair. His short-sleeved shirt revealed shapely biceps and triceps. With the eagerness of a cocker spaniel, he gave me a firm handshake, and in a full-bodied voice, said, "I'm Rupert Pole, Anaïs's husband."

I started to giggle, thinking he was joking; his chiseled good looks made him almost cartoonish. Immediately, I noticed that no one else in the group had registered amusement.

Anaïs said to the others, "We went dancing one night, Tristine and Caresse Crosby and my book illustrator Ian Hugo." Then she said to me, "Aren't you attending that college in Westwood?"

"No, I'm downtown at USC."

A lot of people confused UCLA with USC because both universities were in LA, but I was surprised Anaïs didn't remember it was her husband Hugo Guiler who took us dancing, not Ian Hugo.

"I'll probably go to UCLA for grad school," I offered.

"And what will be your major?" asked a square-jawed man in his early sixties standing on the other side of Anaïs.

"English lit," I answered and told Anaïs, "I've been hoping to see one of your books on a syllabus, but the only woman writer I ever see is Emily Dickinson."

"Who's afraid of Virginia Woolf?" the man quipped in his high-pitched, British-inflected voice.

"Have you met Christopher Isherwood?" Anaïs introduced the famous author, who bowed his head and put his hands together like a yogi.

In reverence, I gasped. "I read your *Berlin Stories* in my Twentieth Century Lit class! I loved the structure of separate short stories that together made up the novel."

"Very insightful. Thank you." His hand moved to the shoulder of an adorable mouse-faced boy standing close to him. "This is Don Bachardy." Even though Don was at least thirty years his junior, I could tell by the way Isherwood hugged him that they were a couple.

Don's grin revealed a gap between his front teeth. He asked me, "What year are you in college?"

I told him I was a junior as Renate pulled on my elbow. She said, "I think your good-looking date is getting worried about you." The others followed her gaze through the glass wall to Harry Browne brushing wrinkles out of his suit as he rose from his chair.

I wished I could stay and become a part of their group but reluctantly I let Renate guide me back to Harry. Before we reached him, I whispered, "Anaïs asked me to keep her secret, but I'm not sure what it is."

Renate hissed back, "She thinks you know."

"I guess she got a divorce, but why—"

"Don't speculate. Call me here tomorrow," she whispered, before pulling out my chair opposite Harry.

∞

Later that night, Harry Browne discovered simultaneous orgasm. Although it disproved his Libertarian theory of sex for his next book, it made him obsessed with me. He just couldn't believe that I wanted him to leave after it, but I had to get up to study for my test. He started phoning me the next morning, wanting to see me that evening, and when I said no, he wanted to take me to the Hotel del Coronado the following weekend. I had no interest in ever seeing him again.

I felt victorious for having disproved his Libertarian theory of sex but also chilled at how impersonal the experience had been for me. It bothered me that I'd wielded my acquired ease with seduction as a weapon, leaving him wounded and me indifferent. Anaïs was the only person I knew who would understand the cold satisfaction I'd felt, for it was what she had described in her character of Sabina. I needed to talk with Anaïs again, but first I'd have to get past Renate, her gatekeeper.

∞

Right after my essay test, I phoned Renate and arranged to meet her at Holiday House the following afternoon. When I arrived, she offered me a drink, compliments of the house. I asked for plain tonic water.

Renate took a seat and sipped the iced tea she had brought for herself. "Keeping secrets is something one gets used to, working here." She blinked her impossibly long lashes. "Movie stars have their rendezvous in the motel rooms below the restaurant, so if you see any celebrities you must keep it mum. We offer them discretion."

I nodded, hoping I might see Robert Mitchum or Natalie Wood.

"Actually, that would be a good test," Renate added, "to see if you can be trusted."

"You mean with Anaïs's secret?" I said.

"Do you know what it is?" Renate asked, and I shook my head. I noticed she didn't answer my question. She just wanted answers to her own. "Did you ever run into a student named Peter Loomer at UCLA?"

"I don't go to UCLA," I reminded her. "I might go there for grad school."

"Please accept my apology for forgetting. And pardon me for asking, why you would want to go to UCLA for grad school?" She frowned. "They didn't know what to do with Peter in that big, impersonal place."

"Who is Peter?"

"My son. He's living at home now." She sighed. "He's such a sensitive, artistic boy. Anaïs illustrated her novel *Solar Barque* with pictures Peter drew when he was just seven. Have you seen it?"

"No, but I've read her other novels. Most of them had illustrations by Ian Hugo. That's one of the things I'm confused about. Why did Anaïs say she and I went dancing with Ian Hugo? I've never even met him. It was her ex-husband Hugo Guiler who took us to Harlem."

"You don't know anything, do you?" Renate peered out the window, then turned her attention back to me. "Do you know who Ronnie Knox is?"

"No."

"He was a star quarterback at UCLA. He played professionally for the Rams."

"I don't follow football."

"Yes, it's boring and violent." She examined her buffed fingernails. "I wouldn't know who Ronnie Knox is, either, except that he's my husband. How old are you?"

"Twenty."

"Ronnie is only nine years older than you."

Renate had to be near Anaïs's age, almost sixty, I guessed. She and Anaïs and Christopher Isherwood seemed to be in some sort of cabal where everyone had much younger partners.

"Ronnie's father is his sports manager," Renate continued. "If the old man ever found out that Ronnie married a bohemian twice his age, he'd kill him. Also, Ronnie is bound by product endorsement contracts that require him to remain a heartthrob bachelor. So it's paramount we keep our marriage secret."

"I understand," I said, but I wondered why we were talking about her young husband or her son.

"As for me"—Renate looked at me deadpan—"I'd be ashamed if my bohemian friends found out I married a famous footballer."

I laughed. She smiled, pleased that I'd gotten her humor. She lowered her black lashes, and I could see they were definitely fake as she continued. "Some people live in two different worlds that have to be kept separate and secret." I noticed how skillfully she'd applied her eyeliner to disguise the glue line and extend the wings. "Haven't you at some point had to keep one side of your life hidden from the other?" She raised her artificial lashes, her piercing blue eyes holding mine.

I considered. "I keep secrets from my mother."

"For instance?"

"That I take the pill."

"Why can't you tell her?"

"She'd know I'm not a virgin anymore."

"Well, that's ridiculous. You're an adult woman."

"I know, but if I told her I'd have to deal with her hysteria and worry. It's better for her and for me not to say anything about it."

"So you are protecting yourself and her?"

"Yes."

"It's not so different from Ronnie and me, needing to protect ourselves from others' foolish judgments," she said. "And not so different from Hugo Guiler and Ian Hugo."

"I don't understand."

"Hugo had to protect his bosses and himself."

"Which one? Hugo Guiler or Ian Hugo?"

"They're the same man. When Hugo Guiler decided to become an engraver he invented the pseudonym Ian Hugo so the other artists would think that he was a struggling artist, too, and take him seriously."

I understood having to pretend you were like other artists so they would accept you. "Oh, now something makes sense!" I remembered my inkling that Anaïs had a very close relationship with the engraver of her books. "When I saw Ian Hugo's engravings, they fit Anaïs's writing so well I imagined he might be her lover. And he was, as her husband, I mean, before she married Rupert."

"Not exactly." The way Renate smiled I could see how much she enjoyed being in the know. "When Hugo was Ian, the artist, he and Anaïs pretended they were *not* married. That way Anaïs could promote Ian Hugo's artistic work without it appearing to be self-serving."

They had certainly succeeded in fooling my godmother. I couldn't wait to tell Lenore that her artist friend Ian Hugo was actually Anaïs's wealthy husband.

I felt Renate watching me, as if she could read my thoughts. I puzzled out loud, "I still don't understand, though, why Anaïs said it was Ian Hugo who went dancing with us."

"Perhaps she didn't want you talking about Hugo Guiler in front of Rupert."

"But if they're divorced . . . Is Rupert jealous?"

"Why do you think Rupert should be jealous?" Renate again answered my question with one of her own.

"Maybe because Hugo is so elegant and sophisticated and Rupert seems, I don't know, bland?"

Renate suppressed a smile. "Don't let Anaïs hear you say that."

"Oh, believe me, I wouldn't." I was still confused, though. "If Ian Hugo and Hugo Guiler are the same person, Rupert would be equally jealous hearing either name."

"Perhaps Rupert doesn't know that Hugo Guiler and Ian Hugo are the same person. Perhaps Anaïs wants to be free to talk about Ian Hugo, her book illustrator, without it bothering Rupert."

"Oh, I see." I thought that Anaïs's new husband must be a very insecure man.

Renate said, "May I ask you another question?"

I nodded.

"Do you think that because Hugo uses two names or Ronnie and I have a secret marriage it makes us liars?"

Actually I did, but I knew that wasn't the answer she was looking for, so I said, "Not necessarily. The rules of the worlds we live in can prevent us from openly being ourselves."

"Exactly." Renate nodded.

It seemed my answer had gained her approval, so I seized the moment. "Anaïs once promised me we would be friends. I want her to know she can trust me."

"Well maybe we can all be friends. It depends."

"On what?"

Renate didn't respond. She stared out the window at the ocean. "Look, there's a cormorant." She pointed. "Maybe I'll paint you with a cormorant."

"You're a painter! I'd love to see your paintings."

"You can. I specialize in portraits of people alongside their animal spirit."

"And I remind you of a cormorant?"

"Always fishing." It sounded like a reprimand. As Renate studied me, I tried not to look fishy. Finally she said, "Maybe you will be able to do a service for Anaïs."

"A service? I would. I would love to."

"Depending on how well you can be trusted," she said, watching something behind me. "Now you know quite a few secrets. Let's see how well you keep them."

"I will," I promised. "I won't mention anything to anyone about you being married to a famous football player. Or that Ian Hugo is Hugo Guiler." Damn, now I couldn't tell my godmother.

"Or what goes on at Holiday House." Renate nodded in the direction behind me. "Be discreet when you turn around."

"I'll go to the ladies' room." As I rose and turned, I saw a man seated two tables away who looked so much like Frank Sinatra it had to be him! He was clasping hands with a blond woman who had her back to me.

When I returned from the bathroom, they had left—probably to use one of the apartments below. I saw that Renate was on the phone at the hostess's desk. I'd been trying to think who she reminded me of, and now it dawned on me: it was Vampira, the local TV emcee of midnight horror films. Renate had the same long black hair and witchy beauty.

As I approached, she put down the receiver. "You're invited to my house to see my paintings Wednesday next."

# CHAPTER 5

# Malibu, California, 1964

AS MY BUICK BUMPED ALONG the dirt road on the east side of Pacific Coast Highway, I understood how Renate could afford to live in Malibu on a hostess's salary. There were no ocean views on this side. Her house sat in the gloom on a barren, undeveloped expanse of scrubby chaparral and tilted telephone poles.

The carport under Renate's characterless stucco was empty. Had she forgotten our appointment? I parked in the carport and walked around the house to find an entry door. I saw a faded red Volkswagen parked at the rear of the house but could find no entry other than the one under the carport, so I knocked on it.

Renate welcomed me and proudly showed me around. This was all hers, paid for with her wages. "My ex-husband was a doctor, but when I left him, all I took was my son and my freedom."

Everything in her house looked as if it had been crafted by a class of third graders told to finish their projects before the bell rang. The spiral ladder leading to a sleeping loft seemed so narrow only a monkey could climb it. The huge velvet pillows that substituted for a couch had been basted with thick white thread that had never been removed. Renate's unfinished canvases balanced on off-kilter, homemade easels.

"It must have been difficult being a single mother," I said, thinking of my mother.

"No, I prefer to be my own boss."

"I mean money-wise."

"People always think that. But that's because they aren't artists. The secret to being an artist is to know how to live well without money."

"How?" This was something I really wanted to know.

"With creativity! Plus, I don't covet all those bourgeois possessions people hold so dear."

"I know! My mother can't let go of any possessions, and as a result, I don't seem to want anything. Material, I mean."

Renate's smile was warm even though she didn't show her teeth. "I knew you were copacetic."

One of her paintings on the wall caught my attention. A naked woman, whose long black hair fell to her lovely bare behind, faced a smaller mirror image of herself walking out of a shadowy mountain pass. A raven perched at the naked woman's foot.

"That's my friend Raven," Renate said. "She loved Edgar Allen Poe, so she purchased a pet raven in his honor."

"So that's her raven?"

"Oh, yes. The two of them bonded so deeply that she had her name legally changed to Raven. When her lovers would visit, the bird would screech and peck at them in a jealous rage."

"Did she get rid of the bird?"

"No, she stopped having her lovers over." Renate had the timing of a vaudeville comedian. I laughed, recognizing that I needed to respond to her humor to keep her approval. "My friend," she continued, "then slept over at her lovers' houses, but the bird fell sick with depression and wouldn't eat. So now she doesn't go anywhere, just stays buried at home with the raven."

"It really is an Edgar Allen Poe story!"

"Yes, that's what Anaïs said. Raven is part of our circle." The circle I wanted to be part of.

"Are all the women in these paintings in your circle?" I looked around at the paintings of women in various degrees of undress, each posed with her animal spirit.

"My circle with Anaïs? No. Most of them haven't even met Anaïs." Renate watched my reaction to her work. "Take your time."

I took more time than I really needed to look at the highly saturated, acrylic paintings that recalled Salvador Dali's *trompe-l'oeil* dreamscapes.

"It's the kind of painting nobody does anymore," Renate said, sighing. It was true; her surrealist style was dated and out of sync with the pop and op art of the day. Her paintings, like Anaïs's novels, embodied a European prewar fascination with the subconscious, while Warhol's soup cans and Vasarely's optics were reflecting our surface, modern realities.

I looked at Renate's skillfully executed but somehow naive paintings: a slender woman lying alongside a panther, a woman with blue skin floating on a swan's spread wing, a woman with the same eyes as her Siamese cat, a naked woman sitting lotus in a field, feeding grapes to a little goat.

I recognized Anaïs in a small, framed painting in metallic gold tones. At her feet, two fish swam in opposite directions as in the sign of Pisces. Anaïs was elevated in a recessed alcove like a saint, her body wrapped in a long, continuous strip of paper that bound her legs like a mermaid's tail, or a mummy.

"Why did you paint Anaïs constrained like that?" I asked. "I think of her as such a free person."

Ignoring my question, Renate ducked into her cramped kitchen. I wondered if the painting of Anaïs tightly bound had to do with her new husband's possessiveness. I wanted to ask Renate why Anaïs had married Rupert Pole. Admittedly he was handsome, but he struck me as the male version of a pin-up. I could not understand why she would have given up Hugo for him, especially now that I knew Hugo was an artist as well as a businessman. But I didn't ask why because of what Renate had said about my companion spirit being a cormorant—always fishing. I wouldn't want to be painted next to a cormorant because its big beak would bring attention to my aquiline nose, about which I was self-conscious.

Renate served us green salad with marinated artichokes on Mexican tin plates that she set on a table made from a wooden door. I picked at the darkened, soggy leaves.

She stabbed a baby artichoke with her fork and waved it like a metronome. "The little service that I have in mind for you involves receiving a few phone calls and handling a small amount of mail for Anaïs. Do you think that is something you might like to do?"

"Sure," I said. "Last month there was an ad on the English Department bulletin board looking for an author's assistant. I really wanted the position, but it was filled when I called. Assisting Anaïs Nin would be a great opportunity."

Renate took a bite of the artichoke and said, "I presume you want to be an author."

"I think so," I said, though now that I was majoring in English literature and had read the immortal authors, I realized I couldn't compete.

"You would like to be an author's apprentice?" Renate smiled.

"That would be great."

"Apprentices do services for their mentors."

"Of course."

"I'm afraid to say it would not pay. But it would give you an association with a mentor."

*Mentor.* The word beckoned like blazing Sirius in the night sky. I wanted to be Sirius B, the cool, circling companion of that scorching star. It was a word that belonged to the guys, who referred to a special male professor as "my mentor." I was thrilled to hear the word applied to Anaïs. Her charisma had captured me the first time I'd met her, inspiring a conviction, however unfounded, that she was my destiny. Anaïs as my mentor? What did I care about money?

"I don't need to be paid."

Renate nodded in approval. "Ordinarily, as Anaïs's best friend, I would not give such an important responsibility to anyone else. I would continue to do it myself. But there are complications since I married Ronnie and my son moved home." Renate eyed my plate. "You've hardly eaten anything. Don't you like it?"

"It's good." I fibbed to be polite. "I ate too big a breakfast."

Renate gave me a stern, all-knowing look, but also a nod to credit my manners. With her aristocratic bearing, she carried her empty plate and my full one into the kitchen. "There's a photo of my husband Ronnie on the shelf behind you," she called out.

I located the framed black and white picture of a kneeling football player holding his helmet and smiling at the camera. Renate and Anaïs were marvels, I thought, both of them married to gorgeous, younger men.

"Where is Ronnie? Will I meet him?"

"No, he's at the apartment he still keeps in Santa Monica so his father won't suspect he's living with me." She returned with mints from the restaurant for us. "Ronnie goes there to try to write. He wants to be an author, too, but he keeps rewriting the same page over and over. His perfectionism is driving him crazy."

"I do that," I admitted.

Renate put out a palm for the cellophane from my mint just as a car screeched to a halt outside. Through the living room window overlooking the carport, I watched Anaïs emerge from a powder blue Thunderbird. She removed the kerchief tied under her chin and tousled her permed bob.

"You invited Anaïs!" I cried, delighted as a six-year-old at seeing Snow White coming up the steps.

"Your enthusiasm is charming." Renate smiled.

Anaïs swept through the door, her black cape flapping behind her like the wings of a great crow. I recalled her statement about always dressing the part for an occasion and wondered if she'd conceived this as some sort of clandestine, cloak-and-dagger meeting.

"I had the most terrible drive here," she announced. "I got so entranced by the sight of the ocean that I went through a red light. The other cars honked and an awful man in a pickup truck followed me to the turn-off, yelling at me."

"Here's pure water to relax you." Renate poured a glass from the tap and handed it to Anaïs. "Sip it slowly."

Anaïs perched herself on a stack of large pillows. She released the clasp on her cape and it fell in graceful folds so she appeared to be sitting on a draped pedestal. As Anaïs dutifully followed Renate's instructions to take five little sips of water, Renate said, "Tristine told me that she would be thrilled to help you with some phone and mail issues. My intuition tells me she's trustworthy, but you need to talk with her yourself to see how you feel."

I grinned at Renate. She was trying to help me get the apprentice position.

After Renate offered Anaïs something to eat and Anaïs refused, Renate picked up her imitation crocodile purse and headed for the door. "Ronnie and Peter won't be back until dinner time, so you two should be undisturbed. I have an appointment with my lawyer." Renate explained that because her contractor had built her house with its only view through the carport, she'd stopped paying him, and he was suing her. After she left, we heard the gears of her Volkswagen as she pulled out.

Anaïs and I sat in awkward silence. Finally, Anaïs said, "Renate likes you very much."

"I like her, too." Why couldn't I think of anything more interesting to say?

Anaïs gave me her reassuring smile. "We have so much catching up to do. I remember you wrote to me that you had an Italian boyfriend. What happened with him?" I hadn't known she'd received my letters about Gerardo Palmieri, because she hadn't replied.

"After I got back to LA and had almost forgotten him, he unexpectedly wrote me saying we should marry, and I should ask my father to sponsor him so he could become a lawyer here."

"Do you see your father now?"

"Occasionally. We aren't close."

"Did you ask him to sponsor Gerardo?"

"Yeah. He just guffawed."

"That was rude of him!"

I shrugged. "When I wrote back to Gerardo, he stopped writing me."

"He wasn't the right one." She squeezed my hand gently. I recalled how safe and cared about she could make me feel.

"Is your father still married to the big buxom blonde?"

"You remembered! They got divorced," I said with satisfaction. She asked about my mother and siblings and my lovers after Gerardo, in this way drawing me out, talking with me like a girlfriend, with no sense that she was more than forty years older than me or that it had been two years since we'd last talked. It was as if we were just picking up where we'd left off, even though we were in a different city, she had a new husband, and I was no longer a virgin.

As I brought her up to date on my life, it seemed transformed by her interest. Through her vision I became a young heroine in an exciting drama with sad and funny parts and the promise of great adventure and romance ahead.

"And what about that man I saw you with at Holiday House?" she asked merrily.

"Ugh, I'm getting worried about myself. You told me I'd develop a Sabina, and you were right. In *A Spy in the House of Love* you wrote that Sabina achieved man's detachment from sex. She could take pleasure without needing love, and afterwards she just wanted to leave, to get away. That's how I am now."

"Don't worry. Your Sabina may be dominant presently, but she is only one part of you. You have a wise, clairvoyant self to advise you. You have a Djuna."

I recalled the character of Djuna in Anaïs's novels, the calm, centered one who reminded me of Anaïs herself. "I still don't have a Djuna," I said.

"She may not have fully emerged yet, but she's there. Are you still writing a diary?"

"No, I stopped."

"Oh no, why?"

"I don't have time. My studies. And, I don't know, I don't like to look at my writing."

"You are being too hard on yourself. The imperfections in a diary are part of the form. It's a human document, full of stutterings. I hope you begin again."

"I will." All the learning I'd crammed into my head in college had touched only my intellect. No one spoke to my emotional and inner life as she did.

She said, "When I was your age, I longed for a woman writer to be my friend and guide." Her melodic voice quivered with sadness. "I wrote to Djuna Barnes because I loved the novel she wrote, *Nightwood*."

"Did she write you back?"

"No, she snubbed me."

I wondered if Anaïs realized that I'd felt snubbed when she'd broken off communication with me, but instead I asked, "Is Djuna Barnes's name where you got the name for your character?"

"No! My character is entirely different from Djuna Barnes, but I heard she complained that I used her first name. She also complained that I wear capes as she does. But that's in tribute! In Paris, I admired her so much. I wanted to be part of her lesbian clique, but she rejected me."

Her face looked stricken, but then she straightened her spine and appeared to throw off the rejection, announcing with a professional air, "Djuna Barnes is a wonderful, mysterious writer. You should have her on your personal reading list. I can give you the names of many neglected women writers. I'll type them up for you, and we can talk about them."

"Thank you!" I was delighted she'd begun to mentor me.

We then fell into silence. I was uncomfortable, wanting to fill the space; but she, it seemed, was perfectly at ease, withdrawing into her private thoughts.

After many moments she gave me a Mona Lisa smile and said, "I have to go to New York on business. I wonder if you might write a letter and mail it for me when I go."

"Sure." I whipped out a steno book I'd packed in my bag, ready to take her dictation with the shorthand the nuns had insisted I learn.

Her thin brows furled unevenly, one pinched in while the other lifted, and she added, "The letter should be addressed to me and it should begin formally: 'Dear Anaïs Nin.'"

"Okay." I assumed there was a reason why she was dictating a letter addressed to herself. "What address?"

"Could you get some stationery from your university?"

"Maybe. I could ask the secretary in the English department office."

"Perfect. Why don't we meet here again on Thursday when you have the stationery and I'll dictate the letter then."

"Don't you have your own stationery?"

"Of course, but this requires something else. But if you can't get it . . ." She seemed terribly disappointed. I couldn't risk being cut off because of her displeasure again.

"I want to help you! I just need to understand," I blurted. "I know I must have said or done the wrong thing at your apartment in New York. I really wanted to see you again and you said you were going to take me shopping and put me together with Jean-Jacques, and I still don't know what I did wrong, but I'm afraid I'll mess up again and somehow ruin your secret because I don't know what it is."

"I'm so sorry, Tristine. You didn't do anything wrong in New York. I was just afraid. When you said you wanted to see me in Los Angeles …" She sighed. "My life is so complicated between the coasts."

"Was it Rupert? Were you already having an affair with Rupert?" I couldn't help myself now. "Renate told me he's jealous and that's why you said that Ian Hugo took us to Harlem instead of—"

"That's true." She averted her eyes.

"I want to be your apprentice." I sat upright to look professional. "I'll get the stationery. Whatever you want me to do. You can trust me, Anaïs. I want to help you!"

My declaration captured her attention, and she contemplated me. She held my gaze for a long time, during which it seemed we had been staring into each other's eyes since the beginning of time, connected in an ancient bond of women's sympathy for one another.

Her eyes dropped to her pale, veined hands clenched in her lap. "I'm afraid I will shock you, so I have to think how to explain. I don't know where to begin." She looked at me again, her face now distressed. "This is all so complicated. I don't know how to trust you not to … Even I—" She stopped, helpless with anxiety. She turned her face away, and I saw her sad Pierrot clown face that I recalled from the limo ride to Harlem.

I wanted desperately for her to confide in me, and my desire made me uncharacteristically expressive. "I think secrets are like big hairy apes." I could see I'd gained her attention. "You have to spend all your time guarding them so they don't get out."

"Yes! Because if the ape gets out," she said, "it will be horribly destructive."

I touched her icy hand. "But if you share the secret with someone you can trust, you don't have to guard it all alone."

A surprised smile lifted the corners of her mouth and lingered as she studied me. "Perhaps we have been reacquainted to help each other." She inhaled deeply and began, "Remember I confided in you that Hugo and I had not been sexually compatible?"

"Because you were both inexperienced when you married."

She nodded. "Our lovemaking never really got much better, though we loved each other and tried. It was a terrible thing because I was so happy with him in every other way."

"I could see you were in love. He was devoted to you."

"Devoted, yes, but from the time I was a girl I dreamt of a marriage of passion as well as devotion. Don't you want that, too?"

"Yes . . . I don't expect to find it, though."

"Oh, Tristine, you can't give up hope so young! I never gave up expecting both passion and devotion. And because with Hugo I had only devotion, I was always looking elsewhere for the passion."

I realized she was telling me that she'd had affairs while married to Hugo; it must have been what led to their divorce. So my inkling when I read *A Spy in the House of Love* was correct: Sabina's sexual adventures were autobiographical; the cuckolded Alan was Hugo. I asked, "So were you Sabina then?"

"Yes. In her desperate way, Sabina is hunting for the great passion that can subdue and defeat her."

So that was it! That was why, though I longed for one true passion, I behaved like Sabina, who seduced and discarded men for her own amusement.

Seemingly out of context, Anaïs asked, "Do you know who Gore Vidal is?"

I recalled she had twice dropped his name when she'd shooed me out of her apartment in New York. Was that what she was afraid to tell? She'd been having an affair with Gore Vidal?

I said, "I know that he's a famous writer, but I've never read anything by him."

"He's best known for *The City and the Pillar*, published when he was only nineteen. By that age, he'd already published two other novels."

A cramp contracted my ribs. I was already twenty-one and hadn't published anything. Actually, I hadn't even written anything other than some short stories and term papers.

"Gore was an *enfant terrible*." Anaïs's smile twisted. "I met him in 1946. He was only seventeen then, and I was forty-three."

Had she seduced an underage boy? I had never heard of statutory rape by a woman.

"Was he your lover?" I whispered.

She laughed but not with her high jingling notes. "Everyone knows Gore is homosexual. He never made a secret of it."

"Oh."

"Not that it mattered to me."

I must have looked confused because she sighed. "When I met Gore, he was part of a clique of homosexuals who included me at all their parties in the Village." She looked at me pleadingly. "You must be patient. I am trying to explain so that you can understand."

I waited, and she began again. "I'd befriended the homosexuals because I didn't want to be unfaithful to Hugo anymore. I thought that with the homosexuals, I could find companionship without temptation. I hadn't realized what a hothouse of enticements I would be entering. The talk was all about sex, and everyone fell so easily into each other's beds, the women as well as the men."

Oh my god, how could I have missed it? Especially after she'd told me that she'd wanted to be part of Djuna Barnes's lesbian clique! It just hadn't occurred to me that Anaïs went with women because she was so feminine. That should have been the tipoff, though; she was one of those *femme* lesbians I'd heard about. Renate had to be one, too—all the paintings of her naked girlfriends! Probably Anaïs's and Renate's young husbands were shills. They were probably homosexual, too.

I felt as if one of Renate's artichoke hearts had gotten stuck in my throat. If Anaïs and Renate were lesbians, then they must think I was one, too, and that was why I'd been brought there! Or they believed I was one but hadn't yet recognized it, so they wanted to help me. The secret was about me: that I was a lesbian, too. But how could I be when I liked sex with men? I didn't even know if I could do it with women, especially women as old as Anaïs and Renate.

Making my voice sound both accepting and neutral I asked, "Are you a lesbian?"

"No!" She laughed her delightful jingle.

"Oh." I took a relieved breath but felt some disappointment on the exhale.

Anaïs went on, "After I turned forty, I was having a midlife crisis like a man. I was in a sexual frenzy, especially for young, beautiful boys, hetero or not." Her laugh cracked. "When I met Gore I'd already slept with enough homosexual young men to know it would be a disaster, but I couldn't help myself. He was so brilliant and beautiful when he was young. Once, in a taxi, he grabbed me into a fierce kiss. I responded, inflamed with desire, and that frightened him. He told the driver to stop, jumped out of the cab, and fled to one of his boys."

"Ouch!" I said.

"That wasn't the worst of it." Her face coiled with ire. "He used secret confidences we'd shared to parody me in his novels! And there was nothing I could do about it because I had to remain friends with him."

"Why?"

"He was my only route to a real publisher."

I was confused. "I thought you had a publisher, Gemor Press."

"Those books were self-published. I handprinted all those books myself."

"What about the British Book Company?"

"It was a vanity press in England." Her sigh was more of a groan. "Hugo wasted so much of his capital on vanity publishing for me."

"Well, at least you handprinted some beautiful books."

"That's true." Wistfully, she lowered her delicate chin. Then she looked up and set her beryl eyes on me. "Actually, that is where the story you need to understand begins: in 1947, probably before you were born."

I quickly calculated. "No, I was born. I was three years old."

She took a deep breath, touched my hand lightly, and began the story of her search for passion. She may not have been able to create a plot in her novels, but in person, with her soft, lilting voice, she was as captivating as Scheherazade, dropping one veil, only to entice with another.

# CHAPTER 6

# Greenwich Village, New York, 1947

## ANAÏS

AT FORTY-FOUR, SHE WAS MAD for sex and wild with anxiety. Hugo had given her money to hire someone to set the type for Gemor Press, and she'd hired Gonzolo Mores, one of her impoverished Paris lovers who had followed her to the US. For a time, she was having sex with Gonzolo in the Village studio she kept for him, and with Henry Miller, who had also followed her to New York, and with a half dozen other men, sometimes five different men in a day—younger ones, older ones, soldiers and film directors, men she met at parties, some straight, some not. She paused only when bedridden with bouts of exhaustion.

Her only anchor in this tumultuous period was the tangible work of handprinting her novels. Gonzolo, after a burst of energy, had fallen back on his old habit of drinking wine before noon, and so Anaïs had taken over his task of positioning the type on the old clamshell press.

One freezing winter night, she was working alone in the East Village studio where the hand press was housed. Wrapped in her winter coat with a dirty printer's smock covering it, she locked in letters of Bernhard Gothic Light. Her fingers were blackened from inking the plate. Her back ached from working the pedal. Yet she loved this work for the respite it gave from her abiding restlessness. She had come to the point where she felt she would have to leave both Hugo and the United States. She had not been able to flower as a woman or as a writer in New York as she had in Paris. She was dissipating her time and her talent. Her relationship with Hugo had become a formality of duty and appearance, and she wanted out of its imprisonment. Yet she did not know how she could get Hugo to live without her; nor, when she was honest with herself, how she would get by without him, financially or emotionally.

She put away the type into boxes, removed the ink-stained smock, and checked her face in the wall mirror. It was after 10 p.m., and she was exhausted but didn't want to go home to the empty apartment. Hugo was on business in Cuba; she was free for the night—that is, as free as she had the energy to be. She decided she would make an appearance at the party Hazel Guggenheim was giving. Hazel was one of the wealthy clients for whom Hugo handled investments. She was a painter of minute talent, and because her sister Peggy Guggenheim was an important collector, there were always some interesting artists at Hazel's large parties.

Anaïs splashed her face with freezing water in the utility sink and re-applied her makeup, carefully penciling the arched eyebrows, blackening her eyelids with kohl, drawing the bow on her upper lip in red, and adding rouge to her pallid cheeks. Her hair was still perfectly set from getting a perm at Elizabeth Arden's Fifth Avenue salon.

She raised her arms and stretched from side to side, took some deep breaths for bravery, added some aqua rhinestone earrings dug from her purse to bring out the color of her eyes, exchanged her flat work shoes for high heels, and slipped into her alluring Sabina persona. How many more times could she act the fascinating literary woman of mystery who dropped that her next novel was under consideration at Random House or Dutton or Viking or Ballantine or Farrar, Straus and Company, omitting that each publisher had actually already passed because her precious, surreal style was considered fusty and dated, like herself? Such thoughts left a clammy coating of fear on her skin and a cramp of anxiety under her ribs. So she thrust herself forward yet again to rush to a Manhattan party, drink champagne, flirt, and promote her glamorous, enigmatic image.

The taxi dropped her at Hazel's swanky apartment building, and after giving her name to the doorman, she saw, holding the elevator door for her, a lanky, handsome young man wearing a full-length white leather coat. Another showy, artistic homosexual, she chided herself; what else did she expect going to a party at Hazel's?

As they rode the elevator together, she examined her ink-stained fingers, then noticed the young man watching, and thrust her hands into the pockets of her wool coat. He removed his hands from his pockets, opening them to her, palms up. His fingertips were blacker than hers.

"You're a printer, too!" she exclaimed.

"It's my night job."

"What's your day job?"

"Unemployed actor. What's yours?"

"Unemployed writer."

They laughed, and she noticed his beautiful teeth and classic features. There was the quality of a dreamer, a sensitive face. *If only he weren't homosexual*, she thought, unbidden, *he could be the one*. But that was ridiculous; he was too beautiful and stylish not to be gay.

As they arrived at the top floor, she started to unbutton her coat. He leapt to help her. Expertly removing it, he said, "My name is Rupert Pole." His exhaled breath shot a current from her neck down between her thighs.

They entered the party together and found Hazel, who had grown more plump since Anaïs had last seen her, and blowsier. Hazel tilted her cigarette holder upward as she took in Rupert standing next to Anaïs.

When he went to get drinks, Anaïs quickly made disclaimers to Hazel. "Hugo wished he could be here. He's in Cuba on business for another week."

Rupert returned, handed Anaïs a vodka gimlet, and settled with her on a divan.

"Are you French?" he asked her. She noticed flecks of gold in his blue eyes.

"I was born in Cuba, but my father moved us to France, where I lived until I was eleven. Then my parents divorced, and Mother brought us to New York."

"But your accent seems too pronounced for you to have lived here since you were eleven." She noticed his ascetic temples.

"When I was twenty, the man I was married to was transferred to a bank in Paris. In France my accent came back and now doesn't want to leave."

"The man I was married to" wasn't a lie, though it was something she said when she didn't want to discourage a man romantically. She kept Hugo hidden. She kept the fact that she'd been married for twenty-four years hidden.

They talked about Rupert growing up among Native Americans in a Palm Springs adobe, about her Spanish blood and her famous Cuban musician father, Joaquin Nin, about Rupert having studied music at Harvard, his belief in pacifism and interest in Eastern spirituality. They talked about typefaces and makes of standing presses. All the while her eyes spoke another language: *I want you, do you want me? Do you desire me? Would you hurt me?*

Rupert told her earnestly that he was giving up the theater and returning home to Los Angeles to study to become a forest ranger.

"So we're both leaving New York for gentler pastures," Anaïs said.

"You're leaving, too? Where are you going?"

"I want to move back to Paris. I don't find the United States hospitable to the kind of writing I do."

"Where have you been in the States besides New York?"

"Brooklyn."

"That's New York."

"And I've been to Boston. I gave talks at Amherst and Dartmouth."

"Have you ever been west of the Mississippi? Have you ever seen the mountains in Utah or the Indian lands in New Mexico? Ever been to California?"

"No." She sighed. "All the publishers are in New York."

"But Anaïs, you haven't seen the United States yet! You're going to leave this magnificent land before you've seen it? The US isn't just the East Coast, you know."

"You sound like my friend Henry Miller. He recently moved to Big Sur in California."

"Big Sur is majestic. High cliffs and crashing waves."

She noted he did not seem to know—or perhaps care—who Henry Miller, the sexually explicit banned novelist, was.

Gazing into Rupert's blue eyes, a child's clear eyes, she decided the danger of his being another unformed child-man who would disappoint her in bed was too great. So when Bernard, a man she had casually slept with, came up and asked if he could give her a ride home, she accepted.

As Bernard was helping her with her coat, though, Rupert approached and said directly, "I'd like to see you again."

Despite Bernard's impatience, she pulled pen and paper from her purse, wrote down her number, and handed it to Rupert with an inviting smile.

Although she had rigorous sex with Bernard that night, it was Rupert's sensitive face she held in her mind.

∞

The next day, she did not leave the apartment in the hope that Rupert would call. He did not, but when she phoned Hazel to thank her for the party, Hazel said, "You have an admirer, that handsome young actor. After you left he went on and on about the beautiful, intriguing Anaïs Nin."

*Then why doesn't he call?* Anaïs tormented herself. Had Hazel told him she was married?

Rupert phoned her the next day. Since Hugo was still out of town, she invited him to dinner at her place. She had Millie prepare the ingredients for her to whip up medallions of veal with sliced eggplant. She made a stack of the 78s she wanted to play, lit candles, and prepared herself for Rupert to be late. He was punctual to the minute.

He strode into the apartment, throwing his white leather coat over a chair, and as she fixed him a gin and tonic, he began to sort through her records. He put on Wagner's *Tristan and Isolde*. The fact that the opera was about adulterous love between a young knight and the very married Isolde did not pass by her.

As she handed him his drink, he set it on a table and pulled her into a forceful embrace, a wave that towed her under. When they finally surfaced, she remembered dinner. As she sizzled the veal in the skillet, he wrapped his arms around her from behind and kissed her neck. When, weak with relief and joy, she forgot what she was doing, he took over preparing the meal. He changed the records on the player. He uncorked the wine. And all the while he found new spots on her arms and face and décolletage to cover with kisses.

Through dinner he kept the play of touch alive, intermittently taking her hand, keeping a knee next to hers under the table.

"Do you live here alone?" he asked.

She knew that he might see evidence of Hugo's things. She heard herself say, "My husband and I have been using the apartment alternately until I move to France and the divorce is final." It wasn't really a lie. She wanted a divorce from Hugo; it had been on her mind repeatedly.

"What about you?" she asked. "There must be a special person in your life. Do you live with anyone?"

"I have a girlfriend."

The bite of veal on her fork turned to lint in her mouth. She pulled herself away, erect in her chair. "Oh, I'm surprised. Actually, you surprise me altogether. I had assumed you were homosexual."

"Why would you assume that?"

"Maybe it was the long, dramatic leather coat."

He laughed. "It belonged to my stepfather's father, Frank Lloyd Wright. I thought it might improve my acting prospects. It didn't."

That he was related to the famous architect made him even more alluring, but she decided not to pursue it; she needed to know if his love for another, younger woman meant he'd inevitably reject her. "So you're returning to Los Angeles to be with your girl."

"No, to study at UCLA. I'll live at my mother's place."

*Stop it, Anaïs*, she warned herself. *Don't clutch. Don't scare him off.* But she had to know.

"Is it serious with your girl?"

"I love her, but she's religious. We've never made love because she's waiting for marriage. I think she wants someone who can offer more security than I can."

She saw the pain and confusion on his face and felt relieved. "Does that mean you haven't had sexual experiences with women?"

He laughed. "I was married. I just got divorced."

"You do surprise me. How old are you?"

"Twenty-eight."

She quickly calculated. He was sixteen years younger than she. As she waited for him to ask her age, she deliberated what to say. But he didn't ask. He sprang up from his chair to change the record.

He stopped at her chair on his way back to his seat. "Listen to Wagner's harmonic suspension in the *Liebestod*. It's been rising since the prelude." He wrapped his arms around her just under her small breasts and spoke into her ear. "Hear how it creates desire and expectation? It teases you by taking you right to the brink, expecting the musical climax, and then withholds it, building your desire, your need for resolution even higher so that when the climax of Isolde's death finally comes, it is shattering, explosive. There is nothing like it."

Anaïs rose from her seat into Rupert's arms, her passion rising with the repeated harmonic chord, with increased intensity, again and again, mouth on mouth, his hands moving hungrily on her back, pulling her into him.

He picked her up like an actor in a Western. It was corny, but she laughed as he carried her into the master bedroom, pulled off the satin bedcover, and released her gently on the bed. Urgently he pulled off her clothes and his own, tossing them to the floor. She saw his body in the half-light: his lean, muscled physique; his compact, alert member.

He thrust into her with the speed and agility of an athlete. In a blast of energy, he took her to the brink repeatedly, challenging her strength, and only when she was wild with readiness did he satisfy her with a long, long orgasm.

She was delirious with joy. She had found a man who could meet her passion with his own!

He held her through the night, reaching out for her when she rolled over. She did not want to fall asleep, aware of the touch of his slender thighs next to hers, his sinewy arms enfolding her. In the morning, he took her again in another tidal wave of pleasure and left only after covering her with kisses. She was sure he would call her that afternoon, want to see her again that night. Her body throbbed, remembering: him throwing his coat on the couch, gently lowering the phonograph arm onto the record, carrying her laughing into the bedroom, leaning over her, his penis sprung hard in the half light.

She was mad to be with him again that night. She circled the phone. She let herself look up the number in the phonebook for the printer where he worked. She opened the cigarette box to keep her hands from dialing the number.

The phone rang. She put a smile on her face before answering so that her voice wouldn't betray her anxiety. She heard Gore Vidal's young, Brahmin voice. "I have some good news for you, my dear, but don't get too excited; nothing is ever for sure."

"Did Dutton say yes?"

"Have you finished *Children of the Albatross*?"

"No, but I'm close."

"If you can have a final manuscript in two weeks, they've tentatively agreed to put it on the spring list."

"Oh Gore, that's wonderful. I know this is only because of you."

"I'll sign off now. You don't have time to talk."

She hung up, dazed. Her body was still crying out for Rupert, but now she simply could not listen. She had worked a lifetime for this opportunity with a real publisher. She snapped her fingers to wake herself. *Get to work, Anaïs. It's just as well Rupert hasn't called.*

∞

The spindly arms of her Bauhaus Olivetti typewriter drummed. She typed one last sentence and swung the carriage with satisfaction. She still had to proof the entire book but tonight she wanted to celebrate. Tonight she wanted Rupert.

Ten days had passed and he had not phoned. She could not understand it. How could this man forget her when their rhythms had been so perfectly in sync?

The hell with it! She had to know what had happened. Hugo would be back in two days for the weekend, then off again on another business trip. She had to phone Rupert, she rationalized, so he didn't end up calling when Hugo was home. As the phone at the printer's rang, she tried to ignore the sickening anxiety in her stomach. She needed to sound light, casual when she announced herself.

He sounded nonchalant when he responded, "Oh, hello, darling." He started making excuses: he'd cut his finger in the press, and it had gotten infected.

She expressed sympathy and then let it drop that she would be out of town for several days so if he'd like to get together, it would have to be immediately or not until Tuesday.

There was a long pause before he said, "Why don't I call you on Tuesday then? Would you like to have dinner?"

"I'd love that."

"Good then."

She hung up, confused and aching. He was not in love with her.

∞

She was at her Olivetti, retyping her manuscript, when she heard Hugo's trudging gait. *He moves like an old man,* she thought. *He's only fifty but everything he does is slow and deliberate like an eighty-five-year-old.*

She sprang up to greet him and carry his bag into the bedroom. "You must be exhausted," she offered as she drew him a bath. He flopped on the bed and slowly recounted his visit with her relatives, his delay at the Havana airport, his negotiations with his clients. The steam from the hot water she'd left running suffused the room, making her think of the heavy atmosphere Hugo brought with him. It descended on her like a low, gray cloud, suffocating her until he would leave and she could breathe freely again.

At midnight she gave up typing and slipped into their king bed as she'd learned to do, so smoothly that Hugo registered no change. At 4 a.m. she was awakened by the glare of light in her face. Since he went to bed at 8 p.m., he awoke at dawn and read with the light on. They were completely out of sync. She fumed silently, pulling her pillow over her head.

Because he hadn't slept through the night, he dozed most of the day, and when he finally roused himself, he bore down on her. "We need to go over the budget."

*We need to get a divorce*, she thought. But out of habit and duty she sat by his side at the kitchen table. He'd point to a number in one of the columns recorded in his banker's ledger. "What cost $86.79 on February fourth? Where is the check stub for it, Anaïs? You forgot again!"

It was bad enough that he spent all his time poring over columns of numbers, but he wanted her to waste her life the same way.

On Sunday she was in her study working when Hugo shambled in and muttered, "What did I come in here for?"

Inside she snapped, *You zombie! I can't wait until Monday for you to leave!* After he shuffled out, she lay her head on her folded arms in misery. Life was passing her by while she was buried in this tomb of a marriage.

Tuesday evening, Hugo having departed, she clipped the price tag off her single spring purchase—a Christian Dior evening suit with a bustier jacket that emphasized her small waist and a long full skirt that complemented her narrow ankles. She heard the buzzer and checked her watch. She liked that Rupert was punctual like herself. She ducked into a mist of Chanel 22 before answering the door.

He was wearing a heavy Pendleton shirt and blue jeans, holding bags of groceries in his arms. Her heart sank. He didn't want to spend the money to take her to a restaurant.

He put the groceries down, pulled her to him, and kissed her breasts, which were lifted by the bustier. His shining, thick hair held the aroma of his pipe tobacco.

Dinner forgotten, she led him into the bedroom and undressed herself as he shed his heavy work clothes. When she turned her back to reach for a hanger, he said, "You have the body of a young girl." She turned her head to smile; with him she felt like one.

With his rapid, forceful movements, he took her to climax, and without leaving her, he took her again, and later again, until they were both exhausted and satiated.

"I want to make love to you in the ocean," he said. "I want to make love to you in the desert."

She warned herself: *Don't let him take your heart; he's leaving. Take this for what it is now.* And she was happy, overjoyed to have this beautiful young lover.

Her pleasure coursed through the following weeks. She was flowing in her life again, moving with the tide, not grasping, not anticipating. It had been so long since she had felt this fluidity, this rightness, this excitement of being in life. Even when Hugo returned, this time without plans to leave any time soon, her happiness extended to him. Her gaiety lifted his spirits. He attributed it to her having handed in *Children of the Albatross* to Dutton. To celebrate he surprised her with opening night tickets to Martha Graham's new ballet *Night Journey*.

Excited that she would be seeing in person one of her artistic idols, Anaïs pulled her new Dior evening suit out of her closet, where she'd carefully hung it, safe from Rupert's tearing. She asked Hugo to zip up the snug bustier that she had struggled with alone the night she'd worn it for Rupert. Hugo touched her small breasts raised in it, and she was aroused recalling Rupert's frenzied kisses there.

"You have to be seen in that dress tonight," Hugo said. He called up the maître d' at 21 Club and got them a table for after the ballet.

Feeling a grateful tenderness for him as he refilled her champagne glass after their expensive evening, she toasted, "To my husband, who works so hard to give me our wonderful life. Who saved my whole family by marrying me against his father's wishes. Dear Hugo, my savior."

He grasped her hand. "And to Anaïs, who makes my life worth living."

That night she tried to enjoy him mounting her in his absent, hurried way.

A few days later, she phoned Rupert without fear, with faith in what their bodies had shared. Since Hugo was home for a stretch now, she offered to come to the print shop and take Rupert to dinner at a little Spanish cantina she knew.

Once they'd settled in a corner booth, the dark brick walls and paintings of Flamenco dancers and bullfighters stirred the courage of Anaïs's Spanish blood. She came right out and asked him, "When are you leaving for California?"

"In three weeks. I have to take Cleo for a checkup and then I'm off."

"Cleo?"

"Cleopatra."

"What's wrong with her?"

"She's been very lethargic."

"I suppose you will miss her."

"Oh, no, I'm taking her with me."

"What about your girl in California?"

"Anaïs, Cleo is my car."

"Oh." She laughed. "I never know the makes of cars."

"No, Cleo's just my name for her. She's a Ford. Sometimes I can't tell when you are teasing me."

"Do you think I'm teasing you if I say I'll miss you?"

"No, because I know I'll miss you."

"Well, we can write to each other." She suddenly felt the happiness of the past weeks drain out of her. She lowered her eyes to the shrimp shells in the bowl between their half-eaten plates of paella. She would be left as hollow as those discarded, brittle carapaces. Empty without the sweet pungency of desire.

"Come with me," Rupert said.

She looked up into his steady blue gaze. "To California?"

"Keep me company on the drive. We can make an adventure of it."

"Yes," she said without thinking. She had no idea how she would manage it, what she would tell Hugo. There wasn't a doubt in her mind, though; she was going to run away with this beautiful man.

That night he drove her to his tiny apartment in Cleo, which turned out to be a ramshackle 1931 Model-A roadster. The convertible top was down in the middle of March and the heater didn't work. Not wanting to seem old and fussy, she didn't say a thing. Nor did it matter to her that his room was that of a messy boy. He played the guitar for her and then his viola. Full of assurance, he leapt up and pushed her down on the lumpy mattress, his kisses strong and skillful, the caresses of a musician, electric; his hands on her backside kneading in a frenzy that awakened her nerves. Fire and nerves and rhythm building to an assured crescendo. There was, she realized with joy, nothing passive about Rupert's desire for her.

After he drove her home in Cleo, she slipped undetected into bed with Hugo and lay awake, drunk from her passion with Rupert. Until dawn, she auditioned possible stories to tell Hugo so that she could run away in three weeks with her exuberant, young lover.

At breakfast she said casually to Hugo, "You know my friend Thurema Sokol?"

"The harpist."

"She's giving a concert in Los Angeles but she's afraid of flying. She asked me to keep her company on her drive across the country to California."

Hugo objected about the money the trip would cost, as she knew he would, but in the end he handed her a stack of bills, insisting that she pay her share of gas and lodging. She threw her arms around his neck and thanked him as a jagged stab of guilt pierced her.

With her guilt came worries: What if Hugo ran into Thurema? What if Rupert didn't show up on their set departure date? What if she got sick from exhaustion on the long drive? Her age would show and scare Rupert away.

She handled her anxiety by keeping busy. She packed and re-packed her suitcase, hiding it with her diaries in the secret closet she'd had a carpenter install in the apartment without Hugo's knowledge.

The morning Rupert was to pick her up at 8:30 a.m., Hugo dawdled over breakfast. "I can be a little late to the office this morning." He gave her a reptilian smile. "I'll wait for Thurema and see you both off."

"Oh, you'd better not. Thurema said she might be late."

Anaïs jumped up and dialed the phone. Turning her back, unseen by Hugo, she disconnected the call. "Oh Thurema, how are you coming?" she said into the dead receiver. "No, that's okay. Eleven would be fine. Hugo wanted to see you, but I'll explain."

Putting down the receiver, she put her arms around Hugo. "I'm sorry, darling. You better get going." She fussed over him, buttoning his coat, repeating how much she would miss him. It was 8:25. If he were coming, Rupert would be there in five minutes. What if Hugo were still in the apartment?

"I don't want you to be late to work, dear." She nearly pushed Hugo out the door, and when he started back for his umbrella, she grabbed it and ran to him holding it out. Once he was in the elevator, she rushed to the terrace.

On the street below, Rupert was backing Cleo into a parking space. Hugo strode from the building and hailed a taxi only six feet away from where Rupert was leaping over the passenger door of his little roadster. *Hurry, Hugo, get in the cab.* He stepped in just as Rupert dashed to the front door. She watched Hugo's taxi turn the corner, then ran to buzz Rupert in.

∞

They emerged from the Holland Tunnel as from the birth canal, the sky expanding into a huge blue dome filled with puffy clouds. The land stretched out from green fields to forests and hills.

She had dressed in shades of purple, the color of new consciousness, with a violet wide-brimmed hat and scarf to protect her face and hair in the open convertible. Rupert looked dapper in a dark blue wool coat and a Tyrolean hat. She imagined they were two vibrant, romantic characters from a Frank Capra road movie running away together.

Cleo chugged past lakes, farmhouses, grazing sheep, and storybook churches. When, at 9 p.m., Rupert pulled the car into the parking lot of a motel, her body was still chugging forward.

He told her they would have to register at the motel as Mr. and Mrs. Pole. She felt a rush of pleasure at the sound of Mrs. Pole. *Stop it,* she reprimanded herself. *This is just casual. It is not meant to last.*

Rupert said, "You'll need a wedding ring."

She caught herself visualizing hands clasped with Rupert, each with matching wedding bands. She reminded herself sternly that she was already married, even though she never wore the engraved gold band Hugo had placed on her finger decades before. Years ago, she'd told him it no longer fit comfortably.

"I bought you a ring from Woolworth's for you to use on the trip," Rupert announced. He dug the band from his coat pocket and placed it in her palm.

"You shouldn't have," she teased, slipping on the almost weightless ring and waving it in front of him. "Mrs. Pole is ready."

As they were finding their bungalow, Anaïs spied a pay phone. "Oh, Rupert, I need to phone my publisher."

"At this hour?" Rupert eyed her doubtfully.

"Yes, he gave me his home number. We have to reschedule some meetings. He said to call whenever I got to a phone."

After calling Hugo collect to assure him she was fine, she returned to the motel room to find Rupert already in pajamas sitting up against the bed's headboard, studying a map in his lap. She bathed and, wearing only her silk nightgown and the cheap wedding band, cuddled up to him.

He raised her chin with his hand. "I'm going to make you very happy with the trip I've planned." He spread the map over her legs and with his finger traced the route he had drawn with a red pen. His finger slid off the map and onto her nightgown, still tracing a path of pleasure.

In the morning, he retrieved the map from the floor and handed it to her. "You can be our navigator." She watched as he instructed her how to measure the miles between towns and what the symbols meant, but her mind was on the calluses on his elegant fingers where he struck the strings of his guitar; gently, knowingly, the way he touched her.

Although she proved useless at navigating from his maps, he complimented her on being a trooper, never complaining about the long hours in the cramped, topless car. She restrained her annoyance when he brought out the little notebook in which he faithfully recorded what they each ordered and owed for breakfast, lunch and dinner. *Hugo's junior accountant*, she thought, but she was not about to let it spoil her romantic adventure.

Contrary to her fears that she would suffer exhaustion, she found herself energized by their morning lovemaking and their play of touch in the car in anticipation of that night's fireworks. She felt younger and healthier with each mile away from Hugo.

They took the southern route via New Orleans so that they could visit Gore Vidal, who had rented a house in the French Quarter. Gore welcomed them and looked Rupert over with an appreciative eye. She knew it was risky to introduce them because Gore was also friends with Hugo, but she couldn't resist making Gore envious of her for a change; Rupert was that gorgeous. While Gore was out in the afternoons, she and Rupert made love on the cool marble floor of his apartment, slivers of light through the slatted shutters falling in fine lines on their skin.

Gore suddenly became the moralist. He who specialized in one-night stands took her aside and reprimanded her for deceiving Hugo.

She used every charm she had to swear Gore to secrecy; he couldn't be trusted with such juicy gossip about her.

The road again: Lake Pontchartrain, Delta country, the Mississippi River, flat regions, cattle ranches, tumbleweeds, the Texas Panhandle, Santa Fe, Indian country, canyons with sculpted turrets, lunar expanses, red earth, the Grand Canyon, immense awe, eons of geological strata, the wind whispering of eternity. America so beautiful, its snowcapped mountains, its deserts, rivers, bison, deer, unfamiliar trees and birds. She loved the land and the young man who knew it, knew its history, told her stories of Navajo legends, Spanish explorers, wagon pioneers. Night and day together. Making love in cabins with fireplaces, in bare rooms with electric heaters, under pine trees in a sleeping bag, on the sloping sand dunes of Death Valley.

She had told herself that she was doing this fling as much for her marriage as for herself. If she did not allow Sabina these excursions, she would not be able to stay in her marriage with Hugo. She'd told herself to keep this affair light. As long as she did not let herself fall in love with Rupert, she would be all right. Her marriage would be all right.

But she had fallen in love with Rupert.

Driving through the last stretch of fragrant orange groves on the way to Los Angeles, Rupert broke a long silence by asking, "Before you and your husband decided on divorce, did you want to have children?"

Her stomach somersaulted. "In the beginning we both thought we would have children," she answered, "but our life was so busy, it didn't seem like a good idea."

"I want children," Rupert announced. She thought she had worried about everything, but she hadn't anticipated this.

"I thought you wanted a life of adventure and freedom. That's why you are choosing forestry."

"I do, but I'm conflicted because I also want a home and a family. I want life to be in harmony like music, and you can't have music without a stable foundation."

She was in turmoil. At forty-four she might still bear him a child but could she take care of one? No, she could not imagine herself in that role now.

They fell into silence again, inhaling the sweet scent of blossoming orange trees.

# CHAPTER 7

# Malibu, California, 1964

## TRISTINE

THE RING OF THE PHONE in Renate's living room brought Anaïs out of her narrative. She lunged for the receiver but changed her mind.

"Hurry, Tristine, we have to leave. We don't want Ronnie or Peter to find us here."

I didn't understand why but quickly gathered my stuff, and we exited through the carport door. In front of our side-by-side cars, both with badly dented fenders, Anaïs gave me a kiss on each cheek. Then she wrapped her arms around me in a hug that held the warmth I'd longed for.

"Do you think I could follow you back to where the highway inclines to Sunset?" she asked. "I have a terrible sense of direction and I'm afraid of missing the exit."

Another similarity between Anaïs and me, I noted. I got lost easily, too, though I chose not to tell her because I could manage the Pacific Coast Highway to Sunset and I wanted her to trust in me.

As we caravanned along the coast, I had to keep my eyes from drifting to the white foam of the waves crawling between the beach houses. I focused on the moonlit dividing line on PCH, glancing back at Anaïs in my rearview mirror, the top down on her Thunderbird, strands of her hair blowing out from under her scarf, her flapping cape fastened at the neck, her pale face intently watching my car. Anaïs's magic had entered my life again, and this time I was determined not to lose it.

Later, as I was eating a plate of freezer-burned corn and peas at my apartment, I realized that nothing Anaïs had told me about running away with Rupert actually clarified anything. Not why I had to get USC stationery for her. Not why she was sending a letter to herself. Not why she'd divorced Hugo and married Rupert. In fact, what she'd shared about her affair with Rupert only raised more questions. How had she gotten Rupert to forget about having children? Or had she? She couldn't have married him until she was divorced from Hugo and that had to have been after 1962, because when I'd met her she was still married to Hugo. Between 1947, when she met Rupert and drove cross-country with him, and 1963 or thereabouts when she divorced Hugo, Rupert might have married and had a kid with someone else. Maybe the Puritanical girlfriend. That would mean Anaïs would now be a stepmom to his kid, though I couldn't visualize that.

My brain felt twisted by trying to calculate her timeline. I took a bath to relax, but a schoolyard taunt ran through my head: *Anaïs Nin is a liar. Anaïs Nin is a liar.* I kept thinking about all the lies she had told Hugo and Rupert, and wondered: if she lied to them, how would I ever know when she was telling me the truth?

I lowered my shoulders into the hot bath water. Anaïs was a liar, and that meant I shouldn't trust her. But for some reason, I did trust her. More than I'd ever trusted anyone. Lying was supposed to be wrong, but Anaïs seemed so right. She knew how to live, she was a writer, she was beautiful and kind, she didn't seem to age like every-body else, and she wasn't a victim. Besides, she had told me the truth about her being a liar. How was it that lying was wrong but keeping a friend's lie wasn't? It bound you together like blood sisters.

∞

When I asked the English department secretary for some stationery, the busy, middle-aged woman just handed me a stack of letterhead and envelopes without asking the purpose. As a second thought, she had me enter in a ledger how many sheets I was taking and the date.

I met Anaïs again at Renate's house, though Renate wasn't there. I presented the blank letterhead protected in a folder. Her reaction was gratifying. "You did brilliantly!"

We got right down to her dictation.

"You can address the letter to me by my pen name, Anaïs Nin, Apt. 14B, 4 Washington Square, New York." That wasn't her address when I'd met her. I guessed she'd moved after the divorce, but still kept a place in the city. "I'll be there in two weeks," she continued. "The letter should arrive before I do. It is an invitation for me to speak at your college."

"From my English department?"

"Yes."

"Did they invite you?"

"No, but I need to have West Coast invitations for the East Coast colleges to offer me engagements."

"Oh." So I was writing a pretend invitation for her to show around.

"The letter should come from you on behalf of the English department. You should say they are offering me an honorarium of $200."

"Alright," I said uncertainly.

"It just needs to seem professional. You should apologize that the college does not have the money to pay for accommodations, but that

I will be welcome to stay with you, as usual, for as long as I wish in your guest room."

"I don't have a guest room! I mean, you could stay with me if you need to, but I only have a single. I don't think you would be very comfortable."

"Oh, don't worry, I'll never stay with you. But it's customary to offer accommodations."

I didn't understand what was going on. I rubbed my forefinger over my lower lip as I do when I'm anxious.

"Oh, never mind. This isn't going to work." She lowered my hand gently and held it with her own surprisingly cool hand. "I'm sorry. Forget all this."

"No! I'll have the letter for you in two days."

"Excellent! Why don't we meet next time at the library downtown, so you don't have to drive all the way out here again. The Central Library is near your college, isn't it?"

We made the arrangements and, hoping to get her to return to her love story with Rupert, I said, "You told me Rupert wanted to have children. You never had a child, did you?"

"No, do you want children?"

"No."

"Why not?"

"Until you, the only women I've known who were happy were my Aunt Anne and my godmother Lenore, and neither of them had a kid."

"Renate is happy and she has a son," Anaïs commented, but I wasn't convinced. Studying me, she said, "I heard a lecture once by Marie Von Franz, who was a student of Carl Jung's, about the *puella aeterna*, the archetype of the eternal ingénue."

The eternal ingénue—that's what Anaïs was and what I wanted to be: forever young and light and carefree. I made a note of the Latin term but later, when I looked it up at Doheny Library, I found that the archetype of the woman who never ages, never loses her sexuality, and never becomes a mother had a dark side too—of being unable to stick to anything, of always being afraid of being trapped, of never growing up.

Anaïs shifted her position on the stacked pillows. "I've been meaning to ask, have you seen your godmother?"

"I stayed with Lenore last Easter break. We went to her show at the American Craft Museum."

"You cannot tell Lenore that you saw me in LA."

"Okay," I said, "But I don't see what harm."

"That's just the point. You don't know what harm!"

"Then tell me. Tell me the rest of the story about you and Rupert. Did he try to find someone else to have children with?"

My question appeared to pierce her like a blade. "I suppose that's a natural question. He was only twenty-eight then."

"But he was in love with you," I said.

"Not yet." She gave a wry smile.

CHAPTER 8

## Los Angeles, California, 1947

## ANAÏS

UPON THEIR ARRIVAL IN LOS Angeles, Rupert insisted they first go
to the beach in Santa Monica. Anaïs sat on the shore shivering as he
played like a puppy in the surf. Charging out of the water, his embrace
wetting her clothes, he whooped, "I could take you right here."

Instead he took her with rough, impersonal sex in a rundown
Hollywood motel room, and she had perhaps the best orgasm of her
life. Putting on his clothes afterwards, he announced, "I have to go
back to my mother's tonight. They're waiting for me."

"I can't stay alone in this dump!" Panic pressed against her
esophagus.

"You'll be safe. Lock the door."

"You expect me to believe that a twenty-eight-year-old man has to
sleep at his mummy's house? It's the girlfriend, isn't it?"

He stepped back as though from a frothing animal. "I'll see you in
the morning."

As the motel door slammed behind him, she knew her uncontrolled anxiety had been ruinous. She ran after him, through the motel courtyard and onto the street, still in her bathrobe. "Rupert, please. Don't leave me here!"

He didn't look back as he slid into Cleo and took off. Anaïs chased the car as it sped down the hill. Slipping on the steep, cracked pavement, she fell and caught herself, scraping her hand. Out of breath, she sat on the road as the last of twilight dimmed and watched as Cleo turned at the corner, huffing dark smoke from the exhaust pipe, and disappeared out of sight.

Pushing herself up on her bleeding palm, she tightened her bathrobe and trudged up the narrow sidewalk of the dimly lit street. On either side were cottages and run-down apartment buildings with window grates that cast threatening shadows onto the small yards. The street was unfamiliar now, but in her bathrobe she could hardly ask directions to the motel.

She heard her own crazy laugh. She was inside her own horror film. Sabina would have swept her cape around her, glad to be rid of Rupert's homespun earnestness. But where was Sabina's bravado now when she needed it? Lost to her, disappeared, leaving a helpless, terrified child.

Trying to control her rising panic, Anaïs ran up the rest of the street and saw the motel. She would phone Hugo; she needed to speak to Hugo. When she discovered that the motel had no phone, she dressed hastily, found a phone booth on Sunset Boulevard, and dialed Hugo.

The unanswered ring intensified to a shriek. Hugo should have been there at that hour. The last two times they had spoken, he'd cut the phone call short, and she'd heard the anger in his voice. He must have learned that she had lied to him about the trip. Hugo was done with her too.

She remembered the sleeping pills in her suitcase. She had brought them to help her fall asleep while on the road, but lovemaking with Rupert had made them unnecessary.

In the motel room, her hand trembling, she emptied the bottle onto the scarred desk. She counted twenty-seven capsules. Enough to silence the piercing shriek cutting through her veins, bleeding into her muscles and nerves.

She'd believed she would not relapse with Rupert because he was younger, because he was not the father image. But she had fallen in love with him, and he had walked out on her. It was enough to set off the cruel mechanism.

She found a chipped drinking glass and filled it from the bathroom faucet. She felt a cold detachment because she had enough pills to end the shriek and the door banging, banging.

She could barely hear the gentle voice beneath the cacophony. *Take three pills, Anaïs. Just three. Try to rest until morning. Wait until daylight.*

She recognized the voice as that of Djuna. She followed its wise instruction like a child who has cried herself into a daze, though she tossed and turned and her blood howled all night.

She gave up hoping for sleep at 6 a.m., showered, and carefully made up her stricken face, on which fine lines had spun overnight. *Whatever happens, whatever Rupert says*, she promised herself, *I will not lose control again.*

She did manage to control the mayhem inside her when he offered to drive her to LAX, saying he had to concentrate now on his studies, and even when he dropped her at the United terminal without a word about seeing her again. As she waited three hours for her flight, though, she wept uncontrollably amongst strangers who avoided looking at her.

∞

When she opened the door to her apartment with Hugo, she saw in the diffused light that Hugo's book, glasses, and slippers lay where he always placed them. She was safe. She was home. Hugo slept, breathing heavily through his mouth, as she slipped past him and shut the bathroom door. She needed to wash off her excesses with Rupert so that when she awoke, she would be Hugo's beloved wife again.

She rose before Hugo the next morning to buy fresh croissants at the corner bakery. At breakfast he winked at her over his *New York Times*. "For a woman who has just driven cross-country and endured thirteen hours on a plane, you look beautiful, Mrs. Guiler."

"Why thank you, Mr. Beguiler." There were advantages to being five years younger than her husband. Of course, the lowered blinds and the soft pink lighting that she'd installed in the apartment helped.

She was thrilled to be in her own kitchen with her own husband, enjoying their Sunday brunch ritual. Hugo perused the arts section of the *Times* while she studied the book reviews.

He turned his narrow, chiseled head to her. "Did you know Thurema Sokol is performing at Weill Recital Hall tonight?"

"Of course. She had to return for the performance." Anaïs was always amazed at how readily an appropriate lie would come to her in a pinch, yet when she tried to write fiction, she couldn't make it up. All she could do was rewrite and disguise her diary entries.

"It says that Thurema also performed at Weill last Thursday night. But how is that possible? Weren't both of you still in Los Angeles then?"

*This is it.* She stopped breathing. He'd caught her. "Oh, Thurema left Los Angeles before me. I decided to stay on for a few days to sightsee."

"But how could Thurema have driven back so quickly?"

"She flew back."

"But you said she had to drive because she is afraid of flying."

"Yes, but she had no choice this time. At least she avoided one flight."

"What about her car?"

"She got another musician to drive it back for her."

Hugo nodded. Did he know she was lying? Was he intentionally giv-ing her enough rope to hang herself? Or was his love and trust so great that he simply accepted whatever she told him? She could never tell. People referred to her as a mystery woman, but he had his mysteries too.

∞

Within weeks, her sense of resilience and security was restored, and she became restless again. In the past, she would have escaped at every opportunity to parties, flirtations, possible new dalliances. But none of that interested her; she had been looking for her ideal partner in pas-sion and she had found him in Rupert. What was the point of looking anymore?

Despite her resolve not to put her security with Hugo in danger again, she wrote Rupert seductive letters reminding him of their pas-sionate days and nights on the road. His replies were discouraging, telling her not to come to Los Angeles.

She had pulled too hard on him. It had made him resist and escape. Now she would have to use reverse psychology to make him chase her. She had learned, and relearned the hard way, that the only way to keep a man smitten was to stay elusive. Like a bird she would have to make spirals around Rupert—swoop, circle, and then fly away.

When Dutton published *Children of the Albatross*, she made a plan. Right after her book parties in New York, she would do a promotional tour west, ending in Los Angeles. She would send Rupert an announce-ment that she would be in Hollywood for a signing but not even suggest they see each other. Then she would wait to see if he took the bait, and if he did, she would have to fly away so he could chase her.

∞

Several months later, Anaïs appeared at Pickwick Bookshop in Hollywood. Her small audience had squeezed together to hear her soft voice.

She returned the smile of a rotund bearded man, and behind him glimpsed Rupert, who had just arrived. She forbade herself to register any response to his handsome, smiling face, but instead turned to the erotic passage she had saved for this moment.

She prefaced it by saying to the group, "In the novel, the young man's parents have forbidden him to see the heroine because she is older and more worldly than he. Secretly he visits her apartment anyway." She read with her musical rhythm:

"He leaned over swiftly and took her whole mouth in his, the whole man coming out in a direct thrust, firm, willful, hungry. With one kiss he appropriated her, asserted his possessiveness. When he had taken her mouth and kissed her until they were both breathless they lay side by side and she felt his body strong and warm against hers, his passion inflexible."

As she continued reading with her French singsong inflection, she could feel the discomfort in her audience; they were unused to an elegant woman celebrating a moment of passion in her writing. But no one left, and when they crowded around to have her sign the copies they'd bought, Rupert included, she treated him with the same charming deference she offered the others. "To whom would you like me to inscribe it?"

"Where are you staying?" he whispered urgently.

*To Rupert Pole*, she wrote in her slanted handwriting. *Looking forward to getting to know you better at Coral Sands.*

That was as much of an invitation as she was going to offer him. If he wanted to see her, he would figure it out.

∞

When Rupert left the Coral Sands Motel at 3 a.m., she was completely satiated. *Don't forget again*, she told herself. *Men want you most when you are most elusive.* She would take one more night of pleasure with Rupert and then she would be gone—the bird who swoops and flies away. But where could she fly? She had no more book signings and she was not ready to be cooped up again with Hugo.

Something new had emerged in her over the three weeks of her book tour: the satisfaction of true independence. She still had some of the advance money for her next novel in her purse, and she needed an adventure. She watched the white window curtain flutter as she lay in her motel room and imagined what her life could be like if *Children of the Albatross* somehow sold enough copies that Dutton would publish another of her novels. She would get another advance, and another, so that she would be financially independent. Then she really could be like the bird she imagined, circling her lover and flying off to freedom, a bird that did not have to migrate dutifully home to Hugo's nest.

# CHAPTER 9

# Acapulco, Mexico, 1947-1948

## ANAÏS

ANAÏS BOUGHT HERSELF A FLIGHT to Acapulco and, with the plea-sure of Rupert's embraces still on her skin, flew there alone. When she checked herself into the El Mirador Hotel, the setting sun tinted everything gold: the beach, the patio of her cabana, the skin of her bare arms and legs. At night she lay in a hammock, a warm breeze caressing her. Above, instead of pinpricks of stars, she saw huge, glowing orbs.

Nature was so present that it annihilated her anxiety. It embraced her so powerfully that the sensuality of her surroundings was the only lover she needed. She was a woman drugged by beauty, and as the days and nights passed, she felt she never wanted to leave. She was at last free from guilt, from worry, from ambition, from memory, from Sabina's hunger, from Lillian's anxiety, from Stella's fear. She was Djuna, her essential self, for once a woman alone experiencing joy.

She spent the rest of her book advance on purchasing a little stucco house perched on the cliffs above Caleta Beach and the vast, sparkling ocean. She believed that in this sweet casita she had found an answer to the confusion of her life. She would not have been able to afford her own home anywhere else, yet she could not imagine a house she would rather have. Now if she left Hugo she would have a home of her own to go to, saving him from the trauma of her leaving him for another man. She'd have a peaceful space to write and not feel restless, a place nestled in nature where Rupert would want to visit her. Acapulco was a sensual feast that would be even richer with a lover.

Rupert accepted her mailed invitation to visit over his semester break, along with some cash for his flight she'd tucked into the envelope. He arrived carrying his forestry textbooks in his suitcase.

Their first night together, they dined at one of the thatched-roof shanties that lined the beach below the cliffs of her house. The delicious grilled fish was so cheap Rupert insisted on paying for both of them. Afterwards he pulled her up the path to her quaint casita where he helped her light lanterns she'd purchased at the market, since the house had no electricity. In the soft light, to the rhythms of the surf, he gently glided his musician's fingers over every part of her. From the jungle behind the house, parrots called and frogs croaked. As he took her to the center of herself, she called back to the creatures of the jungle.

Drifting off to sleep, though, she felt as if she had insects on her skin and wondered if her old anxiety and guilt over Hugo were trying to trick her.

Rupert suddenly jumped out of bed. "Anaïs, don't move!" he commanded, grabbing a flashlight. "Keep your eyes closed."

She closed her eyes and froze, but cried out, "What? What is it?"

She felt him remove something that had been crawling on her arm. She felt another tickle on her leg, a scratch; and then it, too, was gone.

*Whack!* She jumped with fear. She thought of her father's spankings, the whacks that had sexualized her too young because he hit her place of pleasure.

Rupert said, "Okay, you can open your eyes, but I still forbid you to move a muscle." It excited her when he took on that manly, in-charge tone.

She opened her eyes and saw he held a shoe in his hand. Suddenly he dropped the shoe and tore off his Hawaiian shirt. "Move back!"

She did and gasped, seeing a two-inch-long dark crayfish clinging to his bare, muscled torso.

"How did crayfish get in here?" she asked.

"Anaïs," Rupert hissed, "that's a scorpion."

He brushed it off, and before it could escape, picked up the shoe and slammed it on the tile floor.

Her heart jumped again.

Now, with the shoe in one hand and a flashlight in the other, he searched the bedclothes, the walls, and the floor, finding and thwacking four more of the deadly scorpions. He focused the flashlight's beam into a corner crack in the stucco. Tiny red eyes gleamed back.

"Rats! You have scorpions *and* rats in your house." She heard the disgust in his voice.

"What do we do?" she said. "It's too late to go to a hotel."

He dragged the bed out onto the veranda. He ran the flashlight beam over and under the mattress, checking for vermin, and when he was satisfied it was safe he flopped onto the bed and welcomed her into his arms. She lowered herself to him gracefully, feeling him hard against her thigh; he was always ready for her.

"You are my hero," she murmured, making her French accent more pronounced. To reward his bravery, she adored him with her tongue. When he started to turn her over to enter her, she held him in place and mounted him. With his hands on her hips, she rode him, and when she came she threw her head back and saw thousands of glowing globes in the night sky.

They slept restlessly until 4 a.m. when the rooster next door started crowing and a man in the house below started coughing. Already Anaïs was disillusioned with the purchase of her casita, and she suggested that they stay the rest of his visit at the El Mirador hotel. There they spent two weeks of sensuality: he studying his textbooks, she writing in her diary, and together snorkeling in the tropical waters. They barely spoke except for the language of the body.

Underwater she felt as if she had entered her inner self, the eternal feminine, the silky comfort of the womb. Her body met with Rupert's, moving without effort in the soft current. No thoughts here, no conflicts, no time, no past, no guilt, no husband—only the dissolution of water, the fluidity of now.

He left her cheerfully, having repaired the screens of her little house and rid it of vermin.

But when he was gone, her body yearned for him and she could no longer enjoy her solitude or her casita. So when she received a letter from Hugo saying he was coming to Acapulco to visit and that she should make reservations for them at the expensive American hotel, it was not entirely unwelcome. He enclosed a generous money order, enough to pay for a quick round-trip to Los Angeles. With two weeks of freedom until Hugo's arrival, she telegraphed Rupert that she would be visiting LA on business and booked herself a room at the Coral Sands motel.

Upon her arrival at the motel, the desk clerk handed her a note from Rupert, an invitation to dinner at his mother's house. Rupert had warned Anaïs that his mother, Helen, and her second husband, Lloyd, son of the famous architect Frank Lloyd Wright, were guarded about whom they let into their world. Likely they wanted to look her over.

As Anaïs stepped out of a taxi at 858 Doheny that evening, she thought how perfectly the site expressed the family's reserve. She was already forming the metaphors in her mind that she would use in her diary to describe it: The crossed arms of a giant tree guarding the entrance. The high stone wall surrounding the house like a castle moat.

Anaïs tried hard to charm Rupert's mother, but found the short, restrained woman impenetrable. Seated next to Helen at the dinner table, Anaïs could feel her scrutinizing the side of her face, studying her crow's-feet and likely searching for plastic surgery scars.

Helen questioned Anaïs about her life in New York: did they know any of the same people? How long had it been, she asked, since Anaïs had gotten divorced?

Feeling defensive, Anaïs said the first thing that jumped into her head. "I just got my divorce in Mexico."

"And do you intend to continue writing novels?"

"Oh, yes. Dutton is planning on publishing my next one." Well, she hoped they would.

Helen commented, "The artist's life is difficult. It does not create a base for a full life or stable relationships. Rupert has learned that, not only from having been an actor but from marrying an actress."

"So he told me."

"I read one of your books," Helen said as she poured mint sauce from a chrome Bauhaus pitcher for the pink sliced lamb on Anaïs's plate. "The book had a troubling title, what was it? Yes, *House of Incest*?"

Accepting the perfectly presented plate, Anaïs looked across the table to Rupert for help. Where was her brave, manly lover now? Letting her be subjected to his mother's scrutiny and digs without jumping in to support her.

He got the message, finally, in Anaïs's pleading eyes. "Mother," he said, "the title refers to incest as a metaphor for self-absorption, for being able only to see other people as projections of oneself." *So,* Anaïs thought, *Rupert does listen. He can even repeat as his own what I've told him.*

"That's very interesting," said Lloyd.

Anaïs looked at Rupert's stepfather, the famous architect's son, with sympathy. "My father was a world-famous musician," she said.

"Not as famous as Frank Lloyd Wright, of course, but I know what it feels like to be the child of a famous artist. Like you, I have had to work to create my own identity."

Rupert and his brother Eric turned their eyes on Lloyd as he was about to respond, but Helen slid in a question as smoothly as her silver-handled knife through the leg of lamb. "Do you enjoy cooking, Anaïs?"

"Not really. It's not my form of creativity. But Rupert has told me what a superb cook you are, and I greatly admire that."

"We believe it is an important bond for family life," Helen said, nodding to her husband that he should begin eating.

Rupert and Eric followed suit, but Anaïs's throat was so tight that she had difficulty swallowing.

"Delicious as usual, Mother," Rupert enthused. "I love your cooking."

*Better keep Mummy around, then,* Anaïs thought.

When they all said good-bye to her at the front door—Rupert standing in the hallway with his family as though posed as for their annual Christmas card—Helen came straight out and told her that she was not the woman they had hoped their son would find.

So she was surprised when she heard tapping on her motel room door later.

"They're asleep so I slipped out," Rupert said.

She might have objected, but she was hungry for him. Their best language was that of the body, and their lovemaking had become more passionate, more expert, more satisfying each time. With his hands and lips, he directed the tides of her blood, rising in waves, until a huge breaker overcame them, subsiding like bubbling foam. He left at 3 a.m. saying, "I have to get back before they wake up."

For the next eleven days, it became Rupert's pattern to appear at 10 p.m. after his mother and stepfather had gone to sleep and to leave at midnight so he would be fresh for school. He was a phantom lover who came and went in the night, and it suited Anaïs just fine. She had truly achieved what she had not believed herself capable of: a lightness, a total acceptance of the present without anxiety over what would become of their relationship in the future.

In the mornings she would walk to Musso and Frank's Grill for breakfast where, from her booth, she overheard secret deals being made for blacklisted screenwriters. In the afternoons, she worked on her next novel set in Acapulco to submit to Dutton, confident of her phantom lover's nightly visits. On her last night before she was to fly back to Acapulco, though, Rupert seemed reluctant to leave her at midnight.

"I'm going to miss you."

"You see?" She teased him. "You were concerned my being in Los Angeles would interrupt your studies, but I didn't at all."

"When will I see you again?" He had never asked that before.

She lowered her lids, imagined herself flying off, while he chased after, trying to keep her in sight. "I suppose the next time my work brings me here."

"Anaïs, I heard back on the forestry position I applied for. I'll be working in Angeles National Forest near LA."

"Congratulations."

"They're going to give me my own cabin in the woods. We could live there together."

Taken aback, she looked into his eager, open face. "Do you really want to endure your mother's disapproval? I'm hardly the woman she's dreamt of for you."

"But you're the woman I've chosen. I'm in love with you!"

She felt a rush of joy. She had longed to hear those words from the man she had searched for and found. But that warm wave of satisfaction was accompanied by a chill undertow. *What about Hugo?*

"I love you, too," she said.

"I can't imagine my life without you now," he declared.

"Well, we still don't know each other very well."

"That's why I want you to move to California. You said you were going to leave New York anyway and you told me you like it here."

"Yes, but I still have publishing business in New York."

"But you don't have to live there. Now that your divorce is final."

"It's not actually final."

"I heard you tell mother that you got divorced in Mexico."

"Well, there are complications. That's why I have to go back."

His full lips turned downward. "Okay. Come in spring." He raised her chin, forcing her to meet his eyes. "I need to know so I can endure waiting for you. Promise me."

She laughed, remembering how glad she had been that she'd said yes when he'd asked her to run away with him. "Yes."

He gazed at her, blue eyes glowing; his sensitive, young face illuminated with pure love. As he worked his way down from kissing her breasts, to her stomach, to finding the opening of her mound, he murmured, "You've ruined me for any other woman, Anaïs, Anaïs."

∞

Flying back to Acapulco, Anaïs prepared to write in her diary as she often did by closing her eyes and allowing an image to come to mind. She saw herself suspended in space, and Hugo pulling her down by her ankle, a drowning man. Above, Rupert, like Adam on the dome of the Sistine Chapel, extended a muscled arm to lift her into his embrace.

After recording the image in her diary, she came to a decision: She had to divorce Hugo.

# CHAPTER 10

## Malibu, California, 1964

## TRISTINE

I UNDERSTOOD NOW WHY SHE'D chosen Rupert over Hugo. Her story was like that of Lady Chatterley, who'd divorced her rich husband in order to marry a simple man with whom she had great sex. Though I felt bad for Hugo, I admired Anaïs for staking all for the dream of passionate romance. She was my inspiration.

Yet with all she'd revealed to me, I was still more confused about the timing of her divorce than ever. It appeared that she and Rupert had kept up their affair for sixteen years and then she'd finally divorced Hugo and married Rupert. Or could she and Hugo have already been divorced when I met them in 1962? Renate had said that Anaïs and Hugo pretended *not* to be married when he was Ian Hugo; could Anaïs have just been pretending to be married still to Hugo Guiler when I met her?

∞

Writing the pretend invitation letter for Anaïs was torture: typing and re-typing it, checking spellings in the dictionary, laboring the grammar. Knowing it would be read by English department chairs, any error could give it away as a fake—and it would be my fault.

Anaïs and I met as arranged a week later outside the old Beaux Arts central library by the mosaics of sphinxes and snakes. I felt very continental when we rushed to greet each other on the elevated landing, exchanging pecks on both cheeks. We claimed a cement bench, and I presented to her the perfectly typed letter.

She read through it quickly. Afterwards she was pensive. What had I done wrong? "What are these two dots?" she finally said, pointing to the greeting, *Dear Anaïs Nin:*

"You mean the umlaut over the *i* in your name? I found a typewriter that had that key in the library."

"No, after my name." She pointed with a French-tipped nail.

"The colon?"

"Oui," she said impatiently.

"It's a business letter. Isn't it?"

She waved her hand. "I just use a comma."

It was my first inkling of the deficits in her education due to dropping out of high school and receiving no training other than in flamenco dancing. I was troubled by her ignorance of proper punctuation and alarmed when she pronounced, "Renate is right. The letter should actually be for a series of lectures."

"What does Renate have to do with it?"

"The letter is partly her idea. She thinks it would be better if you invited me for a series of lectures covering two years."

Ugh. I would have to re-type the whole thing.

Anaïs could read my face, even though I wasn't aware anything showed on it. "What's wrong, Tristine?"

"I may not have enough stationery to get the typing correct again."

"Oh, we don't have time for that anyway." She took a black and gold Montblanc fountain pen from her large leather purse, uncapped it, and handed it to me. "You haven't signed your name."

I noticed the very fine point on her fountain pen. "I might damage your pen," I said. "I have my own."

"Yes, that would be better."

Anaïs smiled with approval as I pulled out a Bic ballpoint. I looked for something to write on. She offered her purse, but it was too soft. I dug out the Penguin orange-and-white paperback of *Lady Chatterley's Lover* that I'd borrowed from the library to reread, set the letter on top of it, and signed my name. I was eager to have that letter out of my sight. I replaced the plastic cap on the Bic.

"Oh, don't put it away yet," she said. "Just write in 'and a series of lectures over a two-year period.'"

I looked at her askance.

She insisted with a note of sarcasm, "You know, use your little editor's arrow." She took the signed letter from me and studied it again. "Right here." She pointed.

"Are you sure?" I asked.

"Why not?"

"The English department would never send out a revised letter without it being retyped."

"But it's not coming from them. It's coming from you, on behalf of the English department. It says, right here." She pointed to the line that made me the most uncomfortable: *On behalf of the English department at the University of Southern California, I am inviting Anaïs Nin* . . .

I said, "If the letter doesn't look right, it won't impress the East Coast colleges . . ."

"Fine, but it has to go out today."

"Why?"

"So it will get there before I arrive. Why are you asking so many questions? Just write it in. I brought a stamp."

I wrote in as small a hand as I could manage, and as I was writing, she was dictating yet another phrase to add, pointing with her white tipped nail.

"Here add, 'to include screenings of Ian Hugo's films.'" Before I could object, she said, "Just insert it!"

When I finished, she seized the letter and envelope, sealed the flap, affixed the stamp she'd brought, and took my arm, guiding me as a gentleman would. "I'm taking you to lunch to thank you for this little service," she chirped, starting down the flight of steps. "We can look for a mailbox as we walk."

Arm in arm, we made our way down Fifth Street to Olive as unkempt people pushed by us. At the corner of Pershing Square she spied a mailbox into which she dropped the letter.

After that we wandered up and down inclines and through narrow, seedy streets, as she repeated, "I know we're in the right neighborhood, we just have to keep walking." She directed us to an alley with uneven paving and piles of trash. "We'll just cut through here, and it will show up."

But we emerged at a busy intersection I was sure we'd crossed before. She darted across the boulevard full of traffic. I hesitated as the light turned yellow, but then chased after her, cars honking at me before I reached the other side. My anxiety skyrocketed. I was lost and following her, and she didn't know where she was going.

She turned onto a street where disreputable-looking men hung out in stairwells, but she kept up her fast pace with long strides, fearlessly, just as she had described her character Sabina. She stepped over the legs of a wino lying in the street, and I tried to do the same but flinched, paralyzed with sorrow for him. As I watched her ahead of me, I questioned how she could ignore the whimpering man's misery, and something about his angular face made me wonder about Hugo when she'd divorced him. I was flooded with confusion again. When was that?

Catching up with her, I decided just to ask. "At the end of the story you told me, you were going to divorce Hugo. But you were still married to Hugo when I met you."

She swung around to face me. "Are you *trrracking* me, Tristine? Did someone put you up to this?"

"No! I just want to understand—"

"Just say it," she spat. "What do you want to know?"

"Why did you wait so long to divorce Hugo, and what made you finally decide to do it?"

We had emerged into a busy shopping area. She ducked under the canvas awning of a knife shop. "Haven't you heard of those women who marry the same man more than once?"

"Did you marry and divorce Hugo more than once? I love those stories."

She looked away from me. I sensed I'd struck a nerve, that this was something she was embarrassed about. Trying to sound nonjudgmental, I said, "I always wondered how that worked, how a woman who hated a man enough to divorce him could marry him again. I read about a woman who remarried the same man five times!"

"Where did you read that?"

"In a *True Confessions* magazine."

"I don't know that magazine. Do you think they might want something from my diaries?"

"I don't know. It was just trash I read at the Sherman Oaks newsstand when I was thirteen. Besides, I found out the stories aren't even true."

"When I was thirteen, I was reading Proust's *Recherché Temps Perdu* in French."

I wondered if her comment was payback for my pointing out her ignorance of proper punctuation.

She took off in her rapid stride again, and I had to hobble behind because I'd formed a blister on my foot. "Maybe we should have lunch another day," I called to her.

Taking pity on me, she came back and took my arm again. "Let's just walk a little further this way. It will be worth it. The place has the best ceviche in Los Angeles."

"What's that?" We had passed a few Mexican eateries advertising that they served menudo, which I knew was intestines. Ceviche sounded as disgusting.

"It's Mexican prepared raw fish. Delicious. You'll love it. Rupert and I ordered it all the time in Acapulco." With a maternal gesture, she lifted a bleached strand of my hair sticking to my neck. Her voice sweetened. "Now you tell me a personal story as we walk, as I told you my story of meeting Rupert."

I was struck dumb. Much as I had fantasies of becoming a writer, I had no idea how to tell a story. "I can't think of any."

"Then tell me about how you got the university letterhead." She kept us moving through what now seemed a maze of alleys. "Did you steal it?"

I said I had asked for the stationery and the secretary had just given it to me; it wasn't much of a story.

"What were your feelings?" she asked.

"Scared."

"When have you felt that way before?"

That gave me an idea. I did have a story. I decided to tell her about the one time I had stolen something. It had only been the year before.

"You never stole things as a child?" she asked, unbelieving.

"No, never. Did you?"

"Yes, of course. Money from my mother's purse. Candy. It's normal."

"Well, I was sensing that there was something not normal in my never having stolen anything," I began. "I wanted to perform an act of rebellion against authority, just for the sake of doing it. I was tired of always being the good girl."

"That's a promising beginning. Go on." She smiled.

"It was first semester, sophomore year, and we were reading Camus's *The Stranger* in Dr. Inch's world lit class."

"Who is Dr. Inch?"

"He's the chairman of the English department."

"What is his first name?"

"Minor."

"Minor Inch? *Rrr*eally?" She giggled.

I nodded but wanted to get back to the weird, personal story I had never told anyone. "That was when I realized I was an existentialist."

She gave me a look of revulsion.

"Aren't you an existentialist?" I asked, surprised.

"No!" She seemed irritated. "What does it have to do with your story?"

"After reading the end of *The Stranger*, I wanted to prove I was an existentialist by doing an action, like the shooting at the end, that had no reason except my will. I decided to steal one shoe."

"Why just one?"

"Because I would have no use for it. It would be a purely existential act with no motive or self-interest involved."

She stopped where we were, in a little cobblestone square we'd come to, and looked at me as if I were nuts. I tried to explain my thinking, but she pushed me. "Just tell me what you felt when you were taking the shoes."

"Shoe. Singular. First I walked through the shoe department looking for the easiest box of shoes to take without being noticed. I didn't care if they were my size because I would never wear them anyway."

"Yes, but what did they look like? Were they platinum high heels with rhinestone encrusted straps? Were they fine leather loafers such as Greta Garbo would have worn?"

"I think they were pumps. Two sizes too large for me. After I took them into a dressing room with a dress I'd grabbed off a rack, I removed one shoe from the box and hid it in my purse, leaving the other shoe, still wrapped in tissue, with the dress in the changing room. I hurried down the escalator afraid that I would be stopped and arrested for shoplifting. They wouldn't believe I did it to understand existentialism. I burst through the circulating door out onto the street. When I was sure no one would see me, I threw the shoe into a trash bin and resolved never to do anything so stupid again."

She frowned. She did not like my story.

She didn't say anything but turned around slowly in a semi-circle. "There!" She pointed to an archway covered with grape vines, so low we had to duck to enter. Leading the way, she declared, "I found it by intuition!"

The arbor led to a tiny covered patio only big enough for two cafe tables. We sat at one; two men in business suits occupied the other.

Anaïs launched into her critique of my story as soon as we were seated. "What was your underlying motivation? We never find out. If you were going to do it, you, at least, should have taken a pair of shoes."

"No, then it wouldn't have been an intellectual experiment."

"But it was a stupid, risky experiment with nothing to be gained. You said so yourself. What were the feelings that made you do it?"

"I don't see what it has to do with feelings!" I heard my voice rise. The businessmen looked up from their meal.

"The story I told you was driven by feelings," Anaïs said. "Feelings are where you find the *trrut!* Your *trrut!*"

The idea was so completely foreign to me that I did a double take. Feelings were the last place I would look for the truth. As far as I could see, feelings misled people, made them screw up at school or at work.

"I don't trust my feelings," I said.

"Do you even know what they are?"

"Yeah." I shrugged.

"I don't think you do," she said gently. Instead of arguing it further, she rose and glided over to where a Mexican woman was cooking. The eyes of the businessmen followed her, and although they were in their mid-thirties, considerably younger than she, they exchanged a look of appreciation as she passed. It was the way she moved: like a dancer, at once delicate and erotic.

Through open latticed doors, I watched Anaïs chattering with the plump woman patting tortillas who, with her hair in a puffy gray bun, reminded me of my mother. I suddenly felt guilty; here I was being taken to lunch by a fascinating novelist, while Mother was serving lunch to the bratty kids she babysat as she cleaned their house.

Anaïs returned to the folding chair opposite me, descending gracefully, crossing her calves, and presenting her narrow ankles to the businessmen. They paid but lingered, clearly fascinated by her. They were in my line of sight, with Anaïs's back to them, when she told me, "We're in luck. They have ceviche today."

"Very fresh," one of the businessmen chimed in.

Anaïs turned and gave him her glorious smile. "Tell my young friend that it's delicious. It's her first time."

With great gusto, the men assured me I would love it, that this was the right place for the first time.

Then Anaïs returned her attention to me as the cook brought us two glasses of Chablis and two plates of ceviche that carried the faint aroma of the sea. I couldn't believe that I was going to have to put those glistening slices of raw fish into my mouth.

"Just try it. It'll be a new experience. If you don't like it we'll order you something else," Anaïs urged.

I hesitated.

"Just do what I do," she instructed. She squeezed lemon over the pale pink flesh on both of our plates. It seemed to shiver as her fork punctured a square slice. She lifted the entire square to her mouth and, without it touching her lipstick, popped it in. She closed her ruby lips and chewed. I copied her every move, girding myself for the worst. The two men were watching me, amused. Mercifully, the fish had been soaked in so much lemon and spices it tasted good and soon I was asking for more.

Sipping her Chablis, Anaïs said, "Let me see your copy of *Lady Chatterley's Lover*."

I tried to indicate to her that the businessmen were watching us and listening, but she appeared not to care. She leafed through the paperback, finding the page she was looking for, and read aloud in her high, undulating voice, loudly enough for the men to hear:

"'In the short summer night she learnt so much. She would have thought a woman would have died of shame. Instead of which, the shame died. Shame, which is fear: the deep organic shame, the old physical fear which crouches in the bodily roots of us, and can only be chased away by the sensual fire, at last it was roused up and routed by the phallic hunt of the man . . .' Lawrence knows how to tell a story through feelings!"

The two businessmen were grinning with astonishment and titillation. They seemed to be enjoying some sophisticated game with Anaïs at my expense, and my cheeks burned like the red salsa on our table.

"Do you know them?" I hissed.

"No, I've never seen them before in my life." She glanced back at one of the men, who lit up in a smile. "Are they bothering you? We can leave." She started to rise.

The two men rose as well. One said, "We have to get back to work . . . unless?" He let the unspoken question hang in the air.

Anaïs's guttural laugh was the throaty sound she'd described in her novels as Sabina's. She gave me a questioning look. I felt paralyzed in the moment; I had no volition of my own. I was like an insect she'd pinned to a board.

I glared at the dawdling pair of men who were too old for me and too young for her. Finally, they took the hint and left.

As soon as they were gone Anaïs's laughter, like a temple bell, cleansed the air. "I was just playing with them. I thought you were participating. No? Nothing would have happened. I am completely faithful to Rupert now."

"They thought we were prickteases," I said.

"Prrrickteases? I've never heard that one! Prrricktease! I have to tell Renate."

"It's not a compliment."

"No? How is it used?"

"When a guy is mad because you acted sexy but won't follow through. I used to get called it all the time."

"Give me an example of a time you were a prrricktease."

I recalled again, as I had at her Greenwich Village apartment, my pubescent hunt for boys. "When I was just twelve, my girlfriend and I would put on makeup and look for boys to make out with at miniature golf or the movies. When I refused to go past kissing, the guy would call me a pricktease."

"So that's what happens when girls don't have chaperones," she mused. "You were fortunate. At that age I couldn't go anywhere without one of my older brothers."

"You think that was lucky? I think you were lucky to have older brothers."

"Perhaps." She shrugged. "What's interesting is that you were already a baby Sabina."

She went to pay the check rather than wait for the cook to bring it. Returning to our patio table, she leaned down, set her hands lightly on my shoulders, and said into my ear, "But where did Sabina go today, Tchrristine? Nowhere to be found! Into the ether like a genie! You should have flirted with them, had some fun, watched to see what would have happened. It would have given you a better story than a stupid shoe. You should write about being a prrricktease."

∞

Thursday morning, after Anaïs had left for New York, I intended to sleep in. I'd been up late studying and didn't have a class until the afternoon. But the phone jangled insistently at 8:30 a.m.

It was the English department secretary who had given me the stationery. She told me that Dr. Inch wanted to meet with me in his office. I had never been called into a professor's office before and I assumed it was because the secretary had conveyed a question I'd asked, about how I'd apply for a Fulbright scholarship to Italy. My heart took flight with fantasies of getting a Fulbright. I could live in Rome with Gerardo Palmieri as my lover or maybe in Siena with several Italian lovers.

Dr. Inch, a slight, faded man, seemed dwarfed behind his huge wood desk covered with tall stacks of books and papers. He rose to search for something in one of his piles. After not finding it, he sat again, and peered at me disapprovingly.

"I received a phone call, young woman, from a Mr. Guiler who said he had in his possession an invitation addressed to his wife from you on behalf of the English department."

I was stunned. "How did Hugo get that letter? It wasn't mailed to him."

"So you admit you wrote it?"

"It was for Anaïs Nin. She's a writer. I'm apprenticing to her." I hoped that Dr. Inch, as a literature professor, would look kindly on the fact that I was working for a writer.

"I've never heard of her, and for your information, I choose whom to invite to speak on behalf of the English department!"

"It wasn't a real invitation; it was just for her to show around to eastern colleges." I hoped I wasn't breaking Anaïs's confidence. I had to defend myself.

Dr. Inch crossed his arms. "Now I know you are lying to me."

"I'm not! Why do you think I'm lying?"

"East Coast colleges wouldn't care whom West Coast colleges invite. They aren't impressed by that."

My stomach sank. Of course, he was right. I hadn't thought that taking a few sheets of stationery was a big deal but suddenly I realized that it was everything, my whole future. Dr. Inch could impede my graduation and applications to grad school. "All I did was type the letter for her," I pleaded.

"You didn't just type the letter. You procured the stationery for it. We have your signature on record. This is a case of fraud, and I will see that you receive the consequences you deserve. I looked up your record, young lady. State scholarships are not intended for bad apples."

Oh, my God. I could lose my scholarship, everything I'd worked so hard for! "I'm not a bad apple! I'm not. I'm getting As. You can check. What are you going to do?"

"I haven't decided whether to recommend your suspension to the academic senate or the dean. You will be hearing from me. In the meanwhile, speak of this with no one."

∞

"How did Hugo see the letter?" I heard how out of control my voice must have sounded to Renate through the receiver. Anaïs was in New York and hadn't given me her new phone number there, so I'd phoned Renate as soon as I got back to my apartment.

"You mean the letter you mailed to Anaïs? How do you know Hugo saw the letter?"

I should have known Renate would answer my question with one of her own. I recounted what had just happened in Dr. Inch's office.

I was hyperventilating by the time Renate said gravely, "This is very serious. Let me think about it. Perhaps there's a solution to protect you at that uptight university."

I didn't think there was anything Renate or Anaïs could do about the destruction of my college career; they were so peripheral to that world.

"Anaïs can't show that letter now to any eastern colleges!" I warned.

"She won't. I'll talk to her. Here's what I want you to do. When you next see Dr. Inch, find out exactly what he told Hugo. Then be prepared for a meeting at my house with Anaïs the moment she gets back from New York. Don't worry."

How could I not worry? Questions flew around in my mind like moths, eating holes in my brain. What would I do with my life if I couldn't become a college professor? I didn't want to end up a restaurant hostess like Renate; I'd held enough waitressing jobs to know what a dead end that was. Why had I thrown away everything I'd worked for just to please Anaïs Nin?

Dr. Inch had said Hugo called Anaïs his wife. Was my suspicion right that they pretended they were married now, the way they'd pretended they were not married when Hugo was Ian Hugo? These were not honest people! And what was the truth about the letter, anyway? Dr. Inch had said that even if it really were from the USC English department, it wouldn't impress eastern colleges, so what was the real reason Anaïs had me write and send it? What kind of game had she gotten me mixed up in?

The questions flew around madly and collided with one another for a week. Another week went by, and I didn't hear from Renate, Anaïs, or Dr. Inch. I made myself focus on my classwork, hoping that my good grades would bring me leniency when the university's discipline came down on my head.

Just before Thanksgiving break, I got a call to come back to Dr. Inch's office. As I pedaled my bike onto the campus, I imagined begging Dr. Inch to let my punishment be a public flogging before the Tommy Trojan statue, rather than expulsion, so my humiliation would be over all at once.

I looked at the Romanesque campus with the greedy eyes of the doomed, as the whole student body had during the Cuban Missile crisis in my freshman year. The destruction of my life now felt as unreal as that end-of-the-world scare. I felt the same disconnection from my fate now as I had from the newscasts then of Soviet missiles and bomb shelters. Perhaps this was Meursault's detachment at the end

of Camus's *The Stranger*—his acceptance of the universe's indiffer-
ence. What irony: I was being kicked out of the university now that I
understood existentialism. There was no fair or unfair, only one event
leading to another. I had taken the stationery; I would be punished.
I decided to face my end as Meursault had his execution—with grim
determinism.

The middle-aged secretary waved me back to Dr. Inch's office, her
sympathetic eyes following me.

Without looking up from the PMLA journal he was reading, Dr.
Inch said, "Miss Rainer, let's deal with your case."

"Okay," I said apathetically.

"You will have to perform a service administered by the student
judiciary council."

Not really listening, I said dully, as I imagined Meursault would,
"What charge?"

"Destruction of university property, namely twenty sheets of
departmental stationery. Unless, of course, you can return the
stationery."

"I only have a few sheets left. Four."

"That would be fine, then."

What? Was he playing with me? Had he just said there would be no
consequences if I returned the four unused sheets of stationery? How
could he have done such a 180-degree turn?

There was the hint of a smile on his narrow lips. "I will just leave you
with this piece of advice, because you are a bright and well-connected
young lady. You should choose a mentor who can write. Your Anaïs
Nin is a terrible novelist and a *poseur*. An association with her will only
damage your applications to grad school. You can do better, I'm sure."

I was speechless, not only over his derision of Anaïs, a writer he
hadn't even known existed in our previous meeting, but also because
he was giving me advice about applying to grad school. No one at that

university had ever talked to me about my future. He further surprised me:

"Why don't you take my graduate seminar in seventeenth-century drama next year? With my permission you can enroll for credit as an undergrad."

This was suddenly going very well, and I thought I should take advantage of the new direction. "Are you also the person who could write me a recommendation for a Fulbright?"

"A Fulbright? Oh, don't bother with that. They don't grant them to girls."

I was so relieved at not having been expelled, I didn't even notice a door slamming in my face. Instead, I remembered that Renate wanted me to find out what Dr. Inch had told Hugo.

"Did you tell Mr. Guiler the invitation wasn't real?" I asked.

"No, I simply promised him that I would look into the matter, and I have."

"Has he called you again?" Something had happened to make Dr. Inch do a turnabout towards me.

"No. And I do not wish to get involved. If he phones me again I will refer him directly to you."

If Hugo hadn't phoned Dr. Inch again, what had caused him to go from treating me as a pest to be eliminated, to a pansy to be nurtured? I was pretty sure Renate would know. She had speculated that something could be done. Maybe her Gothic witchiness wasn't all appearance.

When I phoned Renate, she was effusively happy for me and pleased that I'd found out what Dr. Inch had said to Hugo. But when I asked her how Hugo had seen the letter mailed to Anaïs and why he'd made the call to Dr. Inch, she said sternly, "Don't you know it is rude to ask so many questions?"

"What's wrong with it?"

"It's impolite. You make people feel that you are grilling them, like they are on the stand and you are cross-examining them. Where do you get that from?"

"My father, I guess. When my mother fought with him, she'd always say, 'Yes, counselor! No, counselor!' because he fired so many questions at her."

"That's right, Anaïs said your father is a lawyer." Apparently, they talked about me. Then I heard Renate sigh into the phone. "Well, I suppose we cannot change your nature. Hopefully we can help you channel it. You would make an excellent lawyer."

"But I'm going to be an English professor now."

"Good. We Viennese consider professors respectable, unlike lawyers." Then she invited me to her house the day after Thanksgiving when Anaïs would be back, promising that all would be made clear about Dr. Inch.

∞

"Tristine Raiiiner, I would like you to meet my son, Peter Loomer." Renate introduced us when I arrived at her house before Anaïs. Peter had the kind of dark good looks that attracted me, and at the moment I had no one to sleep with, so it passed my mind that Renate intended to fix me up with her son. But Peter didn't make eye contact with me, and I felt no sexual charge with him despite his James Dean looks. Behaving like the actor, his eyes studying the floor, he mumbled to his mother that he wouldn't be home until after midnight and left, grabbing a leather jacket from a hook near the door.

"Peter is shy around strangers," Renate explained, evidently embarrassed that his manners didn't match hers.

Trying to put her at ease, I commented on a collection of masks I hadn't noticed before on one of her walls. They all looked homemade: a red devil's mask, a white ruffled lady's mask, a long-nosed Venetian mask, several grotesque animal masks, and the scariest—a featureless bone-white mask. Renate explained that she'd made the masks out of papier-mâché as decorations for a party she'd thrown at her house where all the guests wore costumes to portray their own madness. She'd hung the masks from sumac branches, and in the flickering candlelight, the swinging masks danced amongst the masks of meandering guests.

"I wish I could have been there. What was your costume for the party?" I asked her.

"I held death masks on sticks in two hands. When I removed one, there would be another mask of death behind it."

I loved that—it was deep like existentialism but, as I was learning about surrealism, much more fun. I was attracted to Renate and Anaïs's playfulness and creativity, yet my recent scare had shown me that they could be dangerous to my future.

Renate went on to tell me that a friend of hers, Kenneth Anger, had directed an experimental film called *Inauguration of the Pleasure Dome* that recreated her party. In it, she, her son Peter, Anaïs, and Rupert had enacted a pagan ritual. She recommended I catch the film when it screened at college campuses on Halloween, rekindling my suspicion that Renate was a witch.

Despite her warning on the phone that my questions were rude, I decided I couldn't wait. "You said something could be done for me at my uptight university. Do you know what turned Dr. Inch around?"

To my surprise, she smiled. "Do you remember meeting Chris at Holiday House?" I assumed she was referring to Christopher Isherwood, but I didn't get any more information because we were interrupted by Anaïs's arrival.

Renate quickly departed to display some of her canvases at an outdoor art show, and Anaïs settled on her floor-pillow pedestal asking how I was.

"I'm okay." Actually my blood was racing. I felt like demanding, *I'm owed some answers!* But Anaïs's warmth was shining on me. I recognized how beloved I felt in her presence, and my anger melted away as she introduced the subject so I didn't have to.

"Renate has kept me up to date on the drama that has gone on in your life since Hugo phoned your Dr. Inch. I am so sorry, Tchrristine. We never intended for it to harm you."

"Did you or Renate fix it somehow with Inch?" She smiled as Renate had, a sign I took as permission to ask my questions. "Why did Hugo phone Inch in the first place? How did he know about the letter I wrote for you?"

"Hugo and I are still the best of friends."

I contemplated that. My mother, after her divorce, would never be friends with my father in this life or the next. "Does that mean you showed Hugo the letter?"

"No, he opened it when it arrived before I did," she said.

Was Hugo housesitting at her apartment or did she receive mail at his place? Whichever, I could not understand why she didn't appear upset over his opening her mail.

"Doesn't he know it's a federal offense to open someone else's mail?" I said, indignant on her behalf.

"Is it? I'll have to remember that."

How could she be so literate, so charismatic, I wondered, and yet so ignorant about the things everyone else knew? She was a puzzle, a mystery, and though I now recognized she was devious and dangerous to my life, I was driven to know her secrets. "Do you still stay with Hugo in New York?"

"Well, yes. New York hotels are impossibly expensive."

So she didn't have her own apartment in New York. Renate had told me that Anaïs flew on holidays to save on the airfare, so I knew she tried to conserve on money, but I'd never heard of a couple being so friendly after a divorce that they could stay under the same roof, especially when one had remarried. If Anaïs still stayed at her ex-husband's apartment, perhaps Rupert's jealousy wasn't so irrational after all. "Does Rupert know you stay with Hugo?"

"Why do you want to know?" Her eyes were full of alarm. "Are you playing Perry Mason on me? I thought Renate talked with you about asking so many personal questions!"

"I just want to know when you and Hugo got divorced," I said. "How is that personal? It's public record." I surprised myself, talking back to her as I would my mother. Much as I was still enthralled by Anaïs's presence, I was no longer intimidated, having heard Dr. Inch describe her as a terrible novelist and a *poseur*. I pushed further. "When you told me your story about falling for Rupert, you said you were going to divorce Hugo when you flew back to Acapulco. Did you get divorced then, and later remarry Hugo and divorce him again?"

"What *are* you talking about?"

"You said you were one of those women who got married to the same man more than once."

"I said I was *like* them."

"What does that mean?"

For a moment she looked so angry I thought she was going to yell at me, but she closed her eyes and was quiet for a long time. Finally, when she opened them, her anger was gone.

"I'll try to explain," she said. "I intended to divorce Hugo when Rupert asked me to come live in his forester's cabin with him." She smoothed the skirt of her soft wool dress and looked down, searching, it seemed, for where to pick up the thread of her story.

## Chapter 11

# Acapulco, Mexico, 1948

## ANAÏS

WHEN THE PROP PLANE CARRYING Hugo bumped to a stop on the beach landing strip, Anaïs trudged through the sand to greet him. A cabdriver waited to take them directly to the American Hotel. It was luxurious compared to the El Mirador, where gossiping maids and the patron had seen her with Rupert. She intended to tell Hugo she wanted a divorce as soon as they were alone in their penthouse suite.

After he'd tipped the hotel porters and appreciated the panoramic view of the ocean from fourteen floors above, he said soberly, "You've heard the news that Gandhi was assassinated?"

"Yes, I'm grieving with the world."

They communed for a moment in silence, cooled by the hotel air-conditioning, he sitting on the king-sized bed, she perched on a settee covered with a tropical print, mourning the loss of a hero who had embodied their shared ideals.

"Well, the world goes on," Hugo said softly. "I brought three little surprises that should cheer you, dear. I hope you like them."

*Poor Hugo,* she thought, *I'm sure I'll like them more than you will like my surprise.*

He pulled a gift-wrapped box from his leather satchel. She could tell by its size and shape what was inside: Chanel 22, Coco Chanel's personal scent that the famous designer allowed only a few select customers to buy. Receiving this almost illicit nectar always gave Anaïs a thrill but accepting it did not make her announcement of wanting a divorce easier.

He leaned back, hands clasped behind his head, and told her his second surprise. "I resigned from the bank. I'm a free man!" He grinned. To her increasing alarm, he explained that the conflict between his banker self and his artist self had reached a crisis and that with his psychoanalyst's help he'd decided to become, as she, a full-time artist.

"But what about money?" Anaïs gasped.

"I took an early payout on my pension."

"No!" Her hands gripped her face. "Your pension was there to take care of us in old age," she moaned.

"Anaïs, it's fine. I've paid off our debts and we still have money to invest."

"Invest!"

"Dearest, that's what I do for other people. I can do it for us. Leave that part to me."

How she hated his patronizing tone. "This affects us both!" she cried. A divorce attorney she had once consulted in New York had told her that half of Hugo's pension would be hers if they separated. Now what could she expect? They had always rented and owned no property, except for the rat-infested shack she'd recently purchased.

A terrifying thought seized her. She had driven him to this disastrous act. Hugo had given up his pension in order to keep her from divorcing him. He had put her in checkmate.

*He knows. He's always known I was cheating,* she realized. *He's telling me that it was the bargain he made, offering me silence, in order to hold onto me.*

He confirmed her thoughts. "I've given you the freedom to explore whatever and whomever you wish in the name of your creativity. I understood. The artist needs to be able to play, to experiment, to try out ideas, and a writer, especially, needs to know lots of different kinds of people." He parroted her words sarcastically, but then smiled. "Now we'll have a chance to play together."

Play? With Hugo? It was hard to imagine. "It's too late," she said.

"No it isn't. You have to give this a chance."

She needed time to think. "What's your third surprise?"

He told her to open a leather satchel in the corner and in it she found a sixteen-millimeter movie camera. He explained that with his new freedom he was going to make experimental films and he wanted her to be his star.

Actually, that idea delighted her. Being in Hollywood, overhearing actors, directors, and producers talk shop, she'd found herself wishing she were younger so that she could be involved in moviemaking.

"Let's just play and see what we come up with." Hugo grinned boyishly. "We can experiment with your idea that film is the best medium for replicating our dream life."

Suddenly, she could see the twenty-three-year-old she had fallen madly in love with and married, the young idealist who wrote poetry and to whom every night she'd read her diary or her untutored attempts at short stories. He had always believed in her talent when she had no faith in herself. How could she deny him the same encouragement now?

∞

Lovemaking with Hugo was not as athletic and physically fulfilling as with Rupert, but it was emotionally fulfilling. All their years of marriage resounded like a 120-string orchestra: all the times they had touched, told each other their dreams at breakfast, decorated new dwellings, packed and unpacked, argued and made up, shared disappointments, consoled each other, helped each other dress to go out, slept side by side, melded as one vibrant harmony. With Rupert, making love was like the *Liebestod*, orchestrated to achieve a huge climax. With Hugo, it was the vibration of an infinite, encompassing resonance.

While Hugo went to straighten out the realtor who had sold Anaïs the romantic shack she no longer wanted, she luxuriated at the hotel spa. Over a lobster dinner at the spotless restaurant of the American Hotel, Hugo told her proudly, "I got the realtor to return half your down payment and tear up the contract."

"He should return the whole down payment! It's all that was left of my advance."

"Don't worry about the money. We'll have plenty of investment income."

"But my book advance was different. It was my own money that I made from my writing. And look what I did, I wasted half of it."

"Listen to me," he said, taking her hand and rubbing the ringless finger where he'd once placed a wedding band. "All these years you've felt subordinate because you had to come to me for your allowance. I think I liked it that way. It made me feel important, kingly. But it made you resent me because you saw me as an authoritarian ruler."

"That's true, Hugo, but I was also so grateful to you. You were such a kind and generous king."

"Now I want to be your equal, though, your fellow artist and companion, so you need to have your own income to manage without me."

What was he saying? Was he cutting her off financially? She had wished to be financially independent so many times. Yet having recently gone over the numbers, she'd figured out that even if Dutton published her next book, and the next, she would not have enough money to live anywhere except the rat-infested beach shack.

But Hugo touched her wrist with his long fingers and added, "I've set up a separate entity in your name. From the interest, you'll have $5,000 a year of your own to spend as you wish."

"Why are you doing this?"

"I want you to be with me because you want to be, not because you have to be."

It was such an authentic gesture of love. She knew that Hugo could see the tears forming in the corners of her eyes.

"Hugo, thank you. I do want to be with you, especially now."

She meant it, even when she later realized that with her own income she could easily purchase plane tickets and pay travel expenses to visit Rupert. Her own money would truly make her free to follow her heart; unexpectedly, her heart had returned to Hugo.

# CHAPTER 12

# Malibu, California, 1964

## TRISTINE

I HADN'T BEEN EXACTLY BORED with Anaïs's account of Hugo's financial finagling, but I wanted her to return to the subject that interested me most. "Did your lovemaking with Hugo get better?"

Her dry laugh cracked. "Sex with Hugo was like dancing with a man who can't keep step. On occasion, to the right tune, he may catch the rhythm, but he will always revert back to his innate clumsiness."

"So if you didn't like making love with Hugo, why did you wait so long to divorce him? You told me that a woman has an equal right to pleasure as a man."

"Exactly, which is why I continued my affair with Rupert. I needed the affair to sustain my marriage to Hugo, whom I loved as my lifelong partner."

"So did you join Rupert at his cabin in the woods?"

She nodded.

"What did you tell Hugo?"

"I explained I wasn't feeling well, which was true. I'd returned from Acapulco, not only to the coldest winter in New York history, but also to reviews of my book so chilly that Dutton dropped me. I was depressed and exhausted and I told Hugo I needed time at a rest ranch in California to be able to write again."

"Which was really Rupert's cabin!" Encouraged by her mischievous smile, I said, "I bet it was romantic staying with a lover in the woods."

"You think that would be romantic?" She looked at me dubiously.

"Yeah, Adam and Eve in paradise."

She exhaled a harsh "Ha!" and told me that the national park was too far from the social life she was used to, and that the few locals there were so square that she and Rupert had to pretend they were married. "The US Forest Service had rules that rangers couldn't have female guests overnight in their cabins so we put on a show that I was Rupert's writer wife who traveled a lot."

I had gotten it all wrong! "So that's why Rupert introduced himself as your husband at the restaurant," I said. "That made me think you'd gotten divorced, but you're still married to Hugo!"

"But, Tristine, we have gotten sidetracked from your recent ordeal with that awful Minor Inch."

"Yes, just before you got here, Renate started to tell me that Christopher Isherwood—"

"—was very impressed when he met you."

"I'm surprised he even remembered me."

"Well, Renate reminded him and told him that a terrible injustice was being done to you at that conservative college because you were helping me with an intimate situation of great delicacy. As fortune would have it, Chris had met your Dr. Inch socially and phoned him on your behalf."

"Christopher Isherwood called Dr. Inch?"

Preening, she continued, "Then, in New York, I told Gore Vidal about the phone call and invited him into our little conspiracy. Gore, who loves a conspiracy but doesn't often get to join one, phoned your Dr. Inch, too, and told him what great promise you have in the eyes of the writers' community."

"But he's never even met me!"

"It is our credo that artists support each other."

"Oh my god. Inch must have pissed himself!" Dr. Inch had lectured reverentially about Vidal's books to our Twentieth-Century Authors class, and I'd seen a new hardbound of *Julian* on Dr. Inch's desk.

Anaïs, enjoying my excitement, added, "Gore likes having his fun at the expense of academics. The more he disdains them, the more they prostrate themselves to him."

Now I understood what had turned Dr. Inch around. He might not respect Anaïs, who wasn't in the Acropolis or even on the marble steps of literary recognition, but he would have been awed and intimidated by calls from her celebrated friends.

"Dr. Inch doesn't like you for some reason," I revealed to Anaïs, but immediately regretted it, realizing that Gore Vidal had probably badmouthed her to Dr. Inch, which was why Inch, in turn, had warned me against Anaïs's writing.

To my surprise, Anaïs shrugged it off. "Minor Inch may not like me but now he fears me, and that is better."

Her statement was so at odds with her feminine delicacy and the sweetness of her ageless face that I did not yet realize how telling it was. Anaïs might not be a great writer or know where to use a colon, but she understood power and had used it to save me.

"What can I do to thank you?" I said in all sincerity, forgetting she had caused the problem in the first place.

"There may be something," she said.

I became alert with caution.

"Renate and I were talking . . ."

*Uh-oh.* That's how the two of them had come up with the lecture series scheme.

She continued, "You said Dr. Inch is going to have Hugo phone you if he hears from him again." She smiled slyly. "You'll have to know what to say if Hugo calls you."

"What do you want me to say?"

"Hugo has to believe that I really am booked for a series of lectures at USC and that I'm currently staying with you."

"You mean confirm what it says in the letter."

"Yes, and you may have to tell Hugo that I'm out at the moment."

"You want me to lie to him."

"Lies of love! I'm trying to protect him. You think your brutal honesty that hurts people is better? You just don't understand, do you?" she retorted.

I felt wounded. "You mean that you are still married to Hugo, and that you and Rupert just pretend you are married, but that Hugo still doesn't know about Rupert?"

She looked at the ceiling, as if all that were so obvious. And then it finally hit me as a rush of cold from an opened freezer door. "And the letter was *meant* for Hugo to see!"

"Precisely." She smiled.

"You should have told me that," I said, indignant that I'd been used in her intrigue without even being asked.

"I'm sorry. I'm still learning how much I can trust you." She reached for my hand. "Since I fell in love with Rupert, I've spun myself into a cocoon of lies. I can't escape now."

I couldn't resist. "What lies?"

She gave me a concerned look. "If I tell you my secrets you'll have to tell more lies to protect me. I still don't know if you are willing to do that." Her blue-green eyes held mine until I answered.

"I'll tell Hugo whatever you want me to say." I was too ensnared in her maze of intrigue to figure a way out. And too excited by it to want to.

She continued to hold my gaze, binding me to her mandate. She began, "Whenever I flew to California to be with Rupert, I told Hugo I was staying at the California rest ranch I'd made up. Even though I hated my life of drudgery with Rupert in the cabin—getting up at 5 a.m. to make his breakfast, washing and mending his clothes, and giving directions to pesky hikers when he was out all day—I couldn't end our affair. I had searched for a man who could make love to me as Rupert did and I knew I would never find his equal. I was enslaved by what we shared in bed." Her words were a complaint, but a connoisseur's satisfaction crossed her face. "Sometimes I think it was the friction of our bodies that caused the forest fire."

"You were in a forest fire? Tell me about it! That must have been exciting."

"Rupert was a real hero. That is always exciting to women. He ran up the mountain toward the descending flames with the firemen. They told me to evacuate, and I packed the car but was too worried about Rupert to leave. Then I saw the saw the wall of fire barreling down the mountain, and Rupert running in front of it into my arms.

"While we were speeding out of there in Cleo, it started to rain, and Rupert stubbornly insisted that we go back to check on the cabin. The rain had doused the fire, so we stayed. But then it rained for weeks, causing the hillsides to collapse. Rivers of mud surrounded the cabin and we were stranded there."

# CHAPTER 13

# Sierra Madre, California, 1954

## ANAÏS

RUPERT AND THE OTHER RANGERS worked eighteen-hour days digging ditches to divert the growing rivers. He came in at night covered with mud and ash, still his buoyant self.

To fill her days while he was out building barricades, Anaïs played with the six-year-old daughter of the ranger family that lived in a nearby cabin. One evening when he got home, Rupert found Anaïs and the child dancing *pas de deux* to a Tchaikovsky record. He ran to get his viola to accompany them, encouraging them on with his energetic bowing.

That night when Anaïs joined him in bed, he was even more tender in his foreplay than usual. As he entered her, he whispered, "I want you to have my child."

He said it again when she served him his morning oatmeal. As she was about to put the milk away, he caught her hand. "Let's get married and have a baby."

"Darling, I'm afraid I wouldn't make a very good mother." She touched the corner of his mouth and wiped away the tiniest piece of oatmeal glue. She heard the instant arousal in his voice from her slightest touch when he urged, "Marry me, Anaïs." His poetic face was earnest and pure.

"I can't." She had been leading him on, letting him think she was getting a divorce from Hugo; after a few years when that no longer held water, she'd let him believe that she had already divorced Hugo. Now she had to tell him the truth. She confessed that she couldn't marry him because she was still married to Hugo, and there was no divorce pending.

He pushed her away. She reached out to him, declaring how much she loved him. He crossed his arms against her.

In the following weeks, his mood turned black. The rain stopped, but the winds began to blow, carrying soot that smarted in their eyes, filled their nostrils, and made their scalps gritty. All around her were twisted, blackened trees, cinder, images of death. Anaïs developed a persistent dry cough and an abdominal pain that stabbed her so severely at night she couldn't sleep.

Renate, out of concern, made the three-hour drive out to Sierra Madre, insisting that Anaïs tell her about the pain.

"It feels like when I was eleven and my appendix burst. In the hospital an abscess formed on my abdomen and wouldn't heal. I think this is just an echo."

Renate frowned. "Possibly, but pain usually carries a message. Wasn't it right after your appendix burst that your father left?"

"You should have studied psychiatry, Renate."

"I don't need to. It was in the soil from which I grew; Sigmund Freud was our next-door neighbor in Vienna. Anaïs, are you afraid of being left now for some reason?"

Anaïs nodded and managed a pained smile. "Rupert has given me an ultimatum: if I don't divorce Hugo and really marry him, he's breaking it off. He keeps telling me he wants a whole life, a family."

"He can't mean children!"

"He thinks I'm near his age. Even his mother, who can't stand me, keeps asking when we're tying the knot."

"Don't you want to marry Rupert?"

Anaïs shook her head. "I just don't want to lose him. I don't want to lose my husband, either."

"But you have to choose one, and therefore, you have to lose one," Renate said, and gently added, "as you lost your father when you suffered this pain as a child."

Tears broke, making Anaïs feel like that helpless, abandoned little girl again.

Renate ordered Anaïs to fly to New York to see an internist. Afraid that an illness would make Rupert think about her age, Anaïs told him that she had to go for a magazine writing job. What was one more lie?

∽

"Anaïs? Can you hear me?"

There was a nurse looking down at her. Tubes in her arms. Nausea. Vomit. Dry heaves. Utter weakness. Pain. So much pain from the incision where she'd had the abscess.

Hugo's face. Hugo, there day and night. His eyes, her beacon. Hugo's hand holding her limp hand. Hugo's love, all that mattered.

"Was it cancer?" she asked him.

"No," he said, lifting her palm, kissing it. "They got everything. You're going to be fine."

But that was not what she read in his eyes.

"I love you so much," he said, kissing her forehead.

Eyelids heavy, she drifted off again.

∽

"Your incision is healing nicely." The doctor smiled.

She was sitting up, had applied her makeup, and was wearing her bright red burnoose for courage.

"Was it cancer?"

"Didn't your husband talk with you?" the doctor replied.

"Yes, he said you got everything. What did he mean?"

"We gave you a hysterectomy."

She was so stunned she was inert and couldn't ask more. No one had told her they could take her female parts. Rupert had begged that she marry him, have his child. That choice had been made for her. Inexorably.

# CHAPTER 14

# Malibu, California, 1964

## TRISTINE

WE HEARD THE SOUND OF tires on the gravel outside, and Renate bustled in carrying a bag of groceries. As she put them in the fridge, she called from the kitchen, "You can't believe how much two young men eat!"

"When will they be back?" Anaïs called.

Returning, Renate assured her, "You have another hour. May I join you?"

Once Renate had assembled some floor cushions for herself, Anaïs touched her hand, the way she had mine. "Tristine has told me what she now understands—that Rupert and I have had to *pretend* we're married because of the Forest Service. That I am still married to Hugo. She's agreed to take his calls to help me save my marriage."

I thought I'd agreed to confirm for Hugo what the letter said about the lecture series and Anaïs staying with me. I had not realized I would be "taking Hugo's calls" to save her marriage. That was a huge responsibility, one I could easily screw up. Yet suddenly the idea filled me with a sense of mission. Believing I had ruined my parents' marriage, I now seized the chance to save Anaïs's marriage to Hugo.

Anaïs gazed on me with hope and trust, and then said to Renate, "I'm afraid that Tristine is troubled about needing to lie to Hugo. She does not fully grasp that these are *misonges de la gentilesse*. I think we should explain to her about Rancho Sosegado."

"What is Rancho Sosegado?" I asked.

Anaïs lowered her voice. "It's the rest ranch in California I made up for Hugo as my excuse to visit Rupert. Renate was the voice of the ranch owner."

Lounging sinuously on the floor pillows, Renate explained, "Hugo would phone my number to reach Anaïs, and I would say that ranch guests were not allowed to come to the phone but that I would convey a message. Then I would phone Anaïs at the cabin, and when Rupert went out, Anaïs would drive to Sierra Madre, the nearby town, and phone Hugo collect from a pay phone. She'd told him that I, the ranch owner, wouldn't let her use the ranch phone for long distance calls."

Anaïs sighed. "It worked well until Renate married Ronnie, and he moved in with her."

Renate seemed to take Anaïs's words as an accusation, for she rose abruptly and strode back into her kitchen. Anaïs marched after her. I couldn't make out their whole argument, but I overheard Renate snap, "The phone company promised to have my number changed next week. I can't get them to do it any faster."

When they returned to the living room, Anaïs said, "Renate is going to explain to you about an unfortunate incident last month."

Renate straightened her posture. "Ronnie was already living with me when my son quit UCLA and moved back home. Anaïs and I didn't tell either of them about Hugo's calls to Rancho Sosegado." Wincing, Anaïs massaged her temples while Renate elaborated. "Last month Hugo called here, and my husband answered. Hugo asked him, 'Is this Rancho Sosegado?' and Ronnie said, 'Wrong number!' and hung up."

Anaïs added in distress, "Hugo phoned back and Ronnie hung up on him again." She stopped to slow her breathing. "Renate, tell what happened next."

Renate said with great dignity, "Several days later, Hugo phoned once more, and this time my son answered. Hugo insisted he speak to the woman who owned the place where Anaïs Nin stayed. Peter told Hugo he knew Anaïs, but that she never stayed here."

I asked Anaïs, "Is that why you don't want to be here when Ronnie or Peter get home?"

"Yes, they're too young to understand," Anaïs said, and Renate nodded in agreement.

I was the same age as Renate's son and nine years younger than her husband, but they evidently thought I was mature enough, which was flattering.

"Tristine, do you understand? Now Hugo knows I've been lying to him about Rancho Sosegado for seven years!" Anaïs cried.

I was stunned at the enormity of her deception, and at the same time impressed that she had been able to pull it off for so long.

She eyed me sternly. "You will warn me before you let anyone move in with you?"

I shrugged. "There's no space for a roommate in my single anyway."

Renate rolled her eyes. "Anaïs means don't let a man move in with you."

"I don't even have a boyfriend."

"That won't last," Renate said, and Anaïs readily concurred.

I grinned, delighted they thought so.

Anaïs placed a folded hand under her delicate chin. "I'm thinking of telling Hugo that the ranch owner was so annoyed at people calling to leave messages for guests that she had the phone disconnected, and that the phone company assigned the number to the men who answered."

"Excellent plan," Renate said. "And with Tristine and the lecture series, you are now covered for the next two years."

So that was why Anaïs had made me change the invitation letter to a *series* of lectures! She could no longer tell Hugo that she was writing at the California rest ranch, but she could say repeatedly that she was coming to give the pre-arranged lectures at USC and staying with me. As this last piece fell into place, the chill I'd felt was encompassed by blackness, as if I were inside the freezer and someone had closed the door. Did they expect me to lie to Hugo for the next two years? I would have to memorize every detail of what Anaïs had told him. Renate had been able to pull off their ruse for seven years, but eventually even she had screwed up.

Anaïs asked me, concerned, "Do you think you can do this?"

"Yes," I said with a conviction I didn't feel. I didn't have sufficient experience with lying. I was unqualified for this assignment, but now it was too late to tell Anaïs.

"So, everything is settled." Renate rose, indicating it was time for us to leave. But when Anaïs and I stood, Renate commanded, "We must make an oath with Tristine."

Alarmed, I looked to Anaïs. She simply shrugged and nodded with a resigned smile that I should humor Renate.

"Put your hand over mine," Renate instructed me.

She extended her elevated right hand. I placed mine over hers. Anaïs placed her right hand over mine. Her hand was soft and cold. Renate stacked her left hand over Anaïs's, and we followed suit until our six hands were piled like pancakes.

Renate began, "Tristine swears not to repeat what she has learned or may learn about Anaïs's life. She may discuss it only with Anaïs or Renate."

I felt a frisson of excitement.

"Say 'I swear,'" Renate urged, and I did. Renate continued, "We vow to keep Anaïs's secrets, revealed now or in the future, under pain of personal disaster. The person who betrays this oath, unless released by Anaïs, shall be visited with betrayals increased in magnitude to the tenth degree. Repeat after me: 'This I swear in the name of Archangel Raphael to the East, Uriel to the North, Gabriel to the West and Michael to the South. So be it. Amen.'"

We repeated Renate's words, but Anaïs's voice was so faint, I heard only my own. The hocus pocus reminded me of the silly solemnity of my ADPi sorority initiation, and I was tempted to giggle—but the chill from Anaïs's hand penetrated mine, and I could tell that Renate was completely serious.

# CHAPTER 15

# Los Angeles, California, 1964

## TRISTINE

HUGO PHONED ME THREE DAYS later. "Hello, Tristine."

I wasn't ready! I went into actress mode. I told myself this was improvisation. The givens were that I was a sophisticated young woman who was friends with Anaïs Nin, such good friends that she stayed in my apartment when she was in LA. *Ready, set, go.*

Perhaps with too much gusto, I responded, "Hugo! It's been a long time. It's great to hear from you."

"Thank you, Tristine. And thank you for helping Anaïs when she's there."

"Oh, no problem. Do you have a message for her?"

"No, is she staying there now?"

"She's not here at the moment, but I can get her a message."

"Well, no. I'll tell you why I'm calling. I hope you won't mind if I ask you some personal questions."

*Uh-oh.* I couldn't figure out whether to say yes, he could, or no, he couldn't.

He must have gotten tired of waiting for me to reply because he went on. "Anaïs told me that you've moved universities. She gave me your new address at USC." Moved universities? I hadn't moved. I wasn't sure how to respond.

"Yes."

"Hmm. I've heard that USC has a good football team."

"That's what everyone says. I don't—"

"Actually, that's not what I wanted to ask you about."

*Oh god, I'm not going to be able to do this!*

"I have a friend whose son was going to enroll there," Hugo continued. "My friend says that the surrounding neighborhood is quite dangerous. A lot like Harlem before the riots this summer."

"But the campus is safe."

"How many blocks would you say your apartment is from campus?"

"Oh, it's only a few blocks from campus," I fudged. Twelve blocks could still be a few. "And my building is safe." I wished.

"I never worried when Anaïs was staying at your apartment near UCLA. Westwood is a good neighborhood. But that rich-kids school you're at now is in the ghetto. Go figure."

I was trying to figure. Hugo thought Anaïs had stayed with me before when I was at UCLA? But I'd never gone to UCLA or lived in Westwood. I just held my tongue while Hugo continued to admonish me to be careful on my "new" campus. Finally, given my silence, he stopped and asked, "So what are you majoring in?"

"English lit."

"Well, why would an undergraduate transfer across town for that?"

I hadn't transferred, but he certainly thought I had. *Okay*, I prompted myself, *go with what the other actor gives you*. Preserve the illusion of reality: Why would an undergraduate transfer colleges? For a great professor! But USC didn't have any. Well, there was one great art history professor who was gay, but they'd fired him. *Think! Think! Got it!*

"I'm applying to UCLA for grad school, and they prefer to take undergraduates from colleges other than UCLA. So I had to leave to be able to come back."

"Hmm. You should come east for grad school. Gotta go. Do take extra precautions, won't you?"

When I put down the receiver, my heart was pounding. I thought it had gone all right. Hugo sounded cheerful when he hung up, but how could I know?

I immediately phoned Anaïs.

"That's interesting Hugo called you so soon," she said. At her request, I recounted my conversation with him, sentence by sentence.

"You are a great actress, Tristine!"

I felt triumphant, as when I'd won first place in a national high school acting competition. I started to ask Anaïs why Hugo believed I'd transferred from UCLA to USC, but she interrupted, "Can you come tomorrow evening to hear Rupert's quintet?"

Was she really inviting me? Or was she covering because Rupert had just walked in? I said uncertainly, "I'll need your address."

"I'm going to put Rupert on the phone to give you directions," she replied. "The music begins at six, but you should come earlier. You and I can go over some correspondence. Plan to stay for dinner before the music."

I was becoming a part of Anaïs's life! "How long do you think it will take me to drive to Sierra Madre?" I asked.

"Oh, we haven't lived in Sierra Madre for two years!"

"Did the forestry service relocate Rupert?" I asked.

"No! He's no longer with the Forest Service. He's teaching secondary school in Hollywood, near our apartment here."

∞

Anaïs's faux Tudor building was in the flats near Fountain, a Nathanael West neighborhood: Swiss chalets next to Egyptian temples,

Mediterranean terraces next to Moorish turrets. As I circled block after block for a parking space, I became increasingly disenchanted with Rupert for having left a cabin in nature for this congested grid of tired apartment buildings. Then it hit me—as I nearly hit an Impala pulling out of a parking space—Rupert was no longer a forest ranger.

From what Anaïs had said, he hadn't been one for several years, so he and Anaïs no longer needed to pretend they were married. Yet Rupert had introduced himself to me as Anaïs's husband at Holiday House. Why? The only people who had heard him had been Christopher Isherwood, his boyfriend, Renate, and me. None of us would have cared that Anaïs and Rupert were shacking up. That's what anyone who was cool was doing these days, according to Hugh Hefner. I added this to my list of things I wanted to ask her.

After I parked and arrived at the apartment, Anaïs opened her cross-beamed door, wearing a long, embroidered caftan.

"Please have a seat," she said, indicating a nubby brown couch not unlike the one buried in my mother's living room. "It's awful, I know," Anaïs apologized, "but Rupert refuses to part with it. He can be impossibly bullish."

There were touches of Anaïs's style everywhere: her Spanish shawl thrown over the grand piano; a fireplace grate with surreal, swirling patterns; books neatly organized in the built-in bookcases. But whereas the eclecticism of the apartment she shared with Hugo in New York harmonized, here her things clashed with the Tudor-beamed ceilings, Rupert's modern bargain-basement furniture, and a few vintage prairie-style pieces.

Anaïs perched herself gracefully on the front edge of a square maple armchair. Pulling out my shorthand notebook, I asked, "Shall we deal with your correspondence first?"

"Oh, I just said we'd do correspondence because Rupert was standing there. I don't have any today. I invited you early so we could have a tête-à-tête. Rupert won't be home for hours."

Nevertheless, I hushed my voice. "I need to know certain things in case Hugo calls again."

Anaïs smiled. "What do you need to know?"

"How come Hugo thinks you *have* stayed with me, and that I attended UCLA and transferred to USC?"

"I had to say that, Tristine. I hope you will forgive me."

She might have been waiting for me to say I forgave her, but I was waiting for her to explain, and finally she did, making Balinese dancelike movements with her hands as she spoke. "Just about the time you and I met in New York, Rupert left the Forest Service, and we moved here to Hollywood. Hugo was used to speaking to Renate as the voice of Rancho Sosegado, and I didn't want to change that pretext. The problem was, it was a four-hour round trip from Hollywood to the Sierra Madre post office to pick up Hugo's weekly letters. It was too much driving!"

"Hugo thought he was mailing his letters to you at the rest ranch?" I asked to clarify.

"Well I'd told him that the eccentric owner wouldn't let guests receive mail at the ranch so he had to mail his letters to a P.O. box at the nearby town. But after Rupert and I got settled here in Hollywood, I told Hugo that the Sierra Madre post office had been shut down. Since Hugo had just met you, and you'd said you would be attending college in Los Angeles . . . Hold on. I want to look this up. You need to get this right, because Hugo, though he has a terrible memory about everything else, recalls in precise detail everything I tell him about my trips out here."

She disappeared from the living room and when she came back she was carrying not her diary as I had expected, but her large purse, from which she pulled a small manila accordion file box. She riffled through the box, finding the index card she was looking for, and held it curved in her palm so that I couldn't see the writing. "November 17, 1962. I told Hugo you were a student at UCLA and doing some typing for me."

Anaïs scanned another card. "I told Hugo that you had agreed to receive my mail at your Westwood apartment address and deliver it to me at the rest ranch along with my typing."

I used my notepad to take notes. It was an alternate history of my life!

She carefully replaced that card and pulled out a card just behind it. "November 28, 1962. I rented a post office box at Flax Stationer's in Westwood, four blocks from UCLA, in Tristine Rainer's name."

She looked up at me. "I thought you were going to college at UCLA because Rupert studied forestry there, and I didn't realize there was another university in Los Angeles."

She returned to scanning the card. "I picked up Hugo's mail, sent in care of you at the stationer's address. Did you know that at Flax's you can put down a P.O. box number so it looks like an apartment number?"

She told me to memorize my fictional previous address on Lindbrook Drive in Westwood. "This last trip to New York, I told Hugo that you had transferred colleges and now your rent was cheaper, so you could afford a phone."

I was taken aback that Anaïs had implicated me in her deception of Hugo over the past two years without my knowledge, yet tickled that, at least fictively, I'd been a part of her life.

"This is beginning to make sense," I said. "Because the letterhead on the invitation we sent was from USC and not UCLA, you had to tell Hugo that I'd transferred colleges, right?"

"Yes, and you made the whole thing believable with your story about universities not wanting to take their own students. Is that true? Familiarity breeds contempt?"

"It's more like fear of incest."

"What!?"

"Nepotism. Universities want diverse points of view, so they prefer students they haven't taught."

"I will never understand those places, but it's wonderful that you do." She refastened the elastic band on her little lie box and returned it to a zippered pocket in her purse. "Hugo being able to reach me through you, and you reinforcing the validity of my trips out here, may restore his confidence in me." Tears appeared in the corners of her eyes. "Please, help me, Tristine. I can't change my story anymore; things are too unstable right now. I think Hugo's having an affair. I have to go right back to New York because I'm afraid he's going to divorce me!"

She quickly wiped away tears that had leaked, leaving streaks of kohl on the sides of her face.

My heart went out to her; I had felt bad for Hugo because she cheated on him, but if he had affairs, what else was she to do? Be a victim? Maybe she should just divorce Hugo and, like Lady Chatterley, marry Rupert for real.

"I was wondering," I asked her, "why Rupert introduced himself as your husband to me if he's no longer with the Forest Service."

She looked down, pensive, as if this were a difficult question. When she looked up again the water in her aquamarine eyes sparkled against the smeared black of her mascara. "Renate thinks I should tell you everything. She thinks I can trust you."

"You can trust me." I gave her my Girl Scout–honor face. "Why don't you just let me read the cards in that box, and then I can ask you about the parts I don't understand?"

"No! I don't think so." She gave me a hard smile. "If you are going to understand"—she let out a sigh—"you have to let me finish my story about Hugo and Rupert." She joined her hands in prayer-like entreaty. "Please do not judge me."

"No, I wouldn't. I won't."

"You must promise not to repeat to anyone what I am going to tell you. You may discuss it only with Renate."

"I already took an oath with you both," I tried to reassure her.

"My life depends upon it!" Her eyebrows knit crookedly again. "It is a terrible secret."

Oh, how I wanted to know. "I swear, and not just that oath we did at Renate's. On the life of my mother whom I love more than anything!"

I felt her studying my face, reading my earnestness. She smiled. "You are very tender."

Embarrassed a little, I added, "Besides, you should tell me everything so I don't mess up with Hugo."

"That's what Renate says. Where did I leave off last time?"

"You'd recovered from surgery and were happy to be married to Hugo."

"That just about brings us to 1955. How old were you then?"

"Eleven. It was the year my father left."

She nodded. "A pivotal year for both of us."

# CHAPTER 16

# Sierra Madre, California, 1955

## ANAÏS

AFTER HER HYSTERECTOMY, ANAÏS REALIZED that since she could not give Rupert the family he wanted; it was unfair to string him along. She had to tell him the truth and let him move on to the full life he deserved. She cared too much for him to tell him over the phone, though. So the next time Hugo flew to Switzerland to transfer client money, she booked a TWA Constellation to Los Angeles. During the eight-hour flight, she tried to prepare herself in her diary for Rupert's rage when she told him she hadn't asked Hugo for a divorce. As her hand flew across the paper, she realized she needed a gentler approach. It would be best to leave Hugo out of it entirely and explain to Rupert that her hysterectomy had thrown everything up in the air and it had all come down in a different place. It was the truth, after all. Not that she seemed to have any lasting physical effects from the surgery. Once she'd regained her strength and obtained estrogen for her hot flashes, she felt healthy, better than she had in years.

Still, she had been reluctant to try intercourse with Hugo again because he was too large and would hurt her when he pounded too hard. Fortunately, he was sympathetic, and with great tenderness they found a way to share affection that worked for both of them, returning to their pattern of the first two years of their marriage, when they were both virgins. When they went to bed, they caressed, kissed, and held each other, sometimes for an hour before Hugo would roll over and go to sleep. At twenty, this kissing and cuddling had frantically aroused her, but she had not known what for, whereas now the heartbreaking past sexual disappointments with Hugo had spoiled her appetite.

Reading what she had allowed her hand to write freely, she admitted to herself that she wanted to experience lovemaking with Rupert one more time. She needed to know that despite the hysterectomy, she could still feel sexual fulfillment. Only Rupert could give her that reassurance. He would intuitively respond to her desire for him to be gentle. She needed Rupert's lovemaking to restore her. One last time.

When Rupert picked her up at LAX and brought her to the cabin, the fireplace was ready to be lit, a mattress positioned in front of it, a bottle of wine and glasses set on the hearth.

She felt shy. She'd forgotten how beautiful Rupert was: his golden skin, his ardent, sensitive face lit by the now-blazing fireplace. He offered her a massage, and she placed herself in his hands. Under his touch, her skin became smooth and elastic; her body came alive as he explored its curves and muscles. Her tightly knotted nerve endings released like sea anemones unfolding. He turned her over and played his hands over her breasts, her stomach, her inner thighs.

As he was entering her, he called, "Anaïs, be my wife, my beautiful wife." She tensed with guilt, but as he continued to caress her, as he moved inside her, she lost all thought. Their bodies spoke only pleasure, only desire mounting, rising, and ringing its great cathedral bell, high and low, proclaiming all the joy in the world. From the perspective of the body, this jubilee was everything, the only truth that mattered. All the rest was a lie.

Rupert ran his fingers over her skin again, bringing her down. She watched the glowing embers in the fireplace. She listened to her slow, relaxed breathing and had no regrets. Rupert had given back to her the life of the body.

Now she had to give back to him his whole life, to free him for what he wanted and deserved—a wife, a child. Her lies were standing in his way. Her best hope was that after she'd told him the truth, he would allow her to remain his friend, that the love between them would not be completely destroyed.

The next day he took her to Sunday brunch at a Greek restaurant in Sierra Madre. There were homegrown roses at each table and faded Kodacolor photos of Corfu on the walls. Rupert ordered two champagne brunch specials, an extraordinary splurge for him. He reached across the table to take her cold hands.

She had observed that Rupert's eyes turned a deeper blue as a measure of his mounting desire. They were royal blue when he whispered, "Did you hear what I said to you last night while I was in you?"

"You whispered, 'Be my wife.' How wonderful that would be," she began and, gathering courage, added, "and how terribly unfair to you."

His thick eyebrows furrowed. The color in his eyes faded, and in them she saw fear. It passed like a squall, and his habitual cheer returned. "Drink your orange juice," he said. "It's fresh-squeezed."

"In a minute," she replied. "There's something I need to tell you." She took a breath and then she told him, with a terrible frankness, about the three-inch-long tumor that had been removed, how she had been given a full hysterectomy, and now the question of her ever being able to bear him a child was settled.

She said, "You have told me how important having a family is to you. It's what you want and what you have every right to. But now it cannot be with me. Darling, I let you go with all my love."

She finished and watched his compassionate face. She could not fathom what she saw. His eyes turned to indigo, and he said in a husky voice, "Drink your orange juice, Anaïs."

"Rupert, this is serious. Why do you keep trying to get me to drink my orange juice?"

"There's something at the bottom of your glass."

Could he mean a ring? *Oh god, what cruel irony.*

She plunged her fingers into the juice, and sure enough, pulled out a quarter-carat solitaire ring covered with orange pulp. She tried to hand it to Rupert. "It's lovely. Please keep it for whichever young woman is lucky enough to give you the family I cannot. I'm sorry. I should have told you sooner about my surgery. I just couldn't do it over the phone."

"Anaïs, I'm in love with you." He wrapped his hand around her sticky fingers holding up the ring. "It doesn't matter about having children. That means nothing to me compared to you."

He lifted her chin and asked her to let him take care of her now by becoming his wife.

His love crested over her and pulled her under. She could not see how she could divorce Hugo. She did not want to give up their cultured lifestyle and shared memories. Without Hugo she would lose the greatest booster of her writing. Without Hugo her very identity would be uprooted; she would fall into an abyss of insecurity.

But if she said no to Rupert's proposal she would lose an emotional and sexual connection so essential it was inexplicable, a love so romantic that her heart leapt in her chest whenever he walked through their dilapidated cabin door. She did not want to live without their engagement with music that took her to a transcendent state. Without Rupert's physical love she would waste away and die. It was live now or live never.

"Yes," she heard herself say.

∞

As Rupert drove, Anaïs, in the passenger seat, pushed her foot down on an imaginary brake. Yet she remained mute, passively willing, carried as in a dream, as he hurtled the car towards the dusty town of Quartzite, Arizona. When they'd first driven cross-country he had noticed a justice of the peace's office there. Sentimental and stubborn, Rupert was certain that Judge Hardly's shingle would still be out and the office open. Anaïs's only hope was that in the eight years since Rupert had spotted that sign board, the judge had retired. No such luck.

She was about to become a bigamist.

As pink-cheeked Mrs. Hardly led them into a little courtroom, Anaïs saw on a desk, next to the judge's King James Bible, a large book titled *Arizona Criminal Record*. She imagined that after the marriage her name would be entered there. But which name? Anaïs Nin, Anaïs Guiler, or Anaïs Pole? They were all guilty.

When the ceremony began, with the judge's smiling wife as witness, Anaïs left her body. Detached, in a state of manic hilarity, she observed her wedding ceremony from up in the courtroom rafters. She had to keep from snickering at the thought of Judge Hardly performing a marriage that could hardly be legal.

There was no one with whom she could share her dark mirth. The surrealists from her Paris days—Breton, Ernst, and Artaud—would have loved this wedding. They would have held a mad party to celebrate her *mariage a trois*. They would have carried her on their shoulders to showers of confetti, shouting, "Hail to *la grande dame de l'absurd!*"

But there was no party, no spurting champagne, no all-night celebration. Instead, she and Rupert walked out of the judge's office into the empty desert street and blinding sun. They sped directly back to Sierra Madre so that Rupert could be up for work the next morning at 5 a.m. As he drove, Anaïs glanced over at his handsome profile and tanned hands on the wheel, and she touched him, repeatedly and provocatively. She stroked his smooth young skin and the golden hairs exposed by his open shirt collar as she wondered what sentence she would get for bigamy.

She recalled that Gore Vidal, when denouncing Virginia's laws on sexual deviance, once said that the sentence for bigamy there was ten years in prison.

"That's progress," he'd chuckled. "Used to be the death penalty."

Having recently faced death anyway, she thought, what did it matter? At least she was making one person happy, and Rupert, with his right hand now cupping her breast, a gold wedding band glinting on his left, was truly, innocently happy. He whistled a Bach sonata, his member rising for her in his good pair of slacks.

∞

Their honeymoon consisted of Rupert taking her hiking in the immolated mountains above their cabin. They tramped past trees with gnarled arms like blackened grape vines and basins of mud hardened into the shape of waves. She gasped when she saw their destination, a valley carpeted with poppies bright as a Buddhist monk's robes.

"It's nature's cycle for the chaparral to burn every century or so." Rupert swept an arm dramatically. "Only after that huge conflagration, Anaïs, do certain rare fire flowers grow."

He bent to pluck a speck of white nestled in the spread of poppies and purple lupine. "This one! I remember seeing a sketch of it in an old book on fire flowers. A few of these might appear next spring, but after that, not for a hundred years or so."

She took the delicate white stem from him and when she held it up, the wind blew it in a frenetic dance. She thought it the perfect metaphor for her own regeneration after her scorching illness. Like this flower born out of ash, she had emerged from her near death as a new bride in white again. Like this rare bloom, hers would be a crazy dance that could not last.

∞

Anaïs had followed her heart leading to an illegal act that, at all costs, she had to keep secret. Any mistake, any slip of the tongue or lapse of attention, would cost her everything. She would lose both Rupert and Hugo, and she knew she would not survive it.

She had chosen not to choose, and in so doing she had entered the land of neither and both, the land of the absurd where no ordinary laws applied. Other women dreamt of having more than one love, of combining the qualities of two men into one perfect husband. But only she had dared to live that dream.

At first, her fear of being found out and arrested by the authorities scared her day and night. But in time, being married to two men felt no different from the years she'd spent traveling between husband and lover. Over the next ten years, her swings between New York and Los Angeles became as regular as a pendulum.

Rupert would greet her passionately, and there would be a honeymoon phase when she was able to appreciate those qualities that made him so lovable: his sensuality, his sweet nature, his optimism. After about two months, however, Rupert's penny-pinching, his persnickety insistence that she do things his way, and his stubborn, provincial view of the world would get on Anaïs's nerves so badly that she knew it would be better to arrange her departure than to release the wounding words on the tip of her tongue: "I can't stand you any longer! You are a small man with a small mind and a small life!" It was kinder to tell him that she had to go to New York for an editing job.

Just as her kinetic rise with Rupert peaked, Hugo's potential energy pulled her back. When she was most fed up with Rupert, she felt most drawn to Hugo's wit and the sight of his elegant fingers picking up the check at Café des Artistes. Reunited with Hugo, she basked in his pampering and reveled in their nights on the town. By the end of her second month with Hugo, however, it would begin to get stale. His flirtatious manners seemed old-fashioned; his obsession with material success, superficial; his artistic ambitions those of a dilettante.

With the few close friends like Renate who held her confidence, she spoke of the pendulum as her "trrapeze!" It was no gay leap through the air, though, no acrobatics of freedom. It was a cage in which she swung precariously, lured by alternate baits, ensnared with her "two blind mice." A trap set to collapse should she miss a beat.

The biggest strain was keeping Rupert and Hugo blind. Her lies became so complex she'd had to design the filing system of her little accordion Lie Box. Each time she invented a new cover story, she dated and wrote it on a card. When the little boxes got too stuffed, she locked them inside heavy metal cash boxes on each coast.

Eventually she began having nightmares about their discovery. She dreamt that Hugo ordered the police to smash open the cash box in her secret closet. Out of it blasted deadly light and radioactive rays as from the exploding suitcase at the end of the noir film *Kiss Me Deadly*.

Alternately, she dreamt that the forest fire raged again, burning Rupert's cabin to the ground. Only her smoldering cash box remained in the ashes, where Rupert knelt and wept over it as if it were her coffin.

Such nightmares, along with panic attacks of guilt, became her way of life. She was the accountant of her bigamy: keeping double books, ever fearful of discovery as a love embezzler.

When Anaïs was most honest with herself, she recognized there were advantages to her trapeze. For one thing, her cyclical appearances and disappearances kept her marriages fresh. Her husbands never tired of her because, unlike the usual wife, she could not be taken for granted. When she was gone, each man longed for her as for an absent mistress.

For another thing, her double life tempered her restlessness. After her affair in Paris with Henry Miller, she had been infected with Henry's lust and taste for variety, a greater threat to her marriage to Hugo than this predictable pendulum. Now she no longer picked up men at parties, no longer engaged in affairs. Her need for adventure, her appetite for wildness, was satisfied.

Sometimes she could even see humor in her high-wire act, and sometimes it gave her an almost insane high. On the ground, she felt acutely and sorrowfully the shortness of life, measured by clocks and charts and heartbeats; but flying, she transcended the limits of time. Thirty thousand feet in the air on a Constellation jet, suspended between her men and safe from their demands, she was released from gravity. Aloft, she was Sabina—who defied life's cruel restrictions of one love, one spouse, one life, one self.

When the moon was a sliver, she eyed it from her window seat and imagined herself as Hecate, the moon's dark face, flying invisibly and freely in the night sky. When the moon was round and bright, she thought of herself as Artemis, the huntress, the goddess owned by no man. And when the planet Venus greeted her at dusk or dawn, she knew herself as Aphrodite, faithful only to the essence of love.

# CHAPTER 17

# Los Angeles, California, 1964

## TRISTINE

A DRY CRACK OF LAUGHTER came from the back of Anaïs's throat. "I believed my absurd double marriage could not last a year, and it has lasted a decade."

I quickly calculated: when I'd met Anaïs in 1962, she'd already been a bigamist for seven years! I was excited by her daring. She was an outlaw like the bad boys I'd always been keen on, dangerous and sexy because they took risks and defied convention. I loved her terrible secret; she'd beaten the system of marriage that kept women down, and now that I knew it, she would have to keep me close.

Her penciled eyebrows pinched irregularly and her eyes sought mine. "Now I'm dangling from the *trrapeze* by a thread and I need your help!"

"I'll help you," I responded. "I think it's great that you're a bigamist!"

"Please don't use that word."

"Why not? I think it's fantastic!"

"It's an ugly word. And besides it's illegal."

"Well, smoking pot is illegal, but I know a lot of people who are doing it. So is refusing military service, but it shouldn't be."

"So you don't think I'm terrible now that you know?"

"Terrible? I'm awed by you! I've never heard of a woman with two husbands. Only men have done it until now." I thought her adventurous leap beyond women's traditional roles as remarkable as walking on the moon. She may not have been a great writer, but she was a pioneer, a breaker of boundaries, a daring explorer!

I could see that she was pleased that I'd recognized her extraordinary courage, but she cautioned in a hushed voice, "You must never reveal it. People don't understand."

"Well, I understand," I said, pleased that I was uniquely qualified to do so. She had figured out how never to be abandoned, never caught short of a man. "It's because your father abandoned you like mine did. By having two husbands you're protected. You'll always have a spare."

"That's not it at all!"

"It isn't?"

"No. I can't leave either man because I know how it feels to be abandoned. I couldn't inflict that on someone I love. I'm trapped by my compassion."

She looked completely sincere, but to me, an extra husband as an insurance policy remained a much more compelling reason.

To emphasize her more altruistic perspective, Anaïs asked, "Don't you recall the terrible pain when your father left? Could you cause someone that pain?"

"No," I said uncertainly. "But remember I told you I was glad my father left."

She was scrutinizing me. "If you cannot understand the cruelty it would wreak on Hugo and Rupert to learn of my double life, how can I trust you to keep my secret?"

"Because I gave you my word." I looked her in the eye. "Once I give my word I'll never break it. It's a matter of honor."

"At twenty-one, you haven't had much opportunity to test your honor."

"Yes, I have. For some reason people have always told me secrets, and I always keep my word."

"What secret did someone ask you to keep?" She leaned into me conspiratorially.

I thought about it. Which secret could I tell that wouldn't harm anyone and might also impress her? "That my father was Jewish."

"Did someone ask you not to tell that?"

"My father. I found out by accident when I was sixteen, when an aunt I'd never heard of came to see a play at the Coronet Theater and recognized my name on the program. She took me out to Canters Deli after the play and told me my father had broken off from his Jewish family and changed his last name. I was thrilled to find out I was half Jewish, because my best friend was, but when I talked with my father about it, he told me never to tell anyone."

"And now you have just told me." She gave me a hard smile.

She had caught me!

Finally, I thought of what to say. "My relationship with you is different. I took an oath with you. We're now like blood sisters who tell each other everything, and it's sacred between us."

She still did not look entirely convinced, so I tried again. "I only told you my father's secret because you asked for an example, and that was the only one I could tell. All the other secrets people have told me will go with me to my grave."

Her face relaxed. "You really are a little soldier, aren't you?"

"If you mean I can be trusted, yes." I was proud that she'd entrusted me with a confidence so radical and dangerous.

"So you will help me save my marriage with Rupert as well as with Hugo? You did so well with Hugo." She looked happy for the first time that day.

Unwilling to disappoint her when it was apparent her happiness now depended on me, I said yes. I had been willing to help her save her marriage with Hugo, and so far I had succeeded. Now she was asking me to help her save both her marriages, to keep her suspended on her trapeze, to partake in her daring feat. I would be the person on the ground, holding her safety line, ever vigilant to keep her from falling. I would have the close-up view of her trapeze, how she worked the pulleys and leapt from husband to husband, both of them reaching for her as she spun in glorious, airborne freedom. There wasn't anything as amazing—not on *Peyton Place*, or *The Addams Family*, or *Bewitched*. Her life had elements of all those TV shows, and it was dangerous and thrilling, but it was real. And I'd been cast in an essential role.

"Before Rupert gets home from teaching," she charged on, "we should talk about how you might keep an eye on him while I'm gone."

"Keep an eye on Rupert? What would that entail?"

"For instance, if Rupert gets suspicious about me in New York, you should phone me, and, well . . ." Her hands waved and seemed to reach for something that wasn't there. She averted her eyes when she said, "I wish I didn't have to mention this. It's so unfair. Ever since I fell in love with Rupert I have been absolutely faithful to him."

"Except for Hugo."

"Well, yes, but I was already married to Hugo. That's different. I've been completely faithful to both of them, but I can't trust either of them when I'm out of town."

I might have pointed out a fault in her reasoning, but as I understood our relationship, she was the mentor and I the apprentice, so it wasn't my place.

Instead I said, "What am I supposed to do, track Rupert like a detective?"

A mischievous smile brightened her face. "Not a detective, a spy. *A Spy in the House of Love.*"

I was confused. "You can't mean you want me to follow him around?" I was, at once, terrified and titillated by the idea.

"Yes, I do," she said, "but in plain sight. You need to befriend Rupert. That is why I asked you to stay for dinner and listen to his music group this evening."

"Is his family coming?" When she'd invited me, I'd fantasized meeting Frank Lloyd Wright's descendants.

"No, Rupert has formed a new chamber group with friends closer to his age. I know you'll like them, and they'll like you. Two of them are teachers at his school. They know me as Mrs. Pole, so that is how you should refer to me, either as Anaïs with no last name or as Mrs. Pole."

Her hands went to reach for something again. She saw my eyes follow. "I quit smoking," she explained. "Rupert and I are both quitting. Do you have the habit?"

I shrugged noncommittally.

"The only time I miss it is after making love." She sighed and returned to her agenda. "Tonight, after the musicians finish playing, you should go up to Rupert and tell him how much you enjoyed listening and that you hope to be invited again." I was furiously scribbling notes; she barely paused for a breath. "Rupert will say you are welcome any time."

"You know he'll say that?"

"Yes. You can then come every Tuesday early enough to hear the gossip."

I looked up. "You just want me to listen for gossip?"

"Yes, get the other musicians to trust you. Just be easy and charming."

"Be an actress," I said.

"You told me when we first met that you wanted to be an actress!" Her laugh jingled. "Tristine, do you think you could spare a few weekend afternoons in addition to the chamber group evenings?"

"I guess so."

"Good. Then when you are saying goodnight next Tuesday, volunteer to help Rupert clear the land he bought in Silver Lake on which he plans to build me a house."

"Rupert is building a house?"

"Yes, unfortunately. His half-brother Eric designed it."

"You don't like the design?"

"Oh, yes I do. Eric is very talented. He's Frank Lloyd Wright's grandson, after all. But I don't want to be tethered to any house. It's Rupert's attempt to bury me in permanent soil."

I nodded; I wouldn't want to be tied down to a house, either.

She continued, "Don't strain yourself when you join Rupert at the building site. He prefers to do the work himself but he enjoys company. Bring him some cold beer. It'll get him to talk." She dug a wallet from her purse, pulled out three twenties, and squeezed them into my hand. "For Rupert's beer."

"That's a lot of beer," I said.

"For your trouble, gas." She waved the money away.

"Okay, but I really don't think Rupert is going to confide in me."

"I wouldn't be so sure," she said. "You're a good listener. And that's all you have to do; just be there to listen. If he doesn't confide in you, that's fine, but stay around to keep your eyes and ears open. There's just one more thing you must promise me."

Another promise. "What?"

"That you won't fall for Rupert even if he makes a pass at you."

"Anaïs! I would never do that!"

"Yes, but Rupert can be irresistible."

"I promise you." I looked into her eyes so she could see my sincerity. "I could never do that to another woman."

"Why not?"

"My father, before he left for Mexico, had an affair with my mother's best friend. I know the pain it caused my mother."

Anaïs nodded, her delicate features taking on her expression of infinite compassion.

I added to reassure her, "Besides, Rupert isn't my type."

∞

Rupert's fellow musicians all arrived on the dot at six o'clock. Anaïs greeted them warmly and introduced me to each, dropping a tidbit that would provide a topic for conversation after she was gone. In no time the instruments and players were in place, forming a semicircle beside the piano.

Anaïs and I sat on the scratchy brown couch, off to the side of the musician's circle. As they tuned their instruments, she picked up the leather journal resting in her lap and her gold-and-black Montblanc and began to write, completely blocking everyone out, including me, as if she had stepped behind a shower curtain and could hear only rushing water. I resolved to bring my diary the next time to write in as she was doing, so I wouldn't have to just sit there and listen, and so I could record any gossip before I forgot it.

Rupert stood and gave a lecture for my benefit about what they were going to play and how they had adapted the score for their instruments and limited abilities. I imagined he must be a good teacher, though his discourse on the Brahms concerto seemed at odds with his Venice Beach tan, white teeth, and toned physique. I found myself imagining Anaïs's robust sex life with him. When I glanced back at her, she seemed annoyed for being pulled from her diary writing by Rupert's theatrical emphasis on certain words and phrases: "The *second* piano concerto, called *The Holy Terror!*"

She capped her pen with a snap. "Tristine is not one of your students, Rupert! Just play."

As the musicians began to play, slightly out of sync, I took it as my cue to get into character. The givens were that I was a highly cultured, ladylike coed, sitting knees together, ankles crossed, hands gracefully folded in my lap. I was so interested in chamber music that I really wanted to be invited again to listen to Rupert's quintet. In my imagination I practiced the lines I would say to him before I left, so that he would invite me back in Anaïs's absence, and I could do my surveillance.

My life had gone from being that of a shy girl from the Valley in hand-me-downs to that of a future college professor, who was also a spy like Mata Hari inside a sophisticated, decadent world. I was doing espionage for the world's only female bigamist. It was surreal, as I now understood surrealism from the woman who'd known the surrealists in Paris. I was living inside her dreamscape and flying with her past ordinary life as though lifted by a sudden wind, free from the grim realism of existentialism.

Anaïs had quieted her breathing and adjusted the rhythm of her diary writing to Rupert's strokes on the cello. The script from the fine point of her Montblanc slanted deeply forward, pulled by the future, her high loops reaching for the sky. I marveled at the serenity of her face, the face of Djuna, wise and centered, calm as the mirrored surface of a lake. How was it possible with the life she led?

# CHAPTER 18

# Los Angeles, California, 1964

## TRISTINE

EVERYTHING WENT ACCORDING TO PLAN. When Anaïs left for New York, Rupert invited me to his chamber music evenings and accepted my offer to help at the construction site. The first Saturday I showed up and desultorily added some small rocks to a wheelbarrow, as Rupert hauled lumber around shirtless and went on about how much he missed Anaïs whenever she was gone. He didn't express any suspicions about her, nor did I have to fight off any advances from him.

At the next chamber music evening he complimented me on looking pretty, but he regularly complimented every woman there. However, the following Saturday, when I wore jeans to help him move rocks, he said, "You should wear skirts. I've seen your legs; you shouldn't hide them." Thereafter, I wore pants, even to listen to Mozart.

I finished my semester-end exams and watched my fellow students cheerfully disperse for the winter holiday. I was already depressed at the thought of going to my mother's house for Christmas. Rupert, too, was blue when I visited him at the building site. Anaïs wouldn't be back until after the holidays.

He took a swig from the beer I'd picked up and asked, "Do you want to go to a party with me tonight?"

"You mean like a date? No."

"No, as Anaïs's friend."

I thought about it. What would Anaïs want me to do? My instructions from her were to keep an eye on Rupert, so I agreed to meet him at their apartment and follow him in my car to the party at film director Curtis Harrington's house.

Later in my old Buick, I followed Rupert up a winding road, and when we arrived at Curtis's driveway, valets ran into the street to take our cars.

Rupert offered me his arm as I struggled up a steep incline in my high heels. A young woman wearing a minidress with pinwheel-patterned stockings passed us as she ran down the hill we'd just climbed, calling back, "Dennis Hopper just left! I'm on to another party! Merry Christmas!"

"How do you know Curtis?" I asked Rupert.

"Anaïs's friend Renate Druks introduced us," Rupert said. "They're part of a Hollywood crowd we used to run with." I wondered if Renate and her football star husband would be guests at the party and what she would think of my being there with Rupert. I had tried to phone her when I'd rushed home to change, to make sure that I was doing what Anaïs would want, but no one had answered.

We entered the hall where a bust of Medusa, snakes sprouting from her head, glowed under a Tiffany lamp. As Rupert and I crossed into a high-ceilinged living room, I felt as if we were entering the House of Usher. There were thick velvet drapes over the windows, ornate Art Nouveau furnishings, porcelain masks, darkly erotic Aubrey Beardsley posters of Oscar Wilde's *Salome,* and a stuffed, mounted raven sitting on an end table. I even saw a man dressed all in black and with a long cape like an Edwardian sorcerer.

"Is that Curtis Harrington?" I whispered to Rupert.

"No." Rupert laughed. "That's Samson de Brier. He's at all these parties and always dresses like an aristocratic sorcerer. He was in *Inauguration of the Pleasure Dome*, along with Renate and Curtis and Anaïs and me."

"The film Kenneth Anger directed!" I hadn't seen it yet but remembered Renate telling me to catch a screening. "Will he be at this party?" I asked Rupert excitedly.

"No, Curtis and Kenneth had a falling out," Rupert said, moving toward a man who had the wide face of a Persian cat and a feline's padded step.

"Merry Christmas, Curtis!" Rupert boomed.

For a man who lived in such a Gothic house, Curtis Harrington appeared remarkably congenial.

"I brought a guest," Rupert said, putting his hand on my back.

"I'm Anaïs's friend," I added to clarify I wasn't Rupert's date.

"Oh, well if you're Anaïs's friend"—Curtis took my hands, turning his back on Rupert, and winked at me—"you are welcome any time."

He turned back to Rupert. "So Anaïs told me she has a job in New York with a new magazine."

"Yes. It's named *Cue*," Rupert said proudly.

Curtis raised an eyebrow at me before guiding us over to Basil Rathbone and Florence Marly, whom he told us were committed for his next film, *Queen of Blood*. I was so excited to meet real movie stars that I would have waited an hour for them to finish their conversation, but when they continued for several minutes without making eye contact, Rupert directed me to the kitchen.

A dour maid was replenishing a large bowl of spiked eggnog and handed us some in gargoyle-faced mugs. Taking our drinks, Rupert and I returned to the expansive living room. We settled on the corner of a burgundy velvet settee.

I kept an eye out for Renate but never saw her, so Rupert and I socialized with some friendly nobodies like us. A fellow in embroidered jeans and a sloppy sweater who apparently knew Rupert came up and offered to fortify our eggnogs with the Remy Martin bottle in his hand. Staring down at me, he said, "Rupert, who's your young friend?"

Rupert responded politely, "This is Tristine. I'm sorry, I know your face. You work in New York a lot . . . off Broadway? I just can't remember your name."

"Bruce Nigel. Nice to meet you, Christine." Bruce winked at me, then asked Rupert, "Where's Anaïs?"

"She's got a gig in New York. It's going to keep her there through the holidays."

"Oh yeah? Where's she staying?"

"She stays in a friend's apartment above the Sign of the Dancing Bear bookstore."

"Bullshit!" Bruce waved a dismissive hand at Rupert. "Anaïs really has you going, doesn't she?"

"What are you talking about?" Rupert bristled.

"You don't know where Anaïs stays, do you?"

My antennae shot up, but Rupert seemed unfazed. "I know she stays with Maxwell, the bookstore owner. He isn't into women."

"No, it's Hugo something," Bruce said.

"Ian Hugo?" Rupert asked, and I could see a splotch of redness moving up his neck.

"No. Hugo is his first name. Her husband, for Chrisakes. His last name starts with a *g*. They have parties at their Village apartment."

Rupert asked, "Hugo Guiler?"

I couldn't believe what was happening. "What plays have you been in, Bruce?" I tried to change the conversation.

Ignoring me, he said smugly, "Hugo Guiler, that's her husband."

"Well your info is about eight years old, Bruce," Rupert retorted. "Hugo Guiler is Anaïs's ex-husband. I'm her husband now."

Bruce waved a hand that said Rupert didn't know shit, and carried his bottle back to the kitchen.

"What a weird guy," I said, and tried to engage Rupert in talking about the Warren Report on President Kennedy's assassination. "Do you believe that Oswald and Ruby were both working alone?"

Rupert began to expound on his latest Kennedy assassination theory, as I knew he would, just as Bruce reappeared with a slip of paper in his hand.

Weaving drunkenly, Bruce interrupted, "You don't believe me that she's living with that Hugo guy? Here's her number in New York. Maybe you don't have it, buddy."

Rupert and I reached for the slip of paper at the same time. I got there first, but Rupert had a better grip and jerked it out of my hand.

I scowled at Bruce, who had a smirk on his face. "Why don't you leave us alone? You're drunk."

Bruce's parting words to Rupert were, "Call the number, buddy. See who picks up."

My thoughts raced as fast as my pulse, but I had to appear cool when I said to Rupert, "Give me that stupid paper. You shouldn't pay attention to a drunk."

"I want to call it." Rupert put the note in his pants pocket, his handsome features taking on the bullishness Anaïs complained about. His stubbornness made me think, *go ahead, call it; it'll serve you right.* But I remembered the repercussions if I didn't stop him. She'd crash off her trapeze, and I, the one who was supposed to be holding her safety line, would be responsible.

I tried again. "Do you want Anaïs to think you don't trust her?"

"You want to know the truth?" Rupert now sounded drunk himself. "I *don't* trust her."

I could see I wasn't going to get anywhere with him. "May we go?"

"You go." He sprung up. "I want to find that guy."

I grabbed his arm. "I don't know how to get home from here without you leading the way."

"Then wait." He pulled his arm back rudely.

He stalked out of the living room and stood in the kitchen doorway, arms crossed. His long legs were braced to pounce, but Bruce had disappeared.

I had to get that piece of paper. I sidled up behind Rupert and slipped my hand into the right pocket of his chinos. I caught the folded note between two fingers, but before I could extract it, I felt something fleshy touch my index finger. I quickly withdrew, the note slipping and remaining in Rupert's pocket.

I didn't dare try again. The maid serving punch had been watching me and waved an admonishing hand.

Pretending nothing had happened, I tapped Rupert on the shoulder and when he turned I pleaded, "Please, can you lead me back to your place?"

∞

He drove the Thunderbird too fast, weaving in and out of traffic. Tailing Rupert was like driving on a motor speedway. While trying to avoid a crash, I mentally raced through options to stop him phoning the New York number. If I could distract him with a kiss, I might be able to slip my hand into his pocket again.

But what if Rupert later told Anaïs that I had made a pass at him? I knew that she'd believe him. She'd cut me out of her life again. It wasn't worth that risk. So somehow I had to warn her that Rupert would be calling. At least then she could make sure Hugo didn't answer the phone. I checked the clock on my dashboard. It was 9:50 p.m., well after midnight in New York, too late to phone Anaïs.

Rupert pulled into the apartment driveway, staggered to the street, and leaned on the driver's side of my double-parked car.

I rolled down the window. "You'll be waking up strangers if you call that number tonight. Wait until morning," I said. "Just go to sleep."

Watching him stumble towards his door, clutching the wrought iron railing, I thought he would.

It was eleven by the time I got home and dialed Renate's number. It rang a long time, and then a man answered. I guessed it was Renate's husband. He said she'd just fallen asleep and that he'd give her the message and he hung up. I phoned back to say it was an emergency.

"Renate is not accepting any calls. Don't call again!" He hung up.

I wasn't going to be able to talk to Renate, so I had to figure this out on my own. I'd had no idea that being Anaïs's apprentice would be this hard.

I located the phone number Anaïs had given me for her New York apartment, set it by my alarm clock, and tried to get a few hours of sleep, though that was futile. At 4 a.m. exactly, I dialed her number. Hugo sounded grumpy when he answered. "It's 7 a.m. on a Sunday morning."

"I'm sorry, Hugo. Anaïs got a call here from someone at Warner Brothers, and I thought she would want to know."

He growled, "What's the message?"

I should have figured that out. "Just have her call me as soon as she can," I managed before hanging up, my guts whirling like a garbage disposal.

I had just made a mistake. While I was waiting for Anaïs to phone me back, Rupert could phone there and Hugo would answer!

I had to call again but needed a better strategy. I didn't have a better strategy.

In my nervousness, I dialed the wrong number and got a pissed-off guy with a Brooklyn accent. When I did reach Hugo again, I said, "Actually, I remembered Anaïs said that I should tell her right away if this executive from Warner Brothers called, even if I had to wake her."

"Hold on."

I waited, my anxiety mounting as I realized this long distance call was costing me more by the minute than my mother earned in an hour cleaning houses.

When Anaïs came on the line, she sounded unnaturally cheerful. "*Ahllo?*"

"Anaïs, I told Hugo that someone from Warner Brothers phoned for you." I lowered my voice and added rapidly, "The real reason is because a guy named Bruce gave Rupert your phone number there!"

"The studio already contacted me here!" She gave an artificial laugh. She didn't sound like herself.

"Are you okay?" I asked.

"No, that film is a disaster!" Her voice was a violin squeak. I assumed Hugo was right there. "Too bad your information came too late."

Rupert had beaten me to the call.

She continued in her high scratch, "If you learn anything more, be sure to let me know. *Au revoir.*"

I hung up the receiver as if lowering my own casket. If I had interpreted her code correctly Rupert had already phoned, the consequences had been disastrous, and I should watch Rupert to warn Anaïs of his next step.

It was only 4:12 a.m., but there was no point in trying to sleep. I percolated a pot of Folgers and planned what to say to Rupert when I phoned him: *How are you doing? Did you call that silly phone number? What happened?*

When I dialed Rupert's number at six, it just rang. Maybe he was still sleeping it off. Maybe he'd gone out for breakfast. Maybe he'd gone to visit a girlfriend!

I was exhausted but made myself do my Canadian Air Force calisthenics. As soon as I finished my sit-ups I dialed Rupert's number again. Still no answer.

This went on for two days. I phoned Rupert and Renate. Neither of them answered. I imagined terrible things. Rupert taking up with a woman. Rupert on a drinking binge somewhere in Hollywood. Rupert attempting suicide over the wickedness of Anaïs's lies.

I wanted to find out what had happened when Rupert phoned Anaïs at Hugo's, but I didn't dare call her without new information. Finally, I decided I'd better drive over to the Hollywood apartment to see if Rupert was refusing to answer the phone or unable to.

I parked in the driveway, ran to the Tudorbethan door, and banged the knocker. I walked around and peered through the stained-glass windows. There was no sign of Rupert anywhere. Then I walked to the garage and saw through a dusty window that the Thunderbird wasn't there.

I drove back downtown in the smoggy winter gloom, feeling helpless. As soon as I entered my disheveled room I threw myself on my single bed, resigned to a full-blown depression. I would lose Anaïs again. She had put her trust in me, and I had failed her. Renate's curse would come down on my head, and there would be no second chance this time.

CHAPTER 19

# Los Angeles, California, 1965

## TRISTINE

*January 17, 1965*

*We are in the shower. The warm water running over our bodies. We can't keep our hands off each other. The flesh is warm, wet. We grab each other, squeeze each other's haunches, lick, explore with our fingers.*

*We play child games. He spits water into my eyes, pulls down my shower cap, and kisses me. I grab his cock. He kisses me for real. When we make love in my bed, my new gray kitten, Jadu, watches us with round green eyes.*

∞

It was a new year, and I wasn't worrying about Anaïs's marriages or the loss of them. I wasn't thinking about Rupert's and Renate's disappearances. I wasn't even suffering the coils of guilt that sprang like serpents from Mother's Christmas gifts, each one adding to her astounding credit card debt.

I wasn't lonely. I wasn't bored. I was in love—madly, lustfully, without reserve.

I wasn't thinking about having to warn Anaïs that I'd let someone move in who might answer my phone. I wasn't concerned that I'd given myself entirely to a twenty-three-year-old college dropout whose only paid job was playing Saturday nights in a jazz combo and whose full-time unpaid gig was as a Marxist/Leninist organizer. The passion that D. H. Lawrence had promised in his novels, I'd found with Neal. He taught me to abandon myself to pleasure without a trace of shame.

Neal was a confident, sexy junior I'd dated in my sophomore year, when I was still a virgin. With his fiery black eyes, straight, shiny black hair, and left-wing rhetoric, he wasn't like the other guys at conservative USC. He was a half-Irish, half-Jewish boy from Georgia who loved jazz as I did and saw the South from the minority perspective. I'd likely have lost my virginity to him had he not suddenly left college for a chance to play jazz on the road.

He phoned just after New Year's to say he was in town, while I was still nursing my depression over having failed Anaïs. He invited me to come listen to him play at a hotel in Beverly Hills.

My depression instantly lifted.

That night I wore my slinky black dress, high patent heels, and my mother's fox-trimmed sweater, which she'd somehow preserved from moth holes for twenty-two years.

Neal was blowing "Tenderly" à la Chet Baker when I walked in, a strand of dark hair falling over his forehead. As I was seated, he followed me with his onyx eyes. I hadn't ordered it, but the waiter brought me a hollowed coconut filled with a tropical drink. As the bassist took the solo, I mouthed, *thank you* to Neal.

At the combo's break, he came over and sat with me, gulping down soda water as we interrupted each other's questions trying to cram everything that had happened to us in the past year and a half into twenty minutes before his next set.

The rest of the night Neal didn't take his eyes off me. He was making love to me as he played—his lips blowing on the delicate reed, his fingers on the gold keys, his hips moving with his instrument as he bent down towards me.

After, he walked me back to my car in the hotel parking lot. I said in a voice that sounded unusually husky, as if I were doing a Lauren Bacall imitation, "Your place or mine." Sabina was in control.

I seduced him that night, but he seduced me right back. I already knew there would never be another like him in my life. Together we felt mythic, our intimate parts keyed to engage by some Dionysian locksmith. That first night, and every night we were together, a volitionless wave of passion lifted and carried us, exploding into another dimension. After the first night with him, I was in love, as Shakespeare's Sonnet 116 says, "even to the edge of doom."

Neal stayed for morning coffee and moved into my single apartment that afternoon, not having any permanent digs of his own. Occasionally he bought groceries, but we basically lived off my scholarship and the federal student loans I'd begun taking.

We didn't think much about money. We thought about sex. In bed, in the bathroom, on the floor, testing Kama Sutra positions, giggling at our pretzel bodies, and then just letting loose in lust.

I was the happiest woman in the world to have Neal as my lover. The problem was that I wasn't the only one to feel that way. Other women—just about every woman he met, from secretaries to the movie stars' wives who would take a table at the hotel bar to ogle him—appreciated Neal's talents.

As Anaïs had predicted, when I fell in love, Sabina fled, taking all her self-possession with her. In her place I found the persona Anaïs had characterized in her novels as Stella, a vulnerable girl-woman who clung to her beloved. Neal found my unexpected possessiveness totally uncool.

With the authority of someone who had read both *Playboy* and Engels's *Origin of the Family, Private Property and the State*, he told me that my sexual jealousy was a remnant of the decadent need for private property. He warned me that my desire for monogamy was an impediment to our true love. It might even make it impossible for us to stay together. I tried valiantly to purge myself of my regressive bourgeois jealousy, but when I suspected Neal was in another woman's bed, acid shot up my throat, scorching me from inside.

The first two months we were together, I sat in the hotel lounge every Saturday night to hear Neal play and to stake my claim to him. Then he told me that "the Man" didn't want me taking up a table; I was a distraction. After that, Neal didn't come home Saturday nights. He would phone after his last set to say he was going to jam all night with the guys. The next day, he would drag in and head wordlessly to the shower. I would yell at him through the shower door about how I hadn't slept all night and why did he make me fall in love with him just so he could break my heart. Getting no response, I'd throw myself on the bed in hysterical tears. Fresh from his shower, a towel around his waist, he'd silently remove his sax from its case and sit on the edge of the bed. Then he'd play just for me. Twice he improvised a tune so beautiful it made me cry all the more because I would never hear it again. Or he'd play Satie's *Trois Gymnopedies*, that spare, lonely melody that takes me to the empty streets of my dreams where all alone, I look through buildings and rooms, searching behind doors, and halls for a passageway out that doesn't exist.

Then he'd place the sax, carefully as always, back in its case and say, "Do you want a massage?" and I would refuse to answer. He'd say, "Roll over. On your stomach." He'd knead the anger right out of me, making my body yearn with desire for him. He'd say, "Turn on your back." Then he'd try to kiss me, but I'd turn my head away. He'd gently turn my face to him and kiss my wet eyelids. When his lips would claim mine, I tasted my tears, his kiss sweeping me, pulling me, into a spiraling black hole. I wanted only him and what he would do with my body.

I was in love, but this was no way to live. I needed to talk to Anaïs. I desperately needed her wise Djuna advice for how to handle my turbulent, self-destructive emotions. But I had failed her and I didn't dare call her again. I wouldn't have known where to phone her, in any case. For all I knew, she could still be in New York, or back in LA, or nowhere. She'd said she would not survive if she lost both her husbands. That no longer seemed an exaggeration to me. I knew I would not survive losing Neal, and she'd have that loss twice over.

I did try repeatedly to reach Renate. Ronnie always answered the phone. Finally I acquiesced to his demand that I quit calling. Anaïs must have instructed Renate, who in turn had instructed Ronnie, to cut me off.

So the last person I thought would be phoning me on a Saturday night, when I was home alone throwing a catnip toy for my kitten, was Anaïs. Her voice was a whisper as if she were trying not to be heard. "Come to my place tomorrow. Be here at eleven."

∞

Driving to Anaïs's apartment, I felt sure she'd blame me for the collapse of her trapeze. My anger flared at the injustice of it; I'd tried to stop Rupert's call.

She greeted me with air kisses on both cheeks.

"I'm so glad to see you!" I said.

"Yes, I've been gone longer than I expected." I heard the blame in her voice.

She told me to have a seat on the nubby couch as she disappeared into the kitchen to make tea. I looked around and tried to determine if the Bekins boxes stacked along the walls contained Rupert's possessions or hers.

Anaïs settled herself with her cup of tea. Despite my intent to wait for her lead, I blurted, "I'm sorry I wasn't able to stop Rupert from phoning you in New York."

She listened as I stammered through my explanation of what had happened at Curtis Harrington's party and after. She took my hands in hers and said soothingly, "Thank you for trying, Tristine."

I had to know. "What happened when Rupert called your New York apartment?"

Her eyes and mouth turned down in her sad, Pierrot clown face. She sighed. "I'll tell you. But first I have to ask, did Rupert make a pass at you?"

"No! He took me to Curtis's Christmas party as your friend. Ask Curtis."

"But you did make a pass at Rupert."

"No! Did he tell you that? It's not true!"

"It's alright. You can tell me the truth. Rupert is young and attractive. I know how these things happen."

"I'm telling you the truth, Anaïs. I don't even find him attractive. I'm madly in love with someone else."

"You are? When did that happen?" Her smile transformed her beautiful, tired face into that of a funny little girl with gopher teeth. "That's wonderful! Who is he?"

I told her of my passion for Neal, and how the overwhelming power of sex that D. H. Lawrence described in his novels now possessed me, how Neal had moved in with me the morning after our first night together, and how, just as she'd predicted, Sabina had fled when I fell in love.

She smiled. "Musicians are the best lovers."

"But Neal doesn't believe in monogamy. He sleeps with other women, and I'm tortured by jealousy!" I begged for her guidance.

She shut her eyes to consider my ordeal, but they quickly flashed open. "Tristine!" she cried. "You let him move in with you!"

I hadn't worried about Neal living with me because I thought I'd never hear from Anaïs again. "Hugo hasn't called my place," I tried to reassure her.

"But he will! I told him I'd be staying with you." She berated me, "How could you be so careless? Right now Hugo could be phoning your apartment, and Neal might answer just like Ronnie did at Renate's!"

"I'm so sorry! I haven't been thinking much since Neal moved in. My brain isn't working well."

Anaïs gave an angry sigh. "Have you told Neal what to say if anyone calls for me?"

"No. I didn't want to tell him anything without your permission. I took an oath not to discuss it with anyone except Renate, remember?"

She scowled. "We can't take the chance of Neal being there if Hugo calls."

Did she expect me to tell Neal to move out? I would do almost anything for her, but not that. My resentment rose like a rogue wave. I'd tried to help her keep two husbands, and she expected me to give up my one lover?

"I don't want him to move out." My voice quavered with defiance.

She looked at me in surprise. A sequence played across her face—outrage, deliberation, resolve—before she said, "We need a creative solution, then." She took a sip of her tea and closed her eyes. When she opened them she said, "Don't tell Neal anything, not even that you know me."

"I did tell him that I went to Harlem with you once and we heard Mango Santamaria."

"Does he know anything about Hugo and Rupert?"

"Nothing."

"Good. Change your phone number. Tell the phone company that you have a heckler threatening you. Call them right now from my phone."

I did as she said. It wasn't easy to persuade the operator that the heckler was dangerous, but Anaïs knew exactly what to say. She rapidly scribbled on her pad of violet notepaper, tore the note off, and handed it to me. Thanks to the many phone pranks I'd pulled in grammar school and my high school dramatic training, I was able to do a convincing cold reading of her note.

"He said he was going to break into my place and tie me up and whip me until I begged him to fuck me." I sort of stammered on the "fuck me," but it worked for the reading.

The phone operator gasped.

Anaïs handed me another square of violet paper. "He said he was going to get all his friends, and they were going to line up and do it to me all night."

I held the receiver so that Anaïs could hear the operator. "Did he say anything else?"

She scribbled another note.

"He said he would hang me from the rafters and force"—I couldn't read the writing—"cunnifungus . . . on me."

"What?"

Anaïs scribbled too fast now.

"He said he was going to bring over three girls who would put a dildo in every horizon."

"Horizon?"

Anaïs mouthed the right word.

"Orifice," I corrected.

"What else?" the operator asked.

"Isn't that enough for you to change my number?" I asked the operator, breathless and flushed. I felt like the butt of the joke, as when Anaïs and the two businessmen in the Mexican café had exchanged smirks over my inexperience.

Putting down the receiver, I asked Anaïs, "How do you know all those dirty things to say?"

"Oh, I've had my own dealings with the phone company. You have to make it sound terrrible or they won't change the number." She shrugged. "And I wrote pornography for a wealthy collector when all the artists in the Village were doing it. The old man always wanted more of the rough stuff. Would you like more tea?"

I hadn't touched my now very brown tea. I took the Lipton's bag out of the cup and took a sip.

We sat in silence until I said, "Once they change my number, how will Hugo get in touch with you?"

"Never mind." She rubbed her forehead with her manicured fingers. "There are other people I can trust."

It took a moment before I noticed my stomach had clenched from the stab wound. She meant she'd replace me and wouldn't need me anymore.

"If there's anything else I can do for you," I offered, hoping to hold onto my apprentice position. "I can still help with your writing and correspondence."

She nodded. "There may be something." Her eyebrows furled in thought. "I'm still conceptualizing this." She studied me for awhile. "If you are going to help, you have to know what happened."

"When Rupert called you at Hugo's?"

"That, but there's so much more. So much has changed."

# CHAPTER 20

# Greenwich Village, New York, 1964

## ANAÏS

WHEN ANAÏS RETURNED TO CONVINCE Hugo that the rest ranch hadn't been a lie, she found the situation to be worse than she'd feared. Hugo had taken a mistress, a Haitian-born dancer he'd met at his modern dance class. Driven by jealousy, Anaïs snuck into the back of the theater where the dancers rehearsed and observed Hugo and his mistress gyrating to wild drums. From the communication of their hips, Anaïs imagined that Hugo had, at last, found a woman attuned to his frenzied rhythms, and she panicked.

Needing to speak to someone, she phoned Renate. Ronnie picked up, but Anaïs heard Renate wailing. Between Renate's heaving sobs and Ronnie's attempts to explain, she finally made out that Renate had found her son unconscious on the living room floor and could not revive him. Peter was dead from a heroin overdose. Renate had had no idea that Peter had been using drugs and blamed herself. Anaïs wanted to return to Los Angeles immediately, but Ronnie insisted that Renate, distraught with grief and guilt, would not see anyone.

Anaïs was overcome with guilt for her own blindness. She and Renate's other friends had considered Peter the child of their artists' community. Yet preoccupied with their romantic intrigues, creative projects, and parties, none of them had noticed that their beloved boy was drowning. They'd let him slip away unseen and alone.

With a devastating clarity, Anaïs recognized that it didn't matter that Hugo was finding satisfaction in another woman's arms. It didn't matter that she also loved and lived with Rupert. People needed to keep watch over one another, so that none were lost; people needed to be reminded that they were loved. She and Hugo had cared for and loved each other for three decades. They should not allow denial and a failure to communicate destroy a marriage that had sustained them both.

Denial was not benign; secrets were not benign. It was time for them to face and accept that they were bonded, but that their marriage could not satisfy their sexual needs. It was time for them to be open with each other, to have an open marriage. She would tell Hugo that she knew about his affair and that it was all right with her; they could love each other and have other lovers in their lives. It didn't have to destroy their marriage.

When Hugo got home late that night and tried to slip under the covers without waking her, she snuggled up and wrapped her arms around him. She told him that he did not need to feel guilty that he had a mistress, because she had someone too.

Hugo flung her off, took his pillow, slammed the bedroom door, and abandoned her for his office.

∞

Although she knew that Dr. Inge Bogner would never intervene on her behalf with Hugo, Anaïs expected to gain some clarity when she arrived at the psychoanalyst's Upper East Side apartment. Dr. Bogner had first been Hugo's analyst. Years before, the German analyst had accepted Anaïs as her patient as well, with the proviso that she would never betray the confidences of either partner. Indeed, although she knew all about Anaïs's bigamy, Bogner had been scrupulous in keeping it secret.

Dr. Bogner greeted Anaïs with a smiling face that was welcoming, yet disconcerting, because only one of her eyes moved. The other eye perpetually gazed into space because it was crafted of glass with a painted gray-green iris. The psychoanalyst settled into her armchair opposite Anaïs and picked up her knitting.

After weeping with grief over Peter's overdose, Anaïs blurted that she had asked Hugo for an open marriage. She expected that Bogner would congratulate her for attempting, at last, to be candid with Hugo. But the analyst, uncharacteristically, broke her rule of not revealing one partner's feelings to the other. "You may be ready to drop your denial, Anaïs, but Hugo is not ready to drop his."

"Why not? I've offered him the perfect solution. Openness for both of us."

"I don't believe Hugo is capable of an open marriage."

"But he's capable of having an affair!"

Bogner seemed to nod, or was she just catching a stitch in her knitting? The analyst then raised her face and looked directly at Anaïs with her functioning eye. "Can you ask Hugo for a divorce now?"

"So he can marry his mistress without me in the way? Absolutely not!"

"Are you prepared to divorce Rupert?"

"No, I need Rupert more than ever now that Hugo has a mistress!"

The solution of an open marriage that could release Anaïs from her abiding guilt and terror of discovery had appeared like a strip of film through Hugo's editing machine window and then flown out with a zip. She had no choice but to continue on the trapeze.

∞

Anaïs was alone in the apartment, and Hugo was out late again, probably dancing with his young mistress. The phone rang.

A nurse at New York Hospital said, "Mrs. Guiler, I'm sorry to tell you your husband has been in an accident."

*No! Please God, not Hugo! Not after Peter's death.*

"He's going to be alright, Mrs. Guiler. Given he's in traction."

It took her a while to sort out that Hugo had fallen from kicking too high in class and had fractured a leg.

The next morning, Anaïs arrived at Hugo's hospital room and spent the day with him, waiting to face down the mistress who never showed. A week later, when Hugo and a traction apparatus were delivered to the apartment, there had still been no sign of the young woman who likely was gyrating with someone else now.

Once Hugo and his pain pills and bedpan were hers to deal with, Anaïs almost wished the mistress would claim him. Millie had gone, inconveniently, on her Christmas leave, and Anaïs found herself having to feed and nurse him day and night.

There was nothing to do but turn Hugo's helplessness into an opportunity. She rented a nurse's cap and mini-skirted white uniform from a costume store and wore it with high heels to attend to him. After several weeks of her flirtatious ministrations, their marriage settled into an affectionate, unspoken understanding that she would continue her periodic trips to Los Angeles and he would hold onto her by remaining in denial.

Anaïs resolved that from then on she would be not just a liar, but the best liar; not just desirable, but unforgettable; not just a bigamist, but the most wonderful wife any two men could imagine, so that neither would ever wander from her again.

That was, unfortunately, when Rupert phoned at 1:20 a.m. Anaïs, who had been sleeping on the daybed in Hugo's office, picked up the receiver. She could hear Hugo pick up the other line from his hospital bed in the master bedroom. She knew he could hear Rupert's drunken rant. "Tell me the truth, Anaïs! Are you still living with Hugo?"

Remaining calm, she said, "Hugo broke his leg, and I'm caring for him." She promised to call Rupert back. He hung up in a huff.

She made up a story for Hugo that the caller was a crazy stalker who showed up at her book signings. She said that Dr. Bogner had told her not to contradict the stalker's fantasies or he could become dangerous.

Three days later, she found out that Rupert would be arriving in New York the following morning to be with her. Her mind went into overdrive. Her first instinct was to keep her husbands as far from each other in the city as possible. God forbid that they run into each other. Then she realized that unless she introduced them, neither husband could recognize the other, and that, actually, it would be easier for her to have them only blocks apart. That way, in an emergency, she could get from one to the other in minutes. So she booked Rupert a room at the Washington Square Hotel, directly across the park from her apartment with Hugo. Washington Square Arch in the middle of the park would be the demarcation between Hugo's kingdom and Rupert's domain.

As soon as she had intercepted Rupert and enticed him to the hotel, she told him she had to leave for her *Cue* editing job. Taking a taxi, she arrived within minutes at the elevator to her fourteenth-floor apartment. When she didn't find Hugo in his hospital bed, she was rattled, until she saw him hobbling around on crutches with Millie's help.

"Oh, Millie, I am so glad you are back." Anaïs threw her arms around the Haitian woman's neck while Millie kept her grip on Hugo. Anaïs stepped in front of Hugo, so he didn't have to twist to see her. "Darling, I have big news!"

Both Hugo and Millie looked at her expectantly.

"*Cue* has given me an assignment to oversee a new French edition! The only thing is, I'll have to work day and night until we go to print."

Hugo pulled away from Millie's support and stepped with his crutches toward the bed. "That's enough, Millie. Let me have a word with my wife, if you would," he said, using the paternalistic tone that got on Anaïs's nerves. She anticipated his speech on how he was the breadwinner in the family, and she was his precious helper, and presently he needed her help.

Instead he asked, "Have you talked to them about salary?"

After reprimanding her for not using his help in the negotiations, he urged her to take the job. Surprised, she asked him why.

"Nothing, just things are just a little slow with my investments right now."

Things had been a little slow for years now, ever since Castro had nationalized the assets of Hugo's wealthy Cuban clients. Bad as she was with numbers, Anaïs thought she was better than Hugo had proven to be with their money since leaving the bank. Every profit he made with his investing, he threw away on extravagant spending.

She asked him gently, "Do you think you could ask the bank for your old job back?"

She was afraid he might explode at this suggestion, but he said, "I already have."

"And?"

"George Moore is going to take it to Rockefeller when he thinks the time is right. We have a dinner scheduled with Moore and his wife a week from Friday."

"What about your leg?"

"I should be able to get around on the crutches by then. I'll need your help, though. *Cue* has to let you go that night."

"You can count on me." She smiled, feeling somehow . . . saintly.

Thus began her frenetic daily swing back and forth across Washington Square Park from Hugo to Rupert, and Rupert to Hugo, a foreshortened trapeze at high speed. During the afternoon, while Hugo thought she was at *Cue*, she and Rupert—along with the other teacher families on winter break—visited the Met, MOMA, and the Natural History Museum. In the evening, she and Rupert made love in their hotel bed, enjoying a honeymoon they had never taken. But at 5 a.m. Anaïs had to wake herself, dress in her skirt and heels, and rush off to her supposed job that began before sunrise.

Since crossing Washington Square Park in the dark didn't feel safe, she would scurry along the park perimeter—Waverly to MacDougal, around the corner to Washington Square South and the entrance to the massive apartment complex where she and Hugo lived. She'd crawl under the sheets with Hugo, and when she heard him rattling his crutches to get up at ten she'd force herself awake to help him, make breakfast, shower, and put on a fresh dress for her supposed late-shift job. When Millie arrived to take over helping Hugo at noon, she'd dash from the Washington Square Park Apartments back to Rupert.

At first, she found this frenzied marathon exhilarating. The same excitement she experienced 30,000 feet in the air on her transcontinental trapeze, she now discovered on her brisk walks just before dawn. Wearing her Sabina cape, street lamps glowing as in a de Chirico painting, she swept past the chess players, for whom commandeering their favorite table was worth arriving before dawn. A short Russian with a Lenin cap and a Trotsky goatee would bow to her and say, "Would her majesty care for a game?"

She would laugh. "Not today, comrade. I'm already in a game."

That was when Sabina thrived. Sabina was back.

For a week, she thrilled to this excitement of danger and beauty. Then she began to get paranoid from lack of sleep, thinking the Russian chess player's narrow eyes were tracking her.

On New Year's Day, after sharing fireworks in bed with Rupert at midnight, toasting mimosas in the morning with Hugo, and rushing back to Rupert at noon, she noticed that the winter weather had suddenly turned clear, as if Mother Earth herself were celebrating the first day of 1965. Rupert suggested a walk in Washington Square Park.

It seemed half of the Village had gotten the same idea. The park was full of people promenading around the fountain in both directions: mothers with baby carriages, old ladies leaning into each other, students with signs protesting American troops going to Vietnam.

She and Rupert were halfway around the circle when she saw Hugo on his crutches, walking toward them with Millie's help. Anaïs quickly shielded her face with her hands and hissed at Rupert, "The sun is burning my skin." She tugged on him to turn around. "Let's go look at the arch so I can show you the inscription by George Washington."

When they got to the marble arch, Rupert read the inscription aloud in his hammy actor's voice: "'Let us raise a standard to which the wise and the honest can repair.'"

Anaïs glanced back. Hugo and Millie were heading in the direction of the arch!

She tried to pull Rupert through to the other side of the arch with her, but he resisted, jerking his arm back. "What are you doing? I'm not finished."

Letting go and positioning herself out of sight behind the arch, she beckoned. "Come on, I'll treat you to lunch at the hotel."

Stubborn as always, Rupert remained on the other side of the arch, determined to finish reading the inscription. She heard him intone, "'The event is in the hands of God.'"

Then she heard Hugo's voice! "Did I ever tell you, Millie, about the night that Duchamp climbed inside a door in this arch, and he and six others from the Art Students League spent the evening sitting at the top, setting off cap pistols and releasing balloons?"

"That's a good story," she heard Rupert say to Hugo.

Hugo, encouraged, answered Rupert, "That's not all. They read a proclamation: 'Whereas, whereas, whereas . . .'" Hugo was hamming it, too. "'We hereby declare the Independence of the Republic of Greenwich Village!'"

Rupert chuckled and asked Hugo, "Do you know where Duchamp's door is?"

"On the other side." Hugo pointed his crutch toward the side where Anaïs was hiding. Rupert walked through the arch.

Anaïs shook her head and mouthed, *Not here.* Had she known where the damned door was, she would have climbed inside it. Then Millie was following Rupert through the arch, Hugo shuffling right behind her! Anaïs stopped breathing.

She thrust a flat hand at Millie, who was startled but nodded that she understood and retreated back through the arch. From the other side she heard Millie tell Hugo, "That's enough for today."

Rupert gave Anaïs a shocked look of disapproval, likely mistaking her signal to Millie as unspeakable rudeness to a black woman with a crippled man. He hissed at Anaïs, "I'm going to bring them back here, so you can apologize," and took off to fetch them.

She seized Rupert's arm, whispering, "Let's go back to the hotel room and make love."

Rupert grabbed her hip and whispered back, "I'm going to fuck the rudeness right out of you, Anaïs," as, to her relief, she heard the scrape of Hugo's crutches on the gravel grow fainter.

CHAPTER 21

# Manhattan, New York, 1965

## ANAÏS

AS SHE WAITED FOR THE teller at the Park Avenue branch of First National City Bank to bring her $1,600 in cash, Anaïs calculated what was left in the proprietary account Hugo had set up for her. She had started with a principal of $50,000 that she was supposed to have left untouched except for the interest, but the last time she'd checked it had dwindled to $14,600, given her many withdrawals as "earnings" from her fictional jobs for each husband.

The teller to whom Anaïs had given her passbook was taking a very long time. Anaïs needed that $1,600 today. Rupert expected her "earnings" to pay for the hotel; Hugo said he needed it to pay rent that month. *Please God, don't let there be a problem.*

The teller was leaning over the desk of a young man in an ill-fitting suit. What business was it of theirs if she was draining her account? Her heart pounding rapidly, she listed the things she had to get done to prepare for the crucial dinner with George Moore and his wife the following evening: hair and nails at Elizabeth Arden, pick up Hugo's dry cleaning, get back to the hotel in time to find a place to hide the dry cleaning, meet Rupert for dinner. Next morning, up at five; remember to take Hugo's cleaned shirts and suit with her to the apartment; into bed with Hugo; out of bed with Hugo; lunch with Rupert; back in the afternoon for final rehearsal with Hugo on his crutches; dress for dinner; phone Rupert from a phone booth to make sure that, as arranged, he was meeting her bookstore owner friend Maxwell for a movie; help Hugo into the taxi; and, finally, charm the bank president into hiring Hugo back.

"Mrs. Hugo Guiler?"

Anaïs looked up.

The teller had brought over the man with whom she'd been in discussion, introducing him as her manager. He asked, "Did you not know that your husband closed this account?"

Anaïs reached for the counter to steady herself. "That's impossible," she said calmly. "That account is in my name only. You must have it confused with Hugo's other accounts here."

The manager had a piece of paper in his hand. "Here is the present balance in that account."

She saw only zeros.

"Can you withdraw from any of your husband's other accounts?" the girl said, trying to be helpful. The manager glared at her.

"I don't believe so," Anaïs said. She thought she might faint in the First National City Bank lobby. The bank president, George Moore, would be informed that Mrs. Hugo Guiler had caused a scene downstairs because her husband had covertly emptied her account. That would not make a good impression in advance of their crucial dinner.

"I'm sure there's some confusion." Anaïs smiled weakly. "I'll talk with Hugo about it." She walked, slowly and with great dignity, out of the bank lobby.

∞

At 5 a.m. the day of the important dinner, she didn't need an alarm clock; her exhausted body was on constant alarm. Through the window of Rupert's hotel room, it looked as if the hotel were under a waterfall. *Get up, dress, take an umbrella for the downpour.*

By the time she rounded the corner of the park where the chess tables were, her pumps and nylons were soaked and her expensive hairdo ruined. The little bearded Russian and his chess partner rose and bowed in unison, holding their umbrellas like Tweedledee and Tweedledum.

She heard the little Russian shout through the downpour, "Not a good day for the game, your majesty."

Just then she realized that she'd forgotten Hugo's suit. The dry cleaning was still in the hotel linen closet where she'd stashed it. She did a 180-degree turn and hurried back in the direction she'd come.

She was running now, into the hotel lobby, up the elevator, to the linen closet. Thank God Hugo's dry cleaning was still there. She plunged out the hotel door into the rain, her umbrella protecting the paper-wrapped suit and shirts.

Now she was behind schedule. Even though she would have to pass the junkies sleeping on the park benches, it would be faster to cut through the park. She ran under the arch with her umbrella angled to shield Hugo's dry cleaning from the downpour.

Large muddy ponds had formed in the potholes around the fountain, so she skirted them. All of a sudden the heel of her left pump hit the ground at a sharp angle and she skated forward on it until she splashed bottom-first into a huge puddle, muddy water up to her waist. Hugo's dry cleaned shirts and suit floated in their paper wrappers on the puddle's surface, beginning to sink. Her wet hair plastered to her face, she moved through the muck to gather up Hugo's soaked dry cleaning. She carried it clutched to her chest, holding her broken umbrella, and stumbled on toward the apartment. Then she stopped dead in her tracks, dropping the umbrella, the rain pouring down on her drenched hair, muddy clothes, and Hugo's ruined dry cleaning.

Dazed, she started for the fountain, rending patches of sopping paper off the dry cleaning as if it were her flesh; as if she were the heroine of a Greek tragedy descending the amphitheater steps.

"I can't do this anymore!" She flung down a dress shirt.

"I don't care!" She threw down the muddied trousers.

"It's over!" She stomped on Hugo's expensive jacket.

The game was up.

She was driven with insane energy and, without purpose, she gathered up again the discarded clothing and stumbled with them to the center of the fountain. "Leave me! Go!" She flung away the men's shirts and trousers as if they were her men themselves.

Hitting the deluge of fountain water, she fell to her knees and collapsed under its torrent. Her nose and mouth filled with liquid.

She was literally drowning in a pool of remorse like Sabina at the end of *A Spy in the House of Love*. She had written her own absurd ending! The thought made her heave out water with hysterical laughter.

She raised herself out of the water, gasping for air. Through the rain she saw a form approaching. Suddenly she was terrified, aware of where she was and how it looked. She would be arrested and questioned. The police would see she had lost her mind and commit her to a mental institution. She tried desperately to think how to explain herself. Then she saw the Lenin cap of the little Russian chess player.

He bent down with the formal bow of a Hapsburg duke, gallantly offering his hand.

Accepting his small hand and rising, she sputtered, "Why did you follow me?"

"I knew when you turned around it was a different move for you. I came to see if you might need some help."

"I do." She shivered.

"I am at your service," the little Russian said, tipping his cap. He offered his elbow as he led her out of the fountain, patting her hand. "A woman like you will always have a man to look after her."

∞

After mopping up the floor, showering, crawling into bed with Hugo, and rising to help him with his crutches, Anaïs told him at breakfast how upset she was that the dry cleaners had lost his order. She told him, also, that she had gone to the bank and learned that he had closed out her personal account.

He pronounced, "You had gone into your capital. That was never the intent."

"And what am I supposed to live on?"

"Your job at *Cue*."

"*Cue* has collapsed. No one is getting paid."

She watched Hugo stoically absorb the lie.

Hugo said, "If I get my position at the bank back, we can return to my giving you an allowance."

An allowance. Like a child again, she thought. She wanted Hugo to get his job back, but she didn't look forward to playing the role of banker's wife again. That battle-ax Betty Friedan, who'd written *The Feminine Mystique*, was right: society made women dependent on their husbands to survive. She felt the craziness that had driven her into the fountain rise again. She wanted to yell at Hugo that he thought he was her superior when really he was a fool who didn't know what went on right under his nose, but she caught herself. She had to hold onto what was left of her frazzled nerves and shaky body for one more day and night, for the dinner with George Moore.

That night she played her old role of Hugo's enchanting wife to the hilt. She entranced Mr. and Mrs. Moore with her practiced Parisian stories about Antonin Artaud, Lawrence Durrell, and Henry Miller.

She squeezed Hugo's hand under the table to reassure him of the good impression they were making. When she and Hugo got back to the apartment, they were hopeful he'd get his old job back. She held it together until the following afternoon, when she broke down in Dr. Bogner's office.

Anaïs gasped for breath between sobs, "I can't do it anymore! I've become my mother!"

"How do you mean?" Bogner asked, looking up from her knitting with her good eye.

"All I do is work to take care of other people. I'm dependent on them and angry at them like my mother."

Bogner nodded, a sign for Anaïs to continue.

"If I'd put the same time and energy into making a living for myself, instead of trying to help the men in my life, I'd be . . . I'd be free. Instead Hugo wants to make me dependent on an allowance again!"

"Perhaps it's not too late for you to be self-supporting."

To Anaïs this was an outrageous idea. She was sixty-two years old. The only real job she'd ever had was as an artist's model before she'd married Hugo. The short time she'd worked as a lay psychotherapist in New York was literally under Dr. Otto Rank in bed. She hadn't finished high school and had no secretarial or cooking skills.

"It is too late." She sighed.

Bogner remained as impassive as her glass eye. "If money were not a problem, what is it that you would want to do?"

"That's impossible to answer," Anaïs said. "Money is the problem."

"Use your creativity," Bogner urged calmly. "Pretend you had all the money you could possibly need. What would you do?"

"I'd just go back to giving money to Hugo and Rupert to prove my supposed jobs, only I'd finally get a raise."

Bogner allowed a flicker of a smile but was not deterred. "Let us imagine, for the moment, that you did not have either husband in your life, you'd never had a husband, and you had all the money you needed. What would you be doing?"

"I'd be living in Paris," Anaïs said without hesitation. "I wouldn't even care if it were in a garret by myself. I'd be like Djuna Barnes and have a small audience of French literary readers. That's what I always wanted."

"Well it doesn't sound like you would need a great deal of money to do that."

"But I would. I'd need money to get settled in Paris and to live on until I could translate my work into French and get it published."

"So you think you could make a living as a writer in France?" Bogner asked.

"Maybe. Eventually. The two of my novels in print there sell more than all my books in English ever did. I don't know why I insisted on writing in English to begin with. It isn't my first language."

"Why do you think you avoided writing in French?" Bogner asked.

"Because the French are so damn judgmental! I so admired French literature, especially Proust, that I thought I could never be accepted in French." Anaïs heard her own hollow laugh. "Instead I wrote in English for an audience who never read Proust and doesn't like the kind of writing I do."

"So it was a lack of confidence," Bogner said.

"Yes." Anaïs pulled a tissue to mop her tears.

"Could it be the same lack of confidence that keeps you from fulfilling your dream now? You have always been very successful at helping others to fulfill their dreams. Couldn't you put that energy into living your own dream?"

"When you say that, I feel terrified."

"Have you ever thought about trying to sell your diaries?"

"I couldn't. Can you imagine Hugo's reaction to being exposed as a cuckold?"

"Not necessarily published. There are libraries that buy the papers of authors prior to their deaths. Perhaps you could convince one to purchase your diaries and keep them sealed until after the deaths of anyone who might be hurt."

"Why would they pay money for my diaries? I'm not a famous writer. I'm a failure."

"Aren't there people who are now famous writers like Miller and Durrell whom you describe in your diary?"

Anaïs looked up. Her tears stopped. "Really, you think I could get enough money to move to Paris?"

"It's a possibility. And there are others. You should not have to stay with either of your husbands for purely economic reasons."

Anaïs stared at Bogner, suddenly feeling calm and clear. Something had shifted inside her. A new idea. A new way of being.

By moving to Paris, she could leave both Hugo and Rupert without having to choose between them. She could refrain from fatally wounding either, because she would not be leaving him for another man. She would be leaving to become her own woman.

She was giving birth to a new self. She was springing out of the chrysalis. Soon she would be airbound, one last swing from New York to Los Angeles and back, and then she would spring off the trapeze for good and fly to Paris, with a financial safety net that, somehow, she would create for herself.

# CHAPTER 22

# Los Angeles, California, 1965

## TRISTINE

WHEN ANAÏS WAS TELLING ME about this swerve in direction, I felt disoriented. So much had changed about her life, and Renate's, and mine, in such a short period.

"Tristine, the trapeze is collapsing," Anaïs cried.

I offered to help her write to libraries as Dr. Bogner had suggested, but she waved that idea aside, saying she'd already phoned them, and none had money to acquire her diaries.

"I need you to help me figure out another way to get money to move back to Paris."

If there was one thing I knew nothing about, it was how to make money.

She surprised me by declaring, "You have what I want. You live independently."

"Well I do it with waitressing, and my scholarship, and student loans. I don't think you would like living as I do. Maybe you could teach?"

"It doesn't pay enough. I see how little Rupert brings home."

"What about getting some kind of grant?"

"I've already tried that." She sighed. "I applied twice for a National Endowment and was denied."

I was out of ideas. I was still trying to grasp her new goal of moving to Paris and leaving the very husbands I had tried to help her hold onto. She would be leaving me as well.

As if she'd read my thoughts, she said, "Maybe you could come to Paris, too. You could study at the Sorbonne."

"I don't think I can leave Neal."

"Bring him to Paris! The Parisians love American jazz."

I knew she was right about that, but I was still trying to adjust to her about-face. I looked at the Bekins boxes along the wall; one was unsealed and filled with books. "Are those packed boxes in preparation for your move to Paris?"

"No. Those are for the move into the house Rupert built us in Silver Lake. It's almost finished. He intends to cement me in place there. Then I'll never get to Paris!" She seemed to be hyperventilating, but she calmed herself and took a very deep breath. Her neon eyes flashed as she reiterated my new assignment: "Tristine, we need a bold idea. Something to get a lot of money quickly."

"Maybe you could write a potboiler bestseller like Harold Robbins?" I tried.

"I have a potboiler story alright. But I don't dare write it."

"How about really getting a movie made from one of your novels?" It was evidence of just how little I knew about the movie business that I would have suggested this.

Anaïs liked that idea, though. "Which of my novels do you think would be best as a movie?"

"Without question, *A Spy in the House of Love.*"

"Yes, I think so, too." She nodded. "We just need a producer to option the book and commission a script."

"I don't know any producers," I said.

"Or a director who can get a movie made," she said.

"What about your friend Curtis Harrington?"

"I thought about Curtis, but he only does horror films and, anyway, he's gone commercial." The way she said "gone commercial," it sounded like heinous treason. She knitted her thin brows. "Renate's the one who knows everybody in the movie industry."

"But she's grieving now," I said, feeling on delicate ground. I'd never known anyone who'd endured tragedy as huge as Renate's, but instinctively I recognized there could be no pain like the death of one's child.

Anaïs was pensive for a long while, and in the quiet, it felt as if we were saying a prayer for Renate.

Finally, Anaïs stated, "It would be good for Renate to take on this movie project with us."

I didn't know which part of Anaïs's pronouncement shocked me more: that she thought getting involved with a movie project would be good for Renate after her son's death, or that I would be participating.

Anaïs continued enthusiastically, "I'll call Renate to see if she'll meet with us."

"I don't think I should be there," I said.

"You have to be there."

"I don't think she's going to want to see me at a time like this."

"How old are you?"

"Twenty-one."

"Peter's age," Anaïs said softly. She looked at me tenderly, and in that moment I understood a momentous thing was about to happen in my life. It was an alarming idea, akin to providing a new kitten for a friend whose beloved cat had died. Anaïs had begun to see me as Renate's replacement for Peter.

∽

The next time Anaïs phoned me she reported, to my relief, that Renate was still refusing any visits. To keep our movie project moving along, she suggested we have lunch at the Chateau Marmont café. She asked if I would pick her up; Rupert no longer allowed her to drive because she'd smashed up the T-bird again.

The Chateau Marmont parking lot was closed off, so I parked on Sunset, and we hiked up the steep driveway to the hotel. A handsome young waiter with gelled hair took our lunch orders, and Anaïs pulled from her purse a nine-by-twelve envelope filled with thermofaxed pages. Handing it to me, she smiled. "It's from my diary of my Paris years. I'll need to have it back, though, so don't let it out of your sight and don't let Neal see it."

"You're going to let me read your diary?"

Seeing my delight, she grinned her big gummy smile. I opened the top flap and riffled through typed pages with scattered dates: *March, 1934; November, 1934; January, 1935.*

"You typewrote it?" I asked, disappointed that the thermofaxed pages weren't of handwritten originals.

"No, I handwrite it first, but I selected and typed out the entries about my relationships with Henry Miller and Gonzolo Mores for you. Gonzolo was my Paris lover who was a Marxist like your Neal. I thought that reading about my sexual frenzy with them might help you with yours."

"That is so great of you! But my relationship with Neal isn't just sex," I clarified. "I'm completely in love with him."

"Oh, I was in love with Henry and Gonzolo, too." The waiter brought our iced teas, and we paused to hydrate ourselves after our uphill hike. "When I first fell for Henry," she resumed, "I thought that I would never desire another man. Henry owned my body."

"Like Neal owns mine."

"But I learned from Henry." Her dry laugh cracked her words. "Perhaps I learned too well how to take sex for its own sake. He taught me a taste for the new and the aphrodisiac of danger."

I had to admit that danger was part of Neal's appeal—the danger of his politics, of his sexual wildness, of not being able to hold onto him. "Why are we attracted to men like that?" I asked.

"It's projection. Do you know what that is?"

"It's when you see yourself in another person."

"It's more covert than that." The waiter delivered our niçoise salads and she picked up her fork with her left hand, and I did likewise. "We choose men who play out parts of ourselves we aren't ready to acknowledge. As I did with Henry and Gonzolo. They were both rebels from convention, like your Neal."

"Are you saying that I feel I can't live without Neal because he's playing out my rebelliousness for me?"

"Exactly, Tristine! So you don't have to! Neal is your man from the earth, as Henry was mine. Neal is your revolutionary firebrand, as Gonzolo was mine."

Urgently, I went to the heart of my dilemma. "But it's swept me away. I don't know who I am anymore. I'm so consumed with what Neal does, where he's going, who he's with. How can I get rid of this jealousy?"

Anaïs shrugged. "If you love someone, you will feel jealous."

So it was that simple. All of Neal's intellectual justifications couldn't change the nature of feelings. "Should I go out with other guys to make him jealous, so he knows what it feels like?"

"No, those are not good games to get into."

"So I just have to suffer?"

She thought, closing her eyes. When she opened them, she said, "In the pages I gave you, you will see that I suffered from jealousy, too. When Henry told me his wife was coming from New York to join him in Paris, I was consumed with jealousy."

As Anaïs spoke, I could tell she was pulling the memories together. "My way of dealing with it was to defuse the enemy through seduction.

But I didn't expect that June, beautiful, mysterious June, would be even better at the game of seduction than I was. Now I was obsessed with them both, Henry and June. I was jealous of Henry's relationship with her and of her relationship with him. I projected different aspects of myself onto them. Henry was the writer I wanted to be. June was the woman I wanted to be. Are you attracted to the woman Neal is sleeping with?"

"I think it's more than one woman and I haven't met any of them." Then I told her something very private. "I have a fantasy image of his other woman, though. She's soft and blond and passive, the opposite of me. In my nightmares she is in the shower with Neal, and he loves her."

"She is also a projection of a disowned self." Anaïs nodded. "How are you even sure Neal really has other lovers, and it isn't all your imagination?"

"Because I pester him with questions, and sometimes he answers them honestly."

"You shouldn't do that," Anaïs said.

"I know, but I can't help myself. What can I do? Tell me, please!" I confessed to her how my obsession with him had extinguished my purposefulness and intelligence. "I'm like the professor in *The Blue Angel* who falls for Marlene Dietrich, and it destroys his life."

She laughed so heartily that the few other people in the café looked up from their copies of *Hollywood Reporter*. "Be careful of exaggeration," she said, but seeing my chagrin, she softened her voice. "I hope you are putting this in your diary."

I nodded. "So I'll remember it someday."

"No, so you can move through it."

I must have looked perplexed because she explained, "It's a process of addition." She put down her fork and raised her hands like a conductor with a baton. She pointed to my left shoulder with the imaginary baton. "You feel this"—she pointed to my chest—"and then you feel this"—and to my right shoulder—"and then this. It doesn't matter if the feelings contradict each other." She swung her graceful arms, bent at the elbow, as if I were her orchestra. "All that matters is that the feelings are true to their moment." She lowered her arms and picked up her fork again. "And don't make judgments on yourself as you write. You have to give yourself that freedom."

This was something I thought I could do. Had she suggested I break it off with Neal, or give him an ultimatum, or try to negotiate ground rules, or any other Dear Abby advice, it would have been useless. I was so adrift in the storm of my passion that to ask me to quit would be like asking a sailor on a bucking sailboat to jump off into the turbulent sea. Anaïs was just asking me to cling to the ride and record it.

As we descended the steep Chateau Marmont driveway, stepping sideways and holding onto each other to keep from falling, she offered one more bit of advice. "You can never be fulfilled through another no matter how much you love him." She squeezed my forearm. "You must complete yourself."

She pulled away from me and, arms outstretched, twirled in circles down the remainder of the incline. "You must own your own wildness!" she called, the skirt of her dress swinging at her knees, her graceful movements those of a slim girl. I imagined her releasing the grip on her trapeze, swooping up and gliding on an air current towards Paris, and I was seized with the same panic I felt at the thought of losing Neal. I couldn't live without her.

∞

In the following weeks, I devoured the thermofaxed pages from Anaïs's diary. Unlike the overworked poetry of her novels, the prose of her diary was so alive it throbbed with a heartbeat. It was hard to believe that someone could write a diary that was so readable; mine certainly wasn't.

Her descriptions of her life in Paris when she was near my age filled me with longing: wearing beautiful clothes, arguing about literature in cafés with Henry Miller and his friend Larry Durrell, Henry throwing her onto the unmade bed of his Clichy apartment, visiting whorehouses in Montmartre with him, embracing his wife June as if falling into a mirror of beauty, taking drugs and staying up all night with June, dashing from husband to lovers in taxis, danger and arousal in a whirlwind rising to a tempest. If she had given me her diary pages to give me perspective, they had the opposite effect. Reading about her sexual frenzy only gave me more appetite for mine with Neal.

The next time Anaïs phoned me, I gushed over her diary, which pleased her, but not enough to let me out of the visit with Renate she'd finally succeeded in arranging. Renate had capitulated because she wanted Ronnie to have a break from his caretaking. Anaïs requested that when I pick her up in Hollywood I return her diary pages, which reluctantly I did.

As I drove us over the bumpy road to Renate's, I only wanted out. I didn't want to witness Renate's tragedy. I didn't want to be Peter's replacement. It was enough that my own mother worried about me obsessively, and while I was drawn to Anaïs's bright, light energy, the shroud of darkness surrounding Renate frightened me.

"I'll go walk on the beach while you talk with Renate," I told Anaïs.

She seized my forearm with the most commanding touch I'd ever felt. "No, I have this all planned."

After Renate answered the door in a pale negligee, she went directly back to her bed, waving a weak hand toward the room where she'd found Peter's body. "I will never open that door again."

Her milky skin was translucent with a sickly pallor and, in a haunting way, she was more beautiful than before. I found myself visualizing her as Mary in Michelangelo's *Pieta*, her dead son stretched over her lap, his knees slouched sideways, his head lolled back.

Anaïs and I settled next to Renate's bed as she reclined against a pile of pillows. On the bed stand were water, medicine bottles, and a small, framed photo of a fat-cheeked man in a monk's robe and turban, whom I later learned was Swami Vivekananda.

"We brought you a custard pie from Du Pars," Anaïs chirped as she opened the cardboard box.

Renate turned away as if the pie's golden skin were offensive to look at. I was too uncomfortable to say anything, but Anaïs chatted away about women in New York wearing boots and heavy eye makeup and all the graffiti in the subways, about her nervous breakdown in Washington Square Park, her decision to break from both Hugo and Rupert, the various ways she'd thought of to make money to move to Paris, and about the artists she was going to look up when she got there.

Tenderly she said, "Renate, you should come too. We'll start over together." Renate didn't even acknowledge her presence, but Anaïs kept right on. "Tristine can come also if she wants, but I don't know if she will because she has big news; she's fallen in love." Anaïs smiled at me encouragingly and put me on the spot. "Tell Renate what you said to Neal when he walked you to your car the first night."

"You mean, 'Your place or mine?'"

"She's our daughter!" Anaïs lilted. Renate made a choking sound before turning her head away and staring into space.

Anaïs continued on with tidbits of gossip about artists they both knew. Eventually, she came back to the topic of raising money and getting a film made of A Spy in the House of Love.

Renate was unresponsive, nearly catatonic.

"I heard that your screenwriter friend Jimmy Bridges is about to direct his first feature," Anaïs said brightly.

Renate set her icy eyes on Anaïs. "It's a Western."

"But with Marlon Brando," Anaïs said.

Renate's white hand squeezed a fistful of the afghan next to her as if she would fling it. "How can you ask this of me, Anaïs?" she cried.

"To help you get a movie made, when I don't want to see anybody. I don't want to talk to anybody. I don't want to live."

Remaining perfectly calm, Anaïs said, "That is exactly why I am asking you to help."

I felt myself pull back, questioning Anaïs's judgment.

She continued gently to Renate, "Do you remember the Artist's Credo we wrote together?"

As if with great effort, Renate said, "No."

"I brought my copy." Anaïs produced from her purse a sheet of onionskin paper rolled like a scroll and held with a thin ribbon. "Do you remember any of the items on it?" she asked, even though Renate had closed her eyes.

Renate opened her eyes and spat, "'Let's celebrate the individuals who struggle to create a world of freedom, beauty, and love.'" She added bitterly, "A lot of good it did."

Anaïs asked, "Do you remember the very first statement?"

"Stop this, Anaïs!" Renate snapped. "I'm going to have to ask you to leave."

"The one we thought was so important we put it first."

Anaïs prided herself on being sensitive to the feelings of others. Why was she being so insensitive now?

"'We celebrate the refusal to despair!'" Anaïs read from her unfurled paper.

"That was then," Renate said indignantly. "Before."

Anaïs replied, "When I wanted to give up living you reminded me about it."

"With all due respect for your pain, Anaïs, this is different."

"Yes, it is different and much harder." Anaïs took Renate's bloodless hand in hers. "That is why we are here—to celebrate your refusal to despair. If you can choose life, it will give Tristine and me inspiration no matter what befalls us in the future."

Renate remained silent, angry and unmoved.

Anaïs urged, "Refusing to despair doesn't mean you don't love Peter. It's just acting as if there were a world worth living in without him. It's an absurd, surrealist act."

At the word "surrealist" Renate's eyelids fluttered. Anaïs tried to press the scroll into her hand, but it fell to the floor as tears rolled down Renate's pale face. She gave Anaïs a helpless, apologetic look. Anaïs held her gaze as if the connection might transmit to Renate her own fierce hope.

They stayed that way for many minutes. I watched, awed, as if at a live birth or a ritual fire being built. Renate straightened and bent forward from her crushed pillows. Anaïs quickly reached behind her to prop them up.

With a note of her old irony, Renate said, "I suppose if I'm going to pretend to be alive, it should be for something as completely illusory as getting a movie made."

I had just witnessed Anaïs raise Renate from the dead.

# CHAPTER 23

# Malibu, California, 1965

## TRISTINE

THREE WEEKS LATER, ANAÏS PHONED me, sounding breathless. "We're going to a party in Malibu on Sunday where Renate's director friend Jimmy Bridges and his producer, Alan Miller, are going to be. Have you heard of Alan Miller?"

"No."

"Well, me neither, but he's the producer on *Apple Lose Her*."

"*Apple Loser*?"

"The Western with Brando."

"*Appaloosa*! Did James Bridges tell Renate he would be interested in directing *Spy*?"

"No, Renate said that Bridges has gone commercial. He told her we should get a European director like Antonioni."

If James Bridges didn't want to direct her novel, I could not understand why Anaïs was so thrilled. "How will you get to Antonioni?"

"Jimmy said we need a big producer first, and that Alan Miller, this producer we are going to meet, is a very cultured man, and while he was not a good producer for *Apple Loose Her*, he could be right for our film, and Jimmy will introduce us at this party! And you're coming!"

"I won't be any help."

"Of course you will. I need Renate to go, and Renate needs both of us."

I was uncomfortable with Anaïs's fantasy that my youthful presence could supplant Peter's absence. But I wanted to see a Malibu party. Besides, if I wasn't home Sunday afternoon when Neal dragged in after his night out, he might not take me so much for granted.

When I arrived at Anaïs's apartment, she said that Rupert's brother had picked him up to visit the construction site so that I could drive us to the party in the T-bird. She glanced at me in the driver's seat. "You look good driving a Thunderbird, Tchr*r*istine. Is that a new dress? It suits you."

I'd fretted over what to wear. I was able to live on my scholarship and loans by almost never buying new clothes. Now, though, I wanted to reflect Anaïs's sense of costume, dressing creatively with an awareness of color and nuance. So, using my aunt's employee discount at Bullocks, I'd bought a new dress—a flowered synthetic in a vintage 1930s bias cut, a dress I imagined Anaïs wearing in Paris when she was having her affair with Henry Miller.

The repaired and repainted T-bird bounced so much on Renate's dirt road that I feared we would end up in a ditch, but Anaïs didn't notice. She was too preoccupied with her plan to present *A Spy in the House of Love* to Alan Miller. She would play hard to get, she said, so it would be my job to talk up her novels. "You're studying English literature. That gives you the most credibility," she assured me.

After we picked up Renate, the three of us cooed over one another's clothes. Renate wore a low-cut black sheath that could be interpreted as mourning garb, and Anaïs was resplendent in a violet A-line dress. I had to park several blocks up the street on Malibu Colony Road, which was really an alley behind the strip of beach houses.

Anaïs, Renate, and I entered the open front door to find guests in shorts and bikini swimsuits milling about. I was immediately self-conscious for being overdressed, but Anaïs and Renate were unfazed. They were used to standing out and carried themselves like regal movie stars of an earlier era.

We wandered around until Renate found her friend, James Bridges. He and his partner Jack Larson enclosed Renate in a long hug. She started to tear up but fought it off and, with her formal Viennese manners, introduced Anaïs and me. I stared at Jack Larson because I recognized him as Superman's sidekick, Jimmy Olsen, from the TV series.

James Bridges, whom I now thought of as Superman's partner's partner, told us that he'd seen Alan Miller earlier, but that the producer had disappeared upstairs for a high stakes poker game. We should just enjoy ourselves and circulate until the game broke up.

Anaïs, Renate, and I settled into director's chairs on the second-floor deck enjoying the ocean view. Several people wandered out to the deck but, not seeing anyone important, moved on. A few people recognized Renate and awkwardly offered condolences about Peter, then rushed away.

Renate shrugged. "People in Hollywood think bad fortune is infectious." She rose to leave. "I'm going to see if Jack will give me a lift home. I'm afraid I will be the kiss of death for your movie quest, Anaïs."

Just then, we heard a group of men guffawing and cursing on their way down the stairs. Someone growled, "You're never getting me into another game, Alan. No one can be that lucky."

Through the open French doors, we could see several men shaking hands. Someone punched the arm of a smiling man. "Hey, Alan, if you make a movie with all the money you just skinned, gimme a job, will ya? I'm gonna need it after today."

Anaïs hissed to Renate, "The winner is Alan Miller. Stay!"

Renate sank back into her chair just as Alan strolled out onto our deck. He sat in a director's chair and started counting a huge stack of bills. He had small, well-shaped hands, though the rest of him was muscular and stocky. We all stared at the cash, waiting for him to finish counting.

When he got to the end, a young actor who'd gotten up to leave said, "How much?"

Alan answered him with a George Raft interpretation. "If I told you I'd have to kill you."

To my surprise, Renate jumped in. "Do you always win?"

"Except when I get slaughtered." Alan laughed. "I should put it into my development fund," he continued good-naturedly as if we were all old friends, "but this is play money. I'll buy my wife a present."

"How thoughtful of you. What will you get her?" I was impressed by Renate's flirtatiousness.

"She's been hawking me to send her to a fat farm so she can lose fifteen pounds. I think she looks great, but it's her thing."

Anaïs asked, "Is your wife here?"

"No, she's decorating our ranch in Arizona. She's not into the Hollywood scene."

"No, we aren't ordinarily, either," Anaïs said.

"What are y' doin' here?" Alan asked.

"I'm a neighbor," Renate said. "I live up the road. Jimmy Bridges invited us. Anaïs is a famous novelist."

We three introduced ourselves.

"I've heard of your work," Alan commented to Anaïs. "You have any novels that would make good movies?"

This was falling into our lap! Jimmy Bridges must have prepped Alan Miller.

I said, "She has lots of novels," complying with Anaïs's request that I talk up her work. "The book we think is a natural for a movie is *A Spy in the House of Love*. It's the story of a woman who loves her husband but feels compelled to have secret affairs with other men. She's followed by a detective who is in some ways her own conscience."

Anaïs and Renate looked at me, impressed, and Alan brightened.

"*A Spy in the House of Love*," he repeated. "Great title. It sounds like James Bond meets *The Naked Kiss*."

"Who directed *The Naked Kiss*?" Renate asked. "I haven't heard of it."

"Sam Fuller," Alan said, pulling a cigar out of the flat side of his jacket. The other side, with all the cash in it, protruded like a breast. "Anyone mind if I smoke?"

I think we all minded, but no one said so. And when Alan blew out his cigar smoke, it didn't smell bad to me.

"I have this development fund," he said, leaning back in his chair. "Bunch of dentists and lawyers in Arizona want to get into the movie game. Buy some books. Develop some scripts. I have an open invitation at Paramount to give 'em first look." He turned to Anaïs. "If you want to get copies of your novels to me, I'll give 'em a read."

Anaïs jumped up. "I have copies in my car!"

Alan followed us out to Malibu Colony Road where I'd parked the T-bird. Anaïs opened the trunk and loaded Alan's arms with her novels.

"How do we reach you?" Anaïs dug in her purse for a purple card to write on.

"Alan Rosen." He gave her his phone number.

"Alan Rosen? You aren't Alan Miller, the producer?"

"Naw, I'm the kind of producer Alan Miller comes to for money."

"So we're going to the horse's mouth?" Renate said.

"That or the horse's ass." Alan Rosen roared and carried the books to his Mercedes.

"You just gave your books to the wrong producer," Renate said to Anaïs.

"No," Anaïs chirped. "My intuition tells me he's the right producer. I liked the way he talked about his wife."

In the T-bird, on the way to drop Renate at her house, we laughed about the confusion caused by Alan Miller and Alan Rosen. We were convinced that everything had happened just the way it was supposed to. We agreed that I would call the number Alan Rosen had given us the next day to make sure he was legit and leave him my phone number and Renate's, but not Anaïs's. She would remain the slightly mysterious, elusive author.

When I got home in my flirty, feminine new dress, Neal was waiting for me. The more evasive I was in answering how I'd been invited to a Malibu party where John Huston, director of *The Maltese Falcon* and *The African Queen,* was a guest, the more Neal wanted to know. He assumed I'd been with another guy, and with his mounting jealousy I felt Sabina's power return to me. That night Neal's lovemaking was sweetened with emotion and, for the first time, he whispered that he loved me; though afterward he withdrew, as if his declaration had stolen something from him, something he wanted back.

∞

The next morning I phoned Alan Rosen's number and got an answering service, but he called right back and asked to have a two-week exclusive so he could read through all the novels. He invited the three of us to lunch at the Old World on Sunset.

The lunch with Alan got rescheduled a few times and when it was finally set, Anaïs couldn't come because she was flying back to New York to prepare Hugo for her move to Paris.

She'd instructed me: "You and Renate are my representatives. Tell Alan that you both should have some participation in the project." She added invitingly, "So you'll have money to join me in Paris. I'm counting on you, Tristine, to keep Renate engaged."

Keeping Renate engaged turned out to be easy, since both she and I were soon living alone and needed each other's company. Renate had asked Ronnie to move out because she could now care for herself, and Neal had packed all his things, excited about an invitation to join up with other civil rights activists in Selma.

During this lonely time, my new closeness with Renate sustained me. We talked for hours on the phone every night. Renate's mind was a garden of strange knowledge; there wasn't an esoteric subject about which she was not informed: Joan of Arc, contraception in the Middle Ages, the culture of the Chumash Indians in Malibu, Jung's book on flying saucers, the Vedantist concept of pain as illusion. Listening to Renate speak was like reading a book by a great writer. It saddened me that her true talent of discourse was just thrown to the wind, given away; never to receive recompense, recognition, or appreciation except by Anaïs, who'd taken sentences from Renate's lips and placed them in her fiction. For my part, I would have been happy simply to listen to Renate's stories all night, especially about Anaïs. But Renate challenged me to keep up with her, making me volley sentences, testing my memory, and heightening my game like a tennis pro with a fledgling. Always our nightly conversations began and ended with our shared business of moving Anaïs's movie project forward.

∞

The Old World was an eatery frequented by aspiring actors and directors. Alan Rosen was waiting for us at a street-side patio table where we almost had to shout to be heard over the traffic.

After we ordered salads, he said, "I talked with my investors, and we think the safest thing would be for us to tie up all the novels."

Renate kicked my leg under the table but kept her voice professional. "That would be quite expensive, to tie up all of Anaïs's work."

"You have to help me here." Alan smiled. "I was thinking $50,000 up front. I'm going to need a five-year option for that price."

I could not believe my ears. $50,000! Renate nodded, not agreeing or disagreeing.

"What about the back end?" I asked. I'd been talking to friends, and this was something they always asked about. I wasn't sure what it was.

Alan said, "Look, I know you two want to be producers but I'm not going to promise you anything I can't deliver. Would you consider taking associate producer if I paid you Writer's Guild minimum to write the screenplay?"

We hadn't actually thought we could be producers, real or associate, nor screenwriters, but we both kept silent. Finally, I said, "You'll have to talk to our agent." We didn't have an agent, and Renate gave me a surprised look, but she went along with my bluff.

Alan said, "I'll have to get all this OK'd by my people, too."

Alan told us to get started on a film treatment for *Spy* and have our agent call him.

Renate and I were as excited as twelve-year-old girls. She phoned the Writer's Guild and found out that at minimum, what we would get paid to write one screenplay was more than I could make in five years of waitressing and more than Renate had ever made in her lifetime as a painter.

"We have to call Anaïs in New York," Renate said. "She might not want us to write the screenplay. Remember she said she wanted Marguerite Duras, who wrote *Hiroshima Mon Amour*."

I hadn't thought about that, or the fact that neither Renate nor I had ever written a screenplay and didn't know how. It all just seemed to be working as magic.

We phoned Anaïs and she was agreeable to everything, including our writing the screenplay. Renate asked a neighbor who was a William Morris agent to negotiate the deal. The agent said he didn't know Alan Rosen, but money was money. In a few phone calls, he'd worked out the terms. All that remained to be done was to sign the papers at Alan's office and collect our commencement check and Anaïs's $50,000 option check.

Renate planned a little celebration party. Alan was to come at two in the afternoon and at four Raven, Bebe, Joan Houseman, Curtis Harrington, and others were to arrive. At a few minutes before two, Renate placed a bottle of Mumm's into an ice bucket, opened the door to the room she hadn't set foot in since Peter's overdose, and set out the champagne and hors d' oeuvres in there.

By 2:20 p.m., she and I sat alone in that haunted room. We had, out of nervousness, eaten all the cheese and crackers. We kept checking the time. Alan was late.

"He must have gotten lost," Renate said. When he was an hour and a half late and it was time for the guests to arrive, I called his number.

An operator with his answering service told me, "We are no longer taking messages for Alan Rosen."

"Do you have another number for him?" I asked.

"That's all I know. His service was discontinued for non-payment."

When I told Renate, she frowned. "This is not a good omen." She phoned the agent.

"Let me do some research," the agent said. "I told you I'd never heard of him."

When Renate's guests arrived, they tried to keep her spirits up. They knew what a big step it had been for her to entertain again. But after several hours of waiting, without any word from Alan or the agent, they made their exits, hugging Renate.

When the agent finally did call back, Renate held the receiver so I could hear. "Well, he told the truth about one thing; he does live on a luxury ranch in Arizona," the agent said. "He's the gardener. Before that he was a card mechanic at a Vegas casino. Once a con man, always—"

"Oh no!" Renate cried.

"Don't feel too bad," the agent said. "He had me going, too. And you're not the first hopefuls duped into thinking he was a rich movie producer."

"But why us?" Renate asked. "I can understand why he'd pose as a producer to get into poker games. He made money that way. But he didn't get money out of us."

"That's the interesting part. The woods are full of these guys posing as producers. They do it to live out the fantasy," the agent said before taking another call.

Renate looked at me, crestfallen. "What are we going to tell Anaïs?"

"We have to tell her the truth," I said.

While Renate agonized over how this cruel hoax might push Anaïs into another breakdown, I worried about how it would affect Renate.

When Anaïs phoned to find out how it had gone, Renate bluffed, "We can't talk right now. A little emergency with the plumbing." She hung up with a sigh of relief. "We have a reprieve until Tuesday. Anaïs wants us to come see the new house."

∞

Even though I'd been to the site before, I got lost driving to the Silver Lake house. By the time we drove up the steep hill to Hidalgo and into the long, narrow driveway, Renate and I were both thoroughly frazzled.

There was still evidence of construction around, piles of bricks and paint cans by the back door. Rupert had apparently taken the Thunderbird to his teaching job, so we parked in the open garage. As we were about to knock on the door, Anaïs came around from the side wearing a Grecian-style white muumuu, her swimsuit straps visible at the neckline. She said we were at the back door and insisted we follow her along a walkway around the low-slung, modern house. When we entered and stepped past the cramped entry hall, the space opened into an expanse that floated above the trees. Anaïs glided toward a long wall of windows and slid open a glass door onto the outside deck. Beyond the rectangular pool where the narrow yard dropped off, Silver Lake Reservoir gleamed.

As we all walked out to the pool, Anaïs said, "We can go swimming later. You don't need a swimsuit; it's private here."

I dipped my hand into the water. "Oh! You haven't turned the heater on yet."

"There is no heater. Rupert insists they're too expensive to run."

"Have you tried swimming in this water?" I asked.

"Oh, yes, it's wonderful once you get used to it."

Anaïs might be able to transform that water from freezing with her imagination, but I wasn't going to try.

We followed her back into the living room, which was really the only room. Folding partitions demarcated the bedroom, but they were wide open, so the locus of the house seemed to be the queen bed with its violet bedspread and new side-by-side lavender backrests.

Renate and I sat on a built-in bench along a brick wall, our legs squeezed behind a narrow coffee table. Anaïs placed a purple cushion on the ledge of the stone fireplace and sat with us.

"I'm afraid to ask," she said. "Do you have a $50,000 check for me?"

"Do you want the check or the story first?" Renate said.

"Is it a good story?"

"Yes, I would say it's a very good story," Renate answered, taking the approach we'd discussed.

"Go ahead then," Anaïs said.

Renate dramatized how we'd waited for Alan Rosen, imagining every possible scenario: he'd been in a traffic accident, he'd had a heart attack, he'd changed his mind when he saw the part of Malibu Renate lived in. And then we learned the awful truth: Alan Rosen wasn't the millionaire producer he'd claimed to be. He was an Arizona million-aire's gardener.

Anaïs was outraged. "He cheated us! That's against the law!"

"What law?" Renate said, "There's no law against swindling people of their dreams."

Anaïs laughed. Encouraged, Renate went on, "You have to admit it makes a good surrealist ending. You convinced me to live for an illusion to get your movie made, and we got robbed of that illusion by an illusory producer. The Vedantists are right; everything in life is just illusion."

I asked Anaïs, "What will you do now without the money to go to Paris?"

"Oh my goodness, we have so much catching up to do. It calls for tea." She prepared Lipton's for us in her sleek new kitchen and began, "I thought with our movie deal I'd be able to dismount the trrapeze."

Renate shot me a mortified look. I knew that, like me, she felt responsible for losing the $50,000 and Anaïs's chance for freedom.

CHAPTER 24

# Greenwich Village, New York, 1965

# ANAÏS

ON THE AIRPLANE, ANAÏS REHEARSED in her diary how to tell Hugo she was moving to Paris: *I'm not leaving you, Hugo, and I would never leave you for another man. I'm moving to Paris to live my dream of being a writer. I'm sure, as a fellow artist, you can understand that.*

This is what she did say to Hugo, before hastening to add, "I'm not going to ask you for any money. I just want a quiet divorce. I'll get started in Paris with the proceeds from the movie rights I wrote you about."

Hugo was silent. He refused to look at her.

"Please say something," she pleaded. "Please say that you'll give me a divorce and we will remain the best of friends."

She saw he was fighting back tears. Why did he have to act as if this were a tragedy? She had good reason to believe he had taken a mistress again. This time she really did not care. There was no tightness in her chest, no jealousy, because she was ready to let go. To be her own woman. Why couldn't Hugo flow forward with the changes in the air, as she did?

She urged gently, "Hugo, I know we believed our marriage would be forever, but it's not good for either of us to keep from growing as individuals."

"I haven't stopped you from growing," Hugo said angrily.

She made her voice softer. "It won't feel any different than when I've been gone in Los Angeles. For the past three months, you haven't mentioned once in your letters that you wanted me to come home."

"I haven't asked you to come back because I have nothing to offer you. When the bank job fell through I tried putting together a syndicate of Miami investors, but that went bust. I'm broke. I have nothing but debts. I can't earn any money."

"Hugo, you're exaggerating."

"I wish I were. I don't know how I'm going to pay next month's rent. I've gone through all our savings. I have a heart condition and doctors' bills. And now you're going to leave me."

He gave no resistance to the tears welling in his eyes. He broke down and wept, a hunched, broken man, his narrow, bony shoulders heaving.

She kneeled next to him and held him. He lifted his head from his hands and looked at her, pleading, "Let me come to Paris with you."

She was horrified to see him this way and she would have said almost anything to save him, short of telling him he could join her in Paris. She kissed the tears from his face. "I won't abandon you."

"Please don't divorce me. We married for better or worse." He clung to her.

"Don't worry, Hugo. I'll fix things for you. Whatever money I make, half of it is yours."

With an efficiency that, to her own surprise, she could rally when necessary, she spoke to the manager of their building and moved Hugo into a smaller, cheaper apartment. Feeling like Galahad on his steed, she flew back to LA, having promised Hugo that with the expected option money she would keep him going until she could start earning from her writing in Paris. She felt like a man, buying her way out of a relationship; she discovered it did not feel bad.

When she returned to the Hollywood apartment, she found Rupert in a state of helplessness almost as acute as Hugo's. Rupert had gotten into an argument with his brother and stepfather about furnishings for the new Silver Lake house that his half-brother Eric had designed in the Wright tradition of Modernist purity. Rupert refused to pay for the Eames chair and Eero Saarinen table that would have set off the home's low-slung lines; he was already anxious over having to pay a mortgage.

Anaïs set out to make peace between the warring sides and creatively furnished the house so that Rupert didn't bring his old furniture, yet didn't have to pay for new designer pieces. She believed that once Rupert was reconciled with his family and installed in the new house, he would manage without her when she left for Paris.

The first night after the move, she and Rupert unpacked and cleaned until eleven. Then Rupert grinned. "I think we better test the shower and the pool before we hit the sack."

He pulled her by the hand into the sparkling new bathroom, turned the shower on full blast so that it billowed with steam, undressed her and himself, and pulled her in. He opened a new bar of soap and gently washed her. She leaned against him with fatigue, but he said, "You'll have to run to the pool so your body retains the shower's heat."

Below them, the pool's bottom, which Rupert had painted black, sank into infinite depths; above them, the night sky was endless. They emerged from the pool renewed and awakened, and Rupert picked her up and carried her to the freshly made bed as he had in their courtship days. He made love to her with a perfection she'd come to expect. Only this time they reached a new plane of connection. In the darkened house with its wall of glass, they were inside and outside at the same time, floating on their bed that floated in the night on the lake below.

Her eyes opened to light pouring in through the wall of windows. She watched clouds and birds through the expanse of glass. With love's moisture still between her legs, she stepped into the bathroom and, through its second door, entered the little study Rupert had built for her.

Through high windows running the length of two walls, the sun filtered through tall pines and cypress. On the opposite wall, shadows of branches danced above the built-in desk where her portable Olivetti typewriter sat. Rupert had inserted a blank sheet of paper and rolled it into position for her. It was sweet. She'd told him about her meeting with an East Coast literary agent who'd promised he could sell her Paris diaries if Henry Miller were in them. Rupert wanted her to pursue the possibility, but Anaïs knew it was impossible because exposing her affair with Henry would humiliate Hugo and she couldn't do that to him, especially in his current state.

Nevertheless, she lowered herself into her secretarial chair and began pecking at the keys with two fingers, holding her elbows high to tone her upper arms.

> *Possible plan for editing the diary: Begin in 1931 with Henry coming up the path to Louveciennes the first time I saw him, as in a novel. It should be a Bildungsroman of universal woman with myself as the protagonist and others as continuing characters. Movement of my internal story will be from captivity, neurosis, and fear—to expansion, growth, fulfillment. Must edit for a central theme, as in a literary work, and cut out repetitions. Rupert not a problem—we hadn't met—but Hugo— LEAVE HUGO OUT ENTIRELY!*

She stared at the last sentence. It would be like murder to eliminate Hugo from her diary, as if she'd never shared her life with him, as if they were never married. But it could be the answer. The first volume of the diary could be all about Henry Miller, as the agent had advised, and she could edit out everything about Hugo. If readers didn't even know a husband existed, he couldn't be seen as a cuckold.

"Don't let me interrupt you," Rupert whispered as he left her a cup of coffee. She worked in the little office until he got home from teaching. Then he brought her a martini and insisted she come watch the sunset from their deck.

As night followed day, the way they lived, together and separately, molded to the contours of the floating glass house. Everything flowed in an easy rhythm, and she discovered that she was happy there, happier than she had ever been. She loved rushing outside at dawn to catch the finches sipping dew from the mulberry bushes, writing in her private little study, and swimming with Rupert in the phosphorescence of twilight.

On Rupert's chamber music night, she lit the house festively and set a fire blazing. Glancing up from her diary as the group played, she saw reflected in the glass doors multiple arms bowing, a violin and cello floating freely as in a Chagall painting, the grand piano permeable as a ghost. She looked past the floating musicians to the dark pool and lake beyond, shimmering in the moonlight. There was nothing in Paris that she wanted, she realized, more than she wanted the present to continue forever.

# CHAPTER 25

# Silver Lake, California, 1965

## TRISTINE

"So I've put off saying anything to Rupert about getting a divorce and moving to Paris," Anaïs confessed to Renate and me.

"Actually, you dropped your plan to move to Paris altogether," Renate said. "The plan for which Tristine and I busted ourselves to help you."

"I suppose I have dropped it," Anaïs responded warily.

"And yet, Anaïs"—Renate sat with her back straight against the brick wall—"you did not bother to tell Tristine and me. For this entire week you have let us suffer agonies of guilt for failing you. Could you not have told us that you no longer were depending on that $50,000?"

"No, because I do need it!" Anaïs protested. "I'm not getting an allowance from Hugo and there's no capital to draw on. And I need money to help Hugo!"

Renate scowled. "You're still trapped between your two men."

"No, I'm not trapped. Now I know what makes me happy. I don't have to be alone and I don't have to leave either of my husbands and move to Paris; I just have to recognize that what I want is what I have. We get to choose what makes us happy, and we get to revise and choose again."

"You are only choosing what you see as possible now," Renate said.

"No, I'm choosing how to see my life. I've realized that all we have to do is get clear about what we want and recognize it when it shows up, even if it doesn't look exactly as we thought it would."

Renate countered, "Like Alan Rosen? We wanted a producer, so we embraced a faux producer when he showed up."

"Yes, because a gardener-producer was just what we needed at the time," Anaïs said.

Renate looked startled.

Anaïs's smile was full of mischief. "He watered our dreams so they would grow. He fed my belief that I could make money from my writing. I needed that. He gave you just what you needed, too, Renate. He gave you back your libido."

"He did not! What are you saying?"

"You were attracted to him." Anaïs smiled.

"You were! You had a crush on him," I chimed in.

"I did not." Renate glowered at me.

I shrugged. "He was charming." I was thinking about what Alan Rosen had brought into my life: He'd given me a taste for the movie business, enough to make me want more.

Ignoring our teasing, Renate demanded of Anaïs, "So, if you still need money to take care of Hugo, what will you do now?"

Anaïs's turquoise eyes shone. "There's always a creative solution if we can just imagine it. My new agent says that Harcourt, Brace and World want my diary if it's about Henry. They're all agog these days for Henry Miller, Henry Miller. So I'm going to have to pay Henry a visit and get a release from him."

"May I come?" I blurted.

Both women scowled at my audacity. Then, perhaps remembering that she was the one who'd taught me not to miss new experiences, Anaïs smiled. "Yes."

Renate shot me a dirty look; she hadn't met Henry Miller either, and like Anaïs, she made it her business to meet famous people in the arts whenever she could.

"Actually, Anaïs, that's very clever." Renate raised an eyebrow. "Your new agent is right; Miller is a household name after all his censorship lawsuits. Your diary about him could be very successful. What will you do then?"

"I'll give money to Hugo," Anaïs said, "and I'll travel with Rupert."

Renate shook her head. "No, what will you do if your diary is so successful it makes you famous? It will be much harder to keep your *mariage a trois* secret if you become a public figure."

Anaïs looked as if the abyss had just opened at her feet.

Renate pressed her point. "You should divorce Hugo now that you've decided you want to be with Rupert."

"I can't. I can't do that to Hugo in his condition."

Renate warned, "If you become well known, people in LA will talk about you with people in New York, and someone will put it together."

"You're right." Anaïs's eyebrows knit crookedly.

For some reason both she and Renate looked at me. "I'll never talk," I assured them for the umpteenth time.

"You probably can trust those of us in LA," Renate conceded, "but what about those in New York who know, like that Caresse Crosby woman, whose loyalties are with Hugo? She's hard up for money now; what's to stop her from going to the *National Enquirer*? You can imagine what kind of monster the tabloids would make you into: '*The lying, cheating bigamist who financially ruined one husband and took the boyhood innocence of Frank Lloyd Wright's grandson!*'"

"I've told you, Renate, Rupert isn't a blood relative of the Wrights."

"That's not the point. The tabloids don't care about the truth. They just want a good scandal—like a woman bigamist!"

Anaïs blanched, but insisted, "Nobody reads those things."

"Some people do." Renate's voice was grave. "The authorities could go after you and arrest you and put you in prison!"

"I know what you are doing. You're trying to scare me."

"Oh, don't be scared, Anaïs. You'll probably just go to federal prison, and I hear they're like country clubs. Neither Hugo nor Rupert will visit you after being publicly humiliated, but Tristine and I will, won't we?" Renate turned to me. She had succeeded in scaring me, too.

"It's not fair!" Anaïs cried. "Now the law is keeping me trapped. I'm a writer. I need to publish when I have the chance!"

"I agree it's unfair," Renate continued, "and so is firing teachers for being homosexual, but it's happening every day. What's to stop them from firing Rupert for moral turpitude when they learn about your *mariage a trois*?"

Anaïs put her hands over her ears. "I'm not going to listen to you, Renate. You're just angry that I didn't tell you about my change of plans sooner. I was so caught up in the happiness of the moment with Rupert in this house that I forgot about you and Tristine. I let you suffer with guilt unnecessarily."

"And just for the sake of your vanity!" Renate cried. "Not wanting us to see your new house until you had it fixed up."

Anaïs put her hands together in supplication. "I'm sorry. Please forgive me."

Renate turned her head away and looked around the room instead of meeting Anaïs's eyes. I could tell she'd accepted Anaïs's apology, however, because she softened her voice. "The house is very nice, by the way."

∞

I wasn't ready to give up my fantasy of moving to Paris and bringing Neal along, even though Anaïs appeared to have changed her mind. I simply jiggered my fantasy so that Henry Miller entered the frame. I imagined that when Anaïs and I visited him he would see how enchantingly beautiful she still was and realize that nothing could ever equal their passion. They would run away together back to Paris and live on Henry's royalties from *Tropic of Cancer*.

Then Neal and I would join them in Paris and the four of us would pal around; and Neal, after long bouts of copulation with me, would play the sax; and I would write, and Anaïs and Henry would argue over my writing in bistros, observers envying our foursome's *joie de vivre*.

In reality, Neal hadn't answered my letters for over a month. Renate assured me that the sickening pain in my gut would lessen and eventually go away, but every time I thought about him forgetting me and enjoying himself with a more congenial woman who wasn't possessive, the same hobnailed boot rammed my solar plexus.

A few days later, I was returning empty-handed from checking the mail when I heard my phone ring upstairs and sprinted up the courtyard steps, hoping against hope it was Neal. But it was Anaïs calling to say that if I wanted to meet Henry Miller, I should be at her house in Silver Lake the following morning. Rupert would drive us together to Henry's house in Pacific Palisades.

I cried, "Oh, don't take Rupert. I'll come get you and drive you to Henry's."

"It's too late to change plans. I told Rupert everything."

"Everything? That you and Hugo are still married?"

"No! Don't even say that out loud. I told Rupert I had heard from old friends that Hugo cannot pay his rent, and that I'm indebted to Hugo for his taking care of my family and me when we had nothing. I explained that I want to help Hugo financially when I get my diary published and Rupert said it was a good plan. Isn't Rupert wonderful?"

"Maybe now you could tell Rupert the truth about—"

"No! But along those lines, I need your help with Henry."

"Of course," I said, though I didn't think she would need my help. I was convinced that the moment Henry saw her, he would be besotted again.

"We have to prevent Henry from telling Rupert that I'm still married to Hugo," she said urgently.

"Does Henry know?"

"Henry met Rupert eighteen years ago when we visited him in Big Sur, and our social circles here overlap so he's probably heard that I'm married to Rupert. Would you believe Henry and Hugo are still friends and talk on the phone?"

"But Henry will protect you, won't he? I'm sure he's still in love with you."

She gave an embarrassed laugh. "Oh, I don't think so. And Henry is completely unpredictable. If he gets riled up he could say anything in front of Rupert."

"Then don't bring Rupert!" I didn't want Rupert standing there when the sparks flew between Anaïs and Henry.

"I have to bring Rupert. He's part of my whole life now," she said with her uncanny ability to remain unperturbed by her contradictions.

∞

Rupert drove the Thunderbird with the top down. Anaïs wore a kerchief and kept the window rolled up on the passenger side while I sat on the rump seat, my long hair blowing into my eyes and mouth. Anaïs bent towards me to speak, the wind whipping away her words.

"Remember, you need to help keep the discussion on track with Henry," she told me.

"I'll do my best," I sputtered through a mouthful of hair.

She turned back to the road, leaving me to savor my anticipation of what would happen when Henry Miller opened the door and saw Anaïs in her new Rudi Gernreich dress. She would start to give Henry a buss on each cheek, and despite Rupert standing there, Henry would take her face in his hands and kiss her mouth, and she would respond.

When Henry opened the door to his surprisingly conventional white ranch house, I saw a bald troll holding onto a walker, and my heart sank. Anaïs air-kissed his wrinkled, sagging cheeks.

Instead of kissing her mouth, Henry shoved a snapshot in our faces. "Look at my new girlfriend." He grinned, sunlight through the paned window of the front door shining on his bald pate. "That's Hoki. She's brought me back to life!"

Rupert said, "She's very beautiful."

Anaïs said, "She's very young."

"Twenty-seven," Henry leered, his face crumpling like a squashed piece of paper. Goosebumps of revulsion crept up my arms as I imagined his young girlfriend touching that old man's wizened body. As if reading my mind, Henry said, "She won't touch me because she thinks, at seventy-five, I'm too old for her. But I'll win her. I won't give up. All for love, heh, Anaïs?"

"Until you win her," Anaïs said under her breath.

"You think I'm deaf, but I heard that." His troll eyes twinkled. "What has happened to your faith in the inspiration of Eros, Anaïs? What does it matter how it ends, heh? It's all the insanely beautiful, hellish and holy chase, doncha know?"

Anaïs made a beeline to a couch and chairs and settled there. We all followed, Henry shuffling on his walker. He lowered himself into his armchair where a profusion of books and his dashed-off watercolors covered a side table.

"So Henry," Anaïs began, "I'm here because the last time we corresponded you begged me to let you pay me back."

"Pay you back for what?" he snarled.

"For all the help I gave you at the beginning of your career."

He immediately softened. "Yes, yes, of course. Anything, Anaïs, I owe you." Grinning lasciviously, he turned to Rupert. "She gave me everything she had, doncha know? Everything." He hummed to himself and added, "Even her typewriter."

He tried to raise himself from the chair. "Do you need money?" His hands went to his pockets as if looking for his wallet, a clown doing mime. His round face looked eager as a child's. "Give me the chance to repay you."

"Thank you. You are a good friend, Henry." Anaïs smiled. "What I need from you is your help in getting my diary published."

"Anything I can do! I'll call Barney Rosset at Grove. I always said that diary was your ticket to fame." His sentences trailed off into the introspective hum that Anaïs had described in the diary pages she'd let me read about her affair with Henry. "But you'll make peanuts from royalties, Anaïs, doncha know, hmm, hmm. Pea-*nuts!*"

"They must be paying you something, Henry; this is an expensive house." Anaïs looked around. I could tell she was not impressed with its bourgeois conventionality.

"Yeah, running it is expensive, too. And so are my children, and my ex-wives, and Hoki's new Jag, and all the hangers-on who come here needing to be fed. Sell your papers to a university, Anaïs, that's where you get the dough."

"I tried that."

"No luck? Those white-gloved special collectors at UCLA bought everything from me. They should pay for your diaries 'cause I'm in 'em."

"Well, actually, what I want is to publish the sections of the diaries you're in. I've decided to start with the Paris years in the 1930s, instead of with the childhood diaries. No one's interested in those. They are interested in you, Henry, as a literary figure. The only gratitude I need from you is your permission to publish my portrayal of you." She whipped out a typed release from her purse.

"Of course, of course." He waved his hand as if that was all there was to it but then added, "I'll need to have final say on what goes in and stays out, of course. Hugo, you know. We both owe a great deal to Hugo." He hummed as he looked from Anaïs to Rupert, who sat straight up, alert and amiable.

Anaïs pointed to the margin of the prepared release. "Why don't I just write that in, 'Henry Miller has the right to review the final edit.'" She scribbled on the three copies, then handed them to Henry along with her Montblanc.

Henry took the releases. "I shouldn't do this without having my lawyer look at it." He eyed Anaïs.

She looked stricken.

"But because it's you, damn the lawyers. They always say no. And I owe you, Anaïs. I really do. And Hugo, of course." He hummed as he signed the three copies. "How is your husband, Anaïs? I haven't talked with Hugo in a while."

Anaïs delicately touched Rupert's hand. "Rupert, dear, could you put up the convertible top before we go? Tristine and I got so blown on the way here."

Rupert clearly did not want to leave, but he scurried off to do her bidding.

Before he was out of earshot Henry said, "What about the sex? You gonna to leave in all the sex? Hugo will know we were both lying to him. I don't care what your arrangement with Hugo is, or with this doltish Rupert fellow, but Hugo is my friend, and I don't want him to know I fucked his wife."

"I'll leave out the sex. That way it will seem we were just friends."

"Ha! You won't have anything left!"

"That's not true. We talked about books and art, our writing."

I exclaimed, "Oh, don't leave out the sex. That's the best part!"

Henry set his mischievous eyes on me; he hadn't noticed me before.

Anaïs explained, "I let Tristine read the diary pages about us."

Henry said, "Very good. The young ones take us as models."

Rupert came back. "Top's up."

Henry muttered loudly to himself, "So Anaïs is gonna take out the fucking so Hugo won't know."

Anaïs shot me an urgent look.

I said, "Henry, can students like me look at your papers at UCLA?"

"If you want to ruin your eyes. Buy my books instead. It took thirty goddamned years to lift the ban on them in this country, doncha know? You should exercise your hard-won right to buy them."

"Yes." Anaïs gave Henry her glorious smile. "I forgot to congratulate you on your Supreme Court victory. Your work was recognized as literary. Thirty years after I recognized it."

Henry said, "You'll be making a mistake, Anaïs, if you cut the sex from your diary. Get your book banned like mine, hmm, hmm. That's what makes the books sell."

Anaïs rose to leave, and I stood, but Henry set his sights on Rupert. "What about you, Rupert? How are you gonna feel when you read about Anaïs in heat with me?"

"That was a long time ago," Rupert said pleasantly. "Before I met Anaïs."

"Good attitude, Rupert kid, very good. Hmm, hmm. Besides, what do you have to complain about? She married you. I asked her to marry me, did ya know that? She wouldn't leave Hugo. She never could leave Hugo, doncha know?"

"We really have to get going." Anaïs swept up two of the signed releases and deposited them in her bag.

Henry raised his voice. "But what about Hugo, Anaïs? He's going to know you are a liar when he reads your diary. A liar! Are you going to ask him for a release? Are you finally going to ask him for a divorce?"

*Oh my God.* Henry had said it! I looked at Rupert for his reaction. He must have been zoning out, or maybe he just dismissed whatever

Henry said as claptrap, because his eyes remained on Anaïs, concerned only by how upset she appeared.

I tried again to derail Henry. "After *Tropic of Cancer*, which of your novels do you think I should read?" I asked.

He ignored me. "Are you going to ask Hugo for a divorce?" he called to Anaïs as she hurried to the door where Rupert was waiting. "Do you want me to talk to him about it?"

"I'll send you the edited pages, Henry," she trilled as we all exited.

"Liar! Liar!" he yelled after us.

As soon as we were settled in the T-bird, Rupert screeched onto Ocampo Drive as if wanting to leave Henry Miller in the dust.

Anaïs said, "It's sad that Henry has gone senile. He was always so much older than me."

"He sure is a crazy old coot!" Rupert responded, darting left onto Sunset.

I chimed in, "Anaïs, I don't know how you can stand that man."

She put up a palm, silencing me. "I'm editing the diary and I can't allow my present feelings about Henry to color how I portrayed him then." Lowering her hand, she took Rupert's free hand. "The problem with Henry is that he's never outgrown his adolescent romanticism. Like with that Hoki girl; he only loves what he cannot have. The moment he gets it, he loses his desire and becomes impotent. He can only perform in the realm of fantasy."

Anaïs was criticizing Henry for living in the realm of fantasy? Usually, everything she said was in celebration of the dream, the artist's vision, and the imagination that she recommended as a better route to the unconscious than drugs. Trying to understand what she was saying now, I offered, "I'm a romantic."

"Oh, we're all romantics." She squeezed Rupert's hand. "But Henry is the neurotic kind, always obsessed with the unattainable, the kind of romanticism that strangles life and real connection to others.

I romanticize what is close at hand, what I can touch and connect with." She leaned over to kiss Rupert's cheek as he turned his head and caught her kiss on the lips.

After meeting Henry Miller, Rupert looked a lot better to me. I wondered what it would be like if instead of being in love with Neal, who didn't really love me, I were in love with a good-looking, not too smart, but loving man like Rupert. He certainly seemed to make Anaïs happy. I remembered that after I'd read her diary pages about her steamy affair with Miller, I'd teased her, "Henry must have been great in bed!"

She'd given me a connoisseur's knowing smile. "Rupert is much better." She had chosen Rupert as I had chosen Neal, for the sexual passion, but she'd gotten devotion as well. I wondered why she received devotion from two husbands, while I'd never received it from any man.

Sitting behind Anaïs and Rupert like their kid in the rump seat, I worried aloud, "I'm afraid I do have Henry's negative kind of romanticism. I love Neal most now that he's gone."

"Of course." Anaïs turned around to face me. "But when Neal was living with you, you loved him just as much, didn't you?"

"I guess so."

"So you see, you're not like Henry. He only loves a woman when he's chasing her and she's unattainable." I thought about my relationship with Neal. I always felt I was chasing him because of his other women. I was the caboose on the roller coaster ride he led, up and down: *He loves me, he loves me not (he spent the night with her). He loves me, he loves me not (he hasn't answered my letters).* Was I really different from Henry with his romantic pursuit of the unattainable?

As if she could read my rumination, Anaïs offered me an encouraging smile. "The important thing is to find a man who can return your love in the present and celebrate that."

"Neal doesn't return my love in the present," I blurted. "I think he's left me for good."

"Oh, Tristine, I'm so sorry. I know it's not the same thing, but Rupert and I love you."

The water in my eyes I'd tried to hold back flooded down my cheeks, and Anaïs discreetly turned back to watch the road. Attempting to stop my tears, I stared through the portholes in the back of the T-bird at the green yards of expensive homes gliding by. I thought about negative romanticism, wanting only what I could not have, wanting Neal, who wasn't coming back.

He'd taken our sexual bond with him, and I knew I would never find its equal. That uninhibited intimacy, shameless, unlimited, had felt like true love. Felt more important than anything on Earth. I had expected that my loss of Neal would be a nuclear holocaust, annihilating everything in its wake: the houses, all the people, the plants, the very air. But here I was curled up in the Thunderbird's rump seat, still alive, frightened as a child jolted awake by a nightmare but with my loving family close at hand.

I realized with sudden, blessed relief that sexual passion, fabulous as it was, had no monopoly on love. The world went on, and all those I loved, except for Neal, had been spared: my mother, Renate and Anaïs, my friends, my cat. We shared the close-at-hand kind of romanticism. Perhaps it was Anaïs's ability to romanticize real life that made her so irresistible. She was the ethereal stuff of dreams, yet so close, so present, so connected.

When she turned around in her seat again, it was to talk excitedly about editing her diary for publication. "I've decided it should begin with a description of the iron gates of Louveciennes and Henry walking up the path to the old house the first time I saw him. I'm going to leave Hugo out, as I did in the version I gave you, only entirely. There won't even be a mention of my having a husband."

"So it will seem like you're alone at Louveciennes?" I asked.

"I'll keep my mother and the housekeeper."

"Won't people wonder how you could afford all that?"

"I don't think that's what readers care about. Is that what you cared about when you read the pages I gave you?"

"No, but I knew you were married to Hugo." I caught my breath for saying it in front of Rupert but then recalled we were talking about her life in the 1930s when Rupert was just a boy. When I glanced his way, Rupert's handsome profile was perfectly composed. I said to Anaïs, "If Hugo is not in the diary, people will think you were a single woman in Paris."

She thought for a moment. "Well, that's how it should have been! I'm going to give my readers a perfect life. My *rrreal* life, only perfected."

Rupert responded to that, offering her an approving smile.

I wondered if she would be able to pull it off after she published her diary—keeping her marriages secret. I wondered if other women would respond as I had to reading about her wild, dreamlike life in Paris. It had made me want to move there and live as she had, but now that Rupert had made her forget about Paris by building her the Silver Lake house, I realized I was happy to stay in Los Angeles. Wherever Anaïs was, that place, that time, would be magical; as in that very moment, the three of us driving together on Sunset Boulevard, gliding through the curve at UCLA where college kids lay on the grass making out, the T-bird pulling alongside a VW bus full of long-haired teens bopping up and down to the Beatles' *Help!*

Anaïs tuned the radio to the same station and raised the volume. The teenagers stuck their hands out the bus windows making peace signs, and Anaïs and Rupert separated hands to make *v*'s with their fingers, turning to me to join them. The three of us danced our fingers in the air as we drove into the age of Aquarius.

# CHAPTER 26

# Los Angeles, California, 1966-71

## TRISTINE

THE 1966 PUBLICATION OF THE *Diary of Anaïs Nin (1931-1934)* was perfectly in sync with the zeitgeist. Thanks to Anaïs having edited out any mention of Hugo, her diary was perceived as the true record of an openly sexual single woman living on her own in Paris with no need of a husband. I knew Anaïs's liberated, independent lifestyle was invented, but that didn't stop me from trying to replicate it along with the young women of the '60s who took it as fact.

The first published volume of Anaïs's *Diary* created a new persona for her—not Anaïs Guiler, the privileged wife of an investment banker, nor Anaïs Pole, the bohemian wife of a sexy younger man, but Anaïs Nin, the independent, unmarried woman who had lovers and wrote about them. She positioned herself as a single woman ahead of her time who championed a woman's right to explore and value her own sexuality. For my generation of early Boomers, Anaïs Nin became the icon for our sexual liberation. Colleges and universities all over the country invited her to speak, accept awards, and attend celebrations in her honor.

Anaïs almost always said yes. I had thought she would limit her public exposure given the risks, but she leapt to it with the same abandon and repertoire of tricks that had kept her aloft on her illegal trapeze for over a decade. Radio interviews, TV appearances, auditoriums full of adoring fans—Anaïs appeared before them all as a joyful, free, compassionate, wise, and accomplished exemplar of the *new woman*. She wasn't about to let fear of exposure prevent her from reaping the rewards of a literary renown that had so long eluded her.

Thanks to academic feminists, such as I soon became, and our promotion of previously ignored women authors, Anaïs gained a genuine self-confidence she had lacked. She was finally, and within her lifetime, recognized for what she had intuitively known from childhood: that she was the foremost diarist of the twentieth century. Her belated success proved to her that she had been right in sticking to the callings of her heart and soul, reaffirming her faith in women's intuition and subjectivity; while I, at the same time, was being trained in grad school to accept only supportable, documented objectivity.

Despite the many accusations from critics that a woman who published her diary had to be a narcissist, Anaïs, unlike most people who achieve fame, proved a better person for it. She became more centered, generous, and kind—and happier because she didn't have to lie to her husbands as much. She now had money from her royalties to pay for her coast-to-coast flights, as well as a lecture agent who booked appearances for her alternately on either coast. What a relief for her to have this help with the trapeze!

It was glorious to see Anaïs in these days of her fulfillment. Hugo made few demands on her because he was now completely dependent on her financially, while Rupert leapt to play the handsome young consort to her elegant priestess. She kept her friends "in the know" close, holding Chablis-and-cheese parties for us at the Silver Lake house.

Anaïs would still panic when one or the other husband overheard something incriminating, and although I remained as tightlipped as a CIA agent, every time I traveled east to visit my godmother, Anaïs would phone to ban me from speaking about her to Lenore or seeing Hugo. After my failure to prevent Rupert's middle-of-the-night phone call to Hugo years before, she never again entrusted me to guard her trapeze, which was fine with me as long as I remained her confidante. The responsibility of collecting Hugo's mail and intercepting his calls fell to a ditzy pair of middle-aged women—"the twins"—friends of Renate who dressed alike and accepted little cash gifts for their services.

I now had a different function in Anaïs's life. Since I was getting my PhD in English literature at UCLA, my new assignment was to legitimize her published *Diaries* and novels within the university, for while the coeds of America celebrated her, the academic establishment still held her in contempt. Anaïs knew that her lasting literary reputation depended upon young feminist scholars, such as myself, teaching and writing about her work. I reveled in my reflected glory as Anaïs's protégée and would have liked to tell everyone. However, Renate advised me to downplay the personal relationship, so I'd receive fewer difficult-to-answer questions and would be taken more seriously as an Anaïs Nin scholar.

I'd gone to UCLA for grad school because it would keep me near Anaïs, and there I joined one of the earliest women's consciousness-raising groups. Initially, my involvement with the group increased my admiration for Anaïs. Our method for raising our consciousness echoed the nonjudgmental intimacy of her *Diaries*. At our meetings, we went around in a circle sharing our personal experiences on a particular theme: mothers, fathers, siblings, lovers, to have or not to have children, professions closed to us, the many putdowns for being female we'd internalized.

We confided to each other our secrets, trusting that anything said within the group would never leave it: a baby given up for adoption, years of spousal abuse, faked orgasms, an abortion, a sexual attraction to another woman, an unrevealed rape. Like snakes, our stories dropped into the pit encircled by our chairs, and we examined them wriggling there along with our shame and guilt. We murmured to each other, "It's not your fault . . . That's why we are meeting, so that someday it will be different for women."

By 1970, though, we had transformed into an action group with the goal of establishing a Women's Studies program at UCLA. Those of us who were grad students put together proposals for classes we believed should be offered to undergraduate women, and our whole group, including faculty wives, university secretaries, and women from the community, pressured the administration to fund the courses. By August 1971, a number of us grad students were scheduled to teach the very first classes at UCLA that acknowledged the contributions of women in our respective fields.

By that time, Anaïs had edited and published three volumes of her *Diary*. I made the first two volumes, then in paperback, required reading for my Identity through Expression: Women Writers class, offered through the English department. When I handed out a draft of my syllabus to my women's consciousness circle for feedback, Clara, the most brilliant and beautiful of our remarkably attractive group, objected.

"I guess you could include Nin for historical reasons, but you can't call her a feminist author as you have it here." Clara snapped her unpainted fingernails against my course outline and pushed back a cluster of copper curls that haloed her flawless face.

With her continental sophistication acquired from having attended the Sorbonne and her impeccably correct leftist politics, Clara awed me as Anaïs once had. It bothered me that when I'd first let drop to Clara that I knew Anaïs Nin, she had been unimpressed, unlike everyone else who marveled that the exotic diarist was living, no longer in Paris, but right there in prosaic LA.

The heavyset provost's secretary asked, "Who's Annis Nin?"

Clara gestured for me to answer, but I nodded back, wanting to hear her take on Anaïs. Clara began, probably borrowing from her prepared class on French women writers: "The French like Nin because they have a tradition for her. She follows in a direct line from the French courtesans who were better known for their lovers and literary salons than their own writing. They were professional muses: Marion Delorme, Claudine-Alexandrine Guerin de Tencin, Marie Duplessis, Ninon de l'Enclos." Clara deferentially flipped a hand to emphasize her ease with these French names. "They were like the Greek *hetaera* or the Japanese geishas," she continued, "experts in the arts of pleasing men. They were oppressed because they could only survive by maintaining the pleasure of their male patrons. They could hold power only as long as their sexual appeal lasted, though some of them were able to make it last well into old age thanks to their beauty tricks."

"Do you know any of those tricks?" the provost's secretary asked.

"They were stupid. They used white powder that gave them lead poisoning." Clara waved away the question. "That's not the point. The point is they were hardly liberated."

"Well, they were for their time," I argued.

Clara took my opinion seriously. "I suppose you could say that. By being parasites on the nobility they had better lives than servant women or farmer's wives, but that was a question of class."

I enjoyed batting ideas with Clara; she always came back with a well-reasoned argument, an intellectual muscularity absent in the feminine subjectivity and intuition Anaïs heralded. I countered to Clara, "In some ways the courtesans were better off than we are. They had the leisure to write. Their time wasn't taken up having children, or working, or managing households."

I realized immediately that Clara would see "leisure to write" as an elitist concern, but the provost's secretary jumped in: "Sounds like a liberated life to me!"

Clara gave her a withering look. "A muse spends her life enabling men's creativity instead of her own."

"Well, Anaïs Nin isn't just a muse." I came to my mentor's defense. "She's a diarist and novelist in her own right. Maybe she was a muse to Henry Miller when they were in Paris, but now she's committed to her own work."

Even as I was saying it, though, I realized it wasn't true. Anaïs had completely abandoned her diary and novel writing, in favor of playing muse to her fans through her prolific correspondence. Clara was right, as well, that Anaïs was like a courtesan in that everything about her was delicate and feminine—her soft voice, her graceful movements, her painstaking appearance—as if she'd been designed to fulfill men's fantasies.

Clara smirked at my defense of Anaïs. "Oh, that's right, you know her, don't you?"

"A little."

"You know her?" the provost's secretary interrupted. "Can you get her to visit our group?"

"I don't think so. She has a lecture agent who books all her appearances."

"Offer the stipend you get for guest lecturers in your class, and we'll all come," the excited secretary urged.

Her unabashed eagerness made me want to show Anaïs off to the group, but Clara said, "She's not going to come to your undergraduate class or visit our little group. It would insult her narcissism now that she's a star."

I was so tired of hearing this accusation of narcissism against Anaïs that I was determined to show Clara she was wrong. I'd get Anaïs to come talk to our group and my class. It would be a feather in my cap, and Clara would see for herself how egalitarian, witty, eloquent—and feminist—Anaïs really was.

I always seemed to be trying to prove something to Clara because compared to her raised political consciousness, mine always came up short. She participated in a dangerous underground for Latin American victims of terror, summered on sugar collectives in Cuba, and stood in solidarity with working class women. So in addition to the UCLA women's group, I joined an on-campus socialist group for grad students and professors. It turned out, though, that our group didn't actually do anything except read and discuss texts by Marx, Lenin, and Engels. One evening, I said to the study group—because my landlord wasn't renewing my lease—"What if, instead of just talking about communism, we tested it ourselves to see if we could make it work?"

"What do you mean?" asked Bob, whose beard was the same orange shade as his long hair. He liked experiments; he had a PhD in nuclear physics and had told us that the only jobs he could find in his field were for the US government, so he'd saved his large salary for three years and dropped out at twenty-six with enough money, according to his calculations, to last the rest of his life.

I proposed, "What if we become a commune and live together in a house where we each pay according to our ability and receive according to our need?" I didn't think anyone would go for the idea, especially since my income as a teaching assistant was near bottom, but to my amazement three of the guys said yes. Bob brought along his girlfriend, so we were five; sufficient, we decided, to call ourselves a commune. After we added up what we could collectively pay for rent, we began to look for a mansion to lease.

We found a Greene and Greene–style manor house in Santa Monica four blocks from the boardwalk. In August we all moved in, the guys unloading salvaged furniture my mother had been happy to clear from her living room and running my mattress up the curved, balustraded stairway. We joined a Venice food co-op for weekly boxes of organic produce and established a nightly ritual of communal dinners in our chandeliered dining room.

I knew that upon Anaïs's return from a European trip, she would want to see my commune. She was avid about keeping up with the alternative culture scene: she'd tramped through a field to see geodesic domes, attended love-ins and sit-ins, and turned me on to Judy Chicago's feminist art installations.

So as I was driving to Silver Lake, I formulated my plan. I'd invite her to the commune for a collectively prepared dinner, and afterwards in our expansive living room, she could address my women's group and class. I'd prove to Clara that Anaïs didn't consider our group small potatoes. I'd offer Anaïs my course speaker stipend, because I knew she would appreciate the resonance that I was proffering her a real invitation, with a real stipend, for a real university event, whereas my apprenticeship had begun seven years earlier by sending a fictitious invitation, with a fictitious stipend, for a nonexistent university event. That's the way it was with Anaïs. Whatever she imagined—her *mariage a trois*, her literary stardom, her financial independence—eventually actualized. She had taught me to dream and to actualize my dreams as she had.

When I entered the open front door, Anaïs and Renate were huddled on the built-in couch, discussing their facelift experiences. They changed the subject, knowing that as a doctrinaire feminist now, I considered plastic surgery to hide a woman's age politically incorrect.

After I'd kissed their lifted cheeks, they insisted on hearing all about my new Women's Lit class. It was the first time anyone had taught Anaïs's *Diaries* in a university. Anaïs wanted to know the other authors on my syllabus, but when I listed Virginia Woolf, Doris Lessing, Maya Angelou, Sylvia Plath, and Nikki Giovanni, she wrinkled her nose in distaste while nodding discreetly.

I described the first meeting of my class, when eager young women had lined up in the hallway and poured out into the courtyard, hoping to get on the waiting list. "They limited the enrollment to thirty-two, and over a hundred women showed up!" I enthused. "One guy pushed his way into the classroom and shouted, 'This is sexism! I should be able to take this class!'"

"What did you say?" Renate was enjoying this.

"I told him, 'This class is for women only. There are plenty of classes you can take that were designed just for men.'"

"Did he leave?" Renate asked.

"No! He threatened to sue me and the university for discrimination against him for being the wrong gender!"

Renate exclaimed, "Oh, no, Tristine!" After her ordeal of being sued and losing her house to her contractor, Renate was terrified of lawsuits.

"That kid won't sue me," I assured Renate. "I told him he could get in line with the women in the hallway and sign up on the waiting list. I said, 'I promise you, you'll have as much of a chance of getting in the class as they do, so you are being treated equally.'"

"That was good." Anaïs smiled. She didn't approve of men being seen as the enemy. She repeatedly reminded me that a woman should be responsible for her own emotional issues and not put them on the man.

I shared with Anaïs and Renate my mother's reaction when I'd told her about my consciousness group's victory in getting funding for our classes.

"That's wonderful, Trissy!" Mother's heavily jowled face, exhausted from overwork, had lifted with a rare smile of hope and pride. It was the same with Renate and Anaïs. Their faces were already lifted, and they were already full of hope because of the success of Anaïs's *Diaries*; but they glowed, too, with pride for what we younger women had accomplished.

This gave me my opening. I invited Anaïs to address my class and women's group.

"Don't you dare, Anaïs!" Renate butted in. "You have to preserve your strength."

Damn, Renate was working at a cross-purpose. I should have talked to her beforehand.

I moaned to Anaïs, "Oh, my students will be so disappointed if you don't come!"

Anaïs looked stricken at the thought of disappointing them. She routinely accepted speaking engagements at remote Midwestern colleges where she had to sleep in associate professors' guestrooms, and she personally answered every letter she received in sack loads because, she said, "I don't want my readers to feel rejected. I know what that feels like."

True, she loved the rock star reception when she entered an overflowing auditorium, but in fairness she loved her admirers back. She invited to her parties at the Silver Lake house the loneliest souls met on her travels, people who had told her their sob stories in their letters and then stalked her for, in their floaty words, "a touch of her magic." She felt it was her job to save them, so Renate and I would find ourselves having to socialize with these airheaded young people—the painfully shy poet who would only speak if asked a question, the girl disfigured in a riding accident who kept one side of her face angled away from you, the runaway with the bad teeth, and the recently released ex-con—all sipping Chablis while standing next to Bebe Barron, a pioneer of electronic music; or James Herlihy, whose novel *Midnight Cowboy* had become an Academy Award–winning movie.

Anaïs would glide over to talk to the most awkward and shy guest at the party and shame the rest of us into following her example. She described herself accurately when she wrote that out of her father calling her ugly as a child had come her x-ray vision. People were made of crystal for her. She saw right through their defects—the humped back, the duck walk, the embarrassing acne—straight to their essence, the shadow of their disappointments, the outline of their desires, the glow of their dreams. She completely lacked snobbery and practiced an almost saintly kindness.

I'd seen photos of her male psychiatrists Rene Allende and Otto Rank, both of whom she'd told me she'd slept with to "help return them to their bodies." The thought of Anaïs giving charity sex to these aggressively ugly men revolted me. Yet, as they had, I was now playing on her saintly impulses to get what I wanted, and Renate knew exactly what I was doing.

"How can your students be disappointed?" Renate chided me. "Did you promise them Anaïs's appearance without even asking her?"

I thought Anaïs would object, "Oh, I enjoy the appearances. They energize me," as she always did when Renate tried to get her to slow down. Instead, she sighed, "I am getting tired of repeating myself. And I'm beginning to feel, I don't know, insincere." This was something new!

In response to Renate's and my double-take, Anaïs explained, "I say I value intimacy, but the crowds of people are the opposite of intimate. I don't think all this celebrity is good for me."

"Now you see the horror of fame," Renate said with satisfaction.

"It's not that bad, Renate." Anaïs's laugh was a tiny cough. "Besides, this would be for Tristine." She smiled on me. "And it's not like I have to get on a plane."

"And it will be intimate," I promised. "It'll only be the fourteen women from my consciousness group, my thirty students, and my five commune members."

"You moved into the commune, Tristine?" Anaïs exclaimed.

"We found a mansion in Santa Monica. We have an acre of grounds and a big rolling lawn in front."

"I've visited communes." Renate wrinkled her aristocratic nose. "I don't object to the polymorphously perverse sex, but the houses are so unkempt."

"Not ours. We have the cleanest, most anally retentive commune ever."

Anaïs laughed, but Renate harrumphed. "Well, that doesn't sound like the Birkenstock communes I've seen. What about Jadu?" Renate was always concerned about my cat. She'd identified him as my "familiar."

"He's the house mascot," I said.

"I assume you play musical beds." Renate raised a penciled eyebrow.

"No! I told you, Renate, it's a socio-political experiment."

Anaïs coaxed, "Come now. You can't tell us that there isn't at least one man in this commune you find desirable."

After Neal's disappearance, Sabina had returned to me, and now my varied sex life provided entertainment for our little cabal.

"Give us the latest installment in the Adventures of Donna Juana," Anaïs commanded gaily.

"Donna Juana has found a Don Juan," I began.

"That sounds promising!" Anaïs sang. "What's his name?"

"Don."

"No, his real name."

"Don Brannon. The problem is he's my brother."

"No, Tristine!" Anaïs cried.

"I thought you were an only child." Renate scowled.

"I told you before, I have a younger sister and a half-brother." I was concerned about Renate; she was struggling financially, doing temp work assisting old people, and I was afraid the stress was affecting her usually impeccable memory.

"Oh! Don is just your half-brother," Anaïs exclaimed. "That's not so bad."

"No, Don isn't actually related to me at all. He's one of my brothers in the commune."

"You call them brothers?" Renate said. "Why?"

"Because we live together like a family, and Don says that because we're brother and sister in the commune it would be like incest if we slept together."

Renate flipped her hand provocatively. "I don't see how he can resist the convenience. He wouldn't have to get in his car and drive, and you'd both get to sleep in your own beds."

"Oh, Renate!" Anaïs scolded.

"I'm serious," Renate insisted. "My perfect lover is one I could lower on cables to my bed from the ceiling when I want. When we're finished doing it, I'd just press a lever and he'd disappear through a trap door into the rafters."

I chuckled, but Anaïs rolled her eyes. She'd warned me privately that Renate had let herself become bitter about men, and I should avoid her example. "Bitterness makes you prematurely old," Anaïs frequently declared. "The secret to my eternal youthfulness is that I forbid myself bitterness."

"What does your Don look like?" Renate wanted to know.

"Like Robert Redford. He runs the Writing Center at UCLA."

"That's the kind of man you should be with," Anaïs said. "Someone who shares your interests in literature. But are you sure he isn't gay?"

"I'm sure. He has different girlfriends spend the night on weekends. Really beautiful ones."

"Don't give up on him then," Anaïs urged. "When Donna Juana and Don Juan come together it creates a lot of fireworks." She described her affair with a Don Juan who was an opera singer. "The thing to remember with a Don Juan is that he loses interest the moment you stop being elusive. You have to sustain the cat and mouse game."

I felt fortunate to have Anaïs as advisor to my love life. There wasn't a romantic liaison with which she didn't have personal experience. I was aware that she took vicarious enjoyment through my Sabina adventures, but it seemed only fair given how I, and thousands of other women, had enjoyed her erotic adventures in her novels and *Diaries*.

Anaïs, Renate, and I often took turns telling tales of our Sabina seductions. As in all our conversations, we looked for the metaphors and myths embedded in our encounters. I learned to include poetic details as Anaïs did and humorous twists as Renate did.

When Anaïs and I would have a private tête-à-tête to seriously discuss my search for the one man who would end my search as Rupert had ended hers, she listened with the concentration of a piano tuner. We compared my raunchy affair with an impoverished writer to hers with Henry Miller, my passion for a handsome poet/revolutionary to hers for Gonzolo, and my seduction of a young, gay film director to her attempts with Gore Vidal. These mirror encounters were not really about the men; they were about Anaïs and me, our game of twinship. They were about watching and being watched, the diarist's obsessions.

Now she gave me specific recommendations to seduce Don, offering before I left, "I'll just have to visit and warm him up for you." So a date was set for her to have dinner at the Georgina Avenue commune and afterwards address my class and women's group.

∞

The morning of the event, she called to say she'd have to postpone dinner for another time, but she would be there at seven for the talk. I had warned my commune members, my class, and my women's group not to tell anyone else about Anaïs's visit or it would get out of hand.

"I promised her an intimate evening, a *furrawn*." I used the odd Welsh word Anaïs was then trying to popularize, my mouth gaping as for the dentist.

"*Furrawn*," she would say at her lectures, avoiding a yawning fish face by rolling the *r* and taking "awwn" in the back of her throat. "It means intimate conversation that leads to deep connection. We don't have a word for it in English, or in French for that matter"—she'd give her guttural half-laugh—"so we have to borrow *furrawn* from the Welsh." Privately she'd added to me, referring to her husbands, both of Welsh heritage, "It's all the Welsh have: a useful word and good-looking men." Her humor, what she had of it, was so dry that it evaporated before most people got it; but I knew to chuckle because her desiccated jokes were always indicated by her little cough-like laugh.

At 6:00 people started arriving. Our commune's spacious living room looked like an anthill, teaming with longhaired guys and braless young women in tight T-shirts, most of them crashers. The chairs I'd arranged in a large circle were insufficient and people sat lotus-style on the floor and sprawled on the stairwell, overflowing into the dining room, kitchen, and pantry. The whole thing felt like a huge, unruly surprise party.

I hoped Anaïs wouldn't be too surprised when she walked in and saw what had happened to the intimate *furrawn* I'd promised her.

When at 7:00 she had yet to arrive, I became concerned. Anaïs was always punctual. I saw Don standing under the wide arch to our dining room, looking more like Robert Redford than ever with the Sundance Kid mustache he'd recently grown. His arm was around a pretty brunette he'd invited. I was annoyed that he hadn't asked me if he could bring her, but then, the house was full of crashers who hadn't asked. They were becoming loud and disorderly. I tried to quiet them by lecturing about Anaïs's work, but they lapsed into side discussions, too excited to pay attention.

They fell silent, though, when we saw through the front windows the Thunderbird double park on the street, and a cloaked, regal woman stride alone up the inclined path to the porch.

Anaïs was making an entrance for me! She swept through the open front door and, loosening the tie of her black cape, let it fall into red-bearded Bob's outstretched arms. I'd thought that Bob, as a nuclear scientist, would have been immune to Anaïs's charm, but he blushed through his freckles and later marveled, "It was like the appearance of a white witch in a Disney film. You could almost see a trail of sparkling fairy dust in her wake!"

Sticking to the evening I'd planned, I ignored the crashers and said, "Before I give the floor to Anaïs, I'd like to introduce my fellow commune members, who are our hosts tonight." They each stepped forward as I said their names. Anaïs looked directly into Don's blue eyes when she said, "Thank you so much for allowing me to visit your beautiful home." I could tell he was smitten.

I then introduced my students, who shot up their hands. "And what about the women in your consciousness group, Tristine?" Anaïs said. "I've wanted to meet them for so long."

The women in my group half-raised their hands, including Clara, whom I'd wanted to impress by delivering Anaïs. Anaïs bowed her head in tribute to them. "You are to be honored for transforming the world by first transforming yourselves. The Women's Movement has been an example of what I have always advocated, proceeding from the dream outward." She quoted herself from the *Diary*: "'The personal life deeply lived always expands into truths beyond itself.'"

Then she ardently addressed the entire audience, making each person there feel as if she or he had the most intimate connection with her of all. She presented the persona they had come to see: the sensual, independent, liberated woman she'd invented in editing her *Diary*. She embodied the myth that her readers had embraced as a goddess of love, intimacy, kindness, generosity, romantic idealism, surrealist imagination, and sexual abandon. I saw her that night in all her glory as the consummate *woman artist*: a practitioner of performance art before it had a name, a visionary of life itself as imaginative theater. I had seen packed auditoriums in a frenzy of adoration, and with this smaller group she likewise played her artist/goddess role to the hilt, quoting herself in her French lullaby rhythm, dropping the names of political friends such as Eugene McCarthy and literary associates such as Rebecca West and Lawrence Durrell, encouraging the women before her to value their individuality, throw off their inheritance of guilt, and live their dreams as she had!

My students eagerly asked questions about her diary writing, which she answered with practiced phrases: "I write to taste life twice," and "It is a thousand years of womanhood I am recording, a thousand women."

Some of the young women from my class made passionate personal testimonials to the liberating impact of having read her *Diary*.

One twenty-year-old proclaimed, "You are the mother of us all!" Everyone present looked dazzled, as if they had been touched in a tent revival and received a genuine miracle.

Everyone except Clara, that is. She'd been leaning against the wall distancing herself from my students. Now Clara came forward, flipping a hand upward for Anaïs to spot her. Seeing how beautiful Clara was with her corona of fiery curls, Anaïs offered her most appreciative smile, but Clara did not return it.

She said, "At the end of the second volume of your *Diary*, you tell us you left Paris because your husband was recalled to the US. But until then there was no mention of you having had a husband. Why is that?"

"My publisher—" Anaïs began, but Clara interrupted her.

"Nowhere do you tell us how you got money for your free life. Yet economic self-sufficiency is the first requirement for woman's freedom, wouldn't you agree?"

Anaïs straightened to her full 5'5" height. Her singsong French accent became more pronounced when she answered, "Economic self-sufficiency is essential for woman, but it is not the only ingredient necessary for her freedom. Americans, in particular, are oppressed by the punishing assumptions of Puritanism." She looked into receptive faces as she spoke, settling on Don's. "America's sexual Puritanism must also be examined and dispensed with." There was a murmur of assent in the room.

"But you haven't addressed the question left unanswered in your *Diaries*." Clara brought Anaïs's attention back. "How did you make a living? Certainly it wasn't from your writing. All you published in those years was a booklet of nonprofessional literary criticism on D. H. Lawrence. Not exactly a moneymaker." There were a few titters from Clara's supporters. She pressed, "Since it was your marriage to an international banker that made your free, privileged life possible, don't you think you're obliged to tell us that? It's not fair to let women think that they can have a life like yours without a rich, permissive husband like yours."

There was a hush in the room, stunned fear for Anaïs as the naked emperor exposed by an insurgent. I could not believe what I was witnessing. Clara and Anaïs were playing out a battle that had been raging inside me: Clara on the left, whom I so admired, brave and honest, who challenged unfairness and hypocrisy wherever she found it. Anaïs on the other side, brave and dishonest, my mentor, whom I loved.

Anaïs remained unflappable in the face of Clara's accusation of deception. "I have given you so much of myself in the *Diary*," she intoned sorrowfully. "No woman has revealed so much. I have given voice to the secrets that most women hide. Why do you demand more of me?"

You could feel the audience, like an armada, slowly turn, guns swiveling towards Clara. She shrugged, as if to say, *What can I do if you Americans, unlike the French, cannot appreciate a good intellectual row?* She shot back at Anaïs, "The question is why you did not ask more of yourself. You intentionally misled your readers into thinking you were self-supporting. All that time you were being supported by Hugo Guiler, a banker!"

Anaïs answered calmly, "Yes, that is why I added at the end of *Diary II* that the bank recalled my husband to America and we had to leave Paris. That much had appeared in the newspaper; it was public record. That is all I could include about my husband because I did not have his permission to portray him."

I knew this wasn't exactly true. It sounded convincing, but not to Clara. She glared at Anaïs accusingly. "You mean that you, the renowned seductress, couldn't get permission from your own husband, the one you still live with in New York?"

How did Clara know about Hugo in New York? I'd certainly never said anything about him to her. But Anaïs would believe I had!

I could tell Anaïs was furious because her voice became soft and controlled. She demanded of Clara, "Who are you?"

"I'm a member of Tristine's consciousness group."

God, Clara was making it sound like I was in on this! Don looked over at me, an eyebrow raised.

Anaïs stood tall and her gemstone eyes bored into Clara. "Where did you get the false impression that I am still married to Hugo?"

Clara said, "*Mon Dieu*, everyone in Paris knows about you and your double life! Hugo still has friends there, you know."

Anaïs's panicked eyes darted to me and back to Clara. "I have no idea what you are talking about," she said coolly.

I glanced around and, to my horror, saw Rupert stationed on the front porch, standing in the cold by the open door. He must have heard Clara say that Anaïs had a double life and still lived with Hugo! Yet his countenance remained blank. An actor playing possum?

I jumped up. "It's getting late, and we don't want to exhaust Anaïs when she's been so generous to meet with us."

There were groans and thirty hands shot up. Anaïs recognized only Don. I felt a charge between them before he asked, "Were you the model for Ida Verlaine in Henry Miller's *Sexus*?"

"You'd better ask Henry that question." She laughed gaily, turning away to scan the room for Rupert. "Ah! I see my escort is here! I'm so sorry I cannot stay longer."

The crowd parted before her as she moved through them to the front door, squeezing proffered hands and returning eager gazes with her radiant, reassuring smile. I tried to catch her eye but couldn't. Bob rushed up with her cape, and she wrapped it around her before sweeping away.

She did not take Rupert's arm as they strode to the T-Bird parked up the street. That night, no one could have guessed they were married, the way she kept her distance.

∞

Later, as I was coming out of the bathroom Don and I shared, I saw that he was at a desk in the ballroom studying. Evidently, he'd sent his date home.

He gestured that I should come join him. I got my books and papers from my room so it would look as if I were studying, too.

Right away Don asked, "Who was the younger guy she called her escort? Is that her rich husband?"

I wasn't sure how to answer. To people in Los Angeles, Anaïs usually introduced Rupert as her husband but since she had identified him as just her escort that night, I said, "A friend, I guess."

"What was all that about her having a double life?" Don gave me his irresistible Don Juan grin, and I noticed how neatly his blond mustache was trimmed over his white teeth. He seemed to be looking at me differently, not as a sister. Perhaps Anaïs's fairy dust had succeeded in bathing me in its flattering light.

"I don't know anything about a double life. I think Clara just has old gossip. Anaïs used to be married to Hugo," I said, though I felt uncomfortable lying to Don; it wasn't something we did in our commune.

Don said, "It's common knowledge she had an affair with Henry Miller. Was she married to Hugo then?"

"I think she was." I had to give Don something, and anyone could figure that out.

He and I stayed up until 2 a.m. talking about Anaïs and her place in twentieth-century literature. We talked about Lawrence's *Lady Chatterley's Lover* and Miller's *Tropic of Cancer*, hot talk, suggestive words falling on top of each other. As it got later, there were longer pauses. I was hoping this was the night Don would come to my room. Renate was right; all he would have to do after was slip back to his bed in the sunroom, and no one would be the wiser.

My heart was hopping in my ribcage with anticipation, but a loop of anxiety ran up and down my spine, recalling Anaïs's look at me during Clara's attack. What if Anaïs thought I'd betrayed her?

Don must have noticed the anxiety on my face and perhaps misinterpreted it. He rose, yawning. "I've got to get some sleep. The damn sun through my windows will be waking me in three hours."

I didn't get any sleep that night, not because I was getting Don's kisses and thrusts, or even imagining them. I was turning on my pillow, twisting with agony at the thought that Anaïs believed I'd purposely lured her into Clara's lair.

The next morning, as Bob and I were determining if our homemade yogurt had set, the phone rang and I grabbed the commune kitchen receiver.

"Something terrible has happened!" I heard Anaïs cry. "Come to the house tomorrow. Renate will be here."

The anxiety that had been running along my spine now circuited into all my nerves. I didn't know how I could face Anaïs's anger, and I feared Renate, who was capable of putting a curse on anyone who dared hurt Anaïs.

When I arrived at Anaïs's house, I saw that the front door had been left ajar for me. Renate was already there. I cried out, "I didn't say anything to Clara about Hugo, Anaïs! I swear!"

She looked at me severely. "Who was that woman who talked about Hugo?"

"Clara Doherty. She was only invited because she's part of my women's group."

"How does she know about my staying with Hugo in New York?"

Renate gasped. "Tristine, did you—"

"No! I don't know how she knows. She has a boyfriend in Paris."

"She probably heard gossip from that troublemaker Jean Franchette." Anaïs frowned. "He's always spreading lies about me."

I was confused for a moment. Who was Jean Franchette? I'd never heard of him. And what lies? Clara had spilled the truth.

"It's always those Marxist women who try to get me," Anaïs flicked her French-tipped nails. "Don't ever let that woman near me again."

"I won't. I promise."

"I told you not to do any more public events!" Renate turned from Anaïs to me, scowling. "It's too much stress."

I moaned, "I'm so sorry, Anaïs. It wasn't supposed to be so public. But thank you for doing it. My students were thrilled."

Anaïs gave me a weak smile. "So, how did it go with Don afterwards? He's terribly handsome."

"It didn't go. He was definitely attracted to you but not me."

"Did you invite him to your room?"

"No, you said to remain elusive."

"Elusive, yes. But you can't expect him to be a mind reader."

My head fell into my hands with relief that her anger had moved to my failure to seduce Don. But I tried again to apologize for Clara's attack. Anaïs put up an impatient hand. "Forget it. I have much bigger problems."

"What now?" Renate asked.

"The I-R-S!" The way Anaïs said the initials made them sound truly frightening.

"Oh no!" Renate shook her head. "I tried to warn you."

"I don't understand," I said.

Renate explained, "Two husbands. Two joint tax returns. One IRS." Her voice was somber when she turned to Anaïs. "You could be facing criminal charges. What if they put you in prison after all you've worked for?"

"It would destroy my literary reputation!"

"Well, maybe not," Renate considered. "It didn't hurt Jean Genet's. But prison would be extremely unpleasant. No privacy at all. You have to get a lawyer."

A lawyer's daughter even though I'd been estranged from my father for years, I echoed, "You have to get a lawyer!"

CHAPTER 27

# Los Angeles, California, 1966–71

## ANAÏS

RIGHT AFTER NEW YEAR'S, ANAÏS met with a woman attorney who advised her to divorce Rupert. Anaïs begged the lawyer for a different, "creative" solution because she was finally happy with Rupert. When the lawyer mentioned an annulment Anaïs grabbed that alternative because the word was softer than divorce.

"Rupert," she began after their punctual five o'clock dinner, as he was carrying their dishes to the sink. "Remember I asked you several times to drive me to an attorney's office?"

He gave her a distracted smile.

"I showed her a notice I received from the IRS. It seems that there is some sort of problem." Now she had his full attention. He came back to the table and sat opposite her.

Anaïs said pleasantly, "We need to dissolve our marriage and sign an annulment, and after the lawyer has cleared up the paperwork, we can get married again."

"An annulment!" Rupert looked in shock. "On what basis?"

"Fraud."

"What fraud?"

She couldn't, she just couldn't go ahead with this. She couldn't tell him she'd had another husband for the past seventeen years. But she was far out on the ice now. She had accused herself of deception and there was no going back.

"I lied to you about my age. You thought I was just a few years older than you." She reached and stroked his cheek, tenderly. "I'm really . . . I'm so ashamed to say it . . . I'm sixteen years older than you!"

A smile broke out on his face like the afternoon sun replacing the morning fog over their house. "Don't you think there's a reason, Anaïs, why I've never asked your age?" He grabbed her cold hand. "I don't care."

"But I do. I've cheated you by taking your youth."

He laughed and lifted her balled fist to kiss it. Oh, why was he being so decent about this? She had to get him to sign that annulment but she could not tell him why.

His clear blue eyes were full of love. "My youth is a small thing to give when I think about all you have given me. All the interesting people and places and ideas you have brought into my life." He stayed close as he whispered, "We don't need an annulment, you silly goose. There isn't any woman of any age I'd rather be with."

Dear Rupert. How had she been so lucky to find a man who could love this way? How could she come out and tell him when, despite everything, he still hadn't figured it out?

But why hadn't he figured it out, she wondered. Why hadn't *either* of her husbands figured it out? There had been so many times it had been right there in their faces. Why had they accepted her blithe and often silly lies? They didn't want to know. And why did they not want to know? Because they didn't want to let her go, ever, just as she didn't want to let go of either of them, ever.

This was the honest conversation she should have with Rupert; with Hugo, too.

"Well, as long as I'm confessing things, there's something else. The IRS has no record of my divorce from Hugo and I can't find my copy of the decree." The tiny veins on Rupert's nose and cheeks turned the color of spilled wine, and she knew his rage would follow.

"Then what proof do you have that you're divorced?" Rupert's eyes were ice.

"Well, I know I'm divorced from Hugo. And Hugo knows we're divorced," she lied. "But the IRS demands paper proof. It could take years to unearth and cost a lot of money. Let's just give them a paper annulment and get married again in Mexico."

In the end, Rupert decided that they didn't need the warmongering US government to be a party to their union. After their annulment and a Mexican marriage, they continued to live and love happily as man and wife.

# CHAPTER 28

# Los Angeles, California, 1971–73

## TRISTINE

HAVING SOLVED HER IRS CRISIS, Anaïs expected that I should also be able to manifest my desires. Whenever I saw her she'd ask, "What about your Don Juan?" grousing that I was doing something wrong by not having seduced Don. I'd come to the opposite conclusion, though. If he and I had violated our house incest taboo, it would have destabilized our commune family, and I would have missed the best two years of my life. I would have missed having genuine friendships with men and the experience of being part of a functioning family.

We had embraced the ideal of community devoid of capitalism, and it had worked. Money was never a problem; we each paid less for food and shelter than before. We had the usual roommate disagreements about decorating and cleaning, and our political discussions occasionally led to shouting, especially about sexism, but I always felt a real equality and trust with the guys.

I never had a steady boyfriend during my years in the Georgina house, but I never felt lonely. It was enough to be part of this intelligent, hip family with whom I shared meals and our earnest political ideals. We kept track of each other at anti-war demonstrations, boycotted grapes and Coors beer, harbored Berkeley Free Speech orator Mario Savio after his psychotic breakdown, and threw huge holiday parties that were the hot invite among the Westside's liberal chic.

On academic breaks the five of us would pile our sleeping bags into Bob's van, bring along some joints, and take off on camping trips to Death Valley, the Santa Barbara hot springs, and the High Sierras. We rented a cabin at Lake Arrowhead where we tried acid together, confident that we would all be safe in each other's company. We hiked, and swam in our birthday suits, and talked deep into the night under the open sky. For a latchkey kid who'd eaten alone in front of the TV and didn't go on vacations, these were days of heaven.

Then one evening I was upstairs in the ballroom working on my doctoral dissertation, which I'd changed three times already from Renaissance tragedy to Restoration comedy to women's diaries. Actually, I had wanted to write about Anaïs's *Diaries*, but my dissertation chair had objected that she was neither important enough, nor dead. He recommended I write about all women's diaries, from the tenth-century Japanese diarists on through to the present, so I would have enough material for a "proper" PhD dissertation.

I'd enjoyed learning about the early Japanese diarists whose aesthetic was to make imperceptible the line between fact and the imagined. But now I was trying to write about boring spinster and invalid Alice James, so instead of writing, I was fantasizing about a pirate with a British accent I'd met at our annual Halloween party. Our eyes had connected over the punch bowl and in less than two hours, his pirate breeches and my Old West saloon girl gown were on the floor of my upstairs bedroom, and we were naked on my mattress. For the life of me, though, I could not recall his name.

I noticed Don standing over me. "Sorry to interrupt, but there's a guy at the front door who says he met you at our party, Philip Forester?"

Right! *That* was his name!

Don and my other commune mates were gawking from the top of the stairs when I greeted Philip. In order to get some privacy, I took him to my bedroom and shut the door. With an adorable grin Philip produced from the pocket of his slinky shirt an expertly rolled joint, lit it, and handed it to me. I knew I shouldn't smoke because it was a weeknight, and in our house pot was reserved for socializing on weekends. But I was entranced again by Philip's Michael Caine-in-*Alfie* accent, his buttery hair and blue eyes, and his beautiful face that matched Anaïs's description of Rupert's sensitive face when they'd met.

I had decided it was high time I found my own Rupert, a lover and devoted domestic partner, whose sensuous nature would keep me connected to the earth. I saw how happy Rupert made Anaïs, and I wanted that. So, copying how she materialized what she desired by writing in her diary, I'd written a portrait of a younger, less cornball Rupert in mine, and now assumed Philip was the manifestation.

However, Philip Forester, who was repping a Carnaby Street fashion line in LA, didn't fit in with my commune. Politicos, like my commune members, and hippies, like Philip, were in opposing camps. My commune family rejected Philip as a new age capitalist. It was *West Side Story* all over again: my leftist-feminist Maria in love with his mercantile, joint-toking Tony; my commune as Maria's disapproving family.

It was just the sort of romantic melodrama Anaïs and Renate would have loved. When it happened, though, Anaïs was on an extended trip to Asia for *Westways* magazine, accompanied by Rupert as her paid photographer, and Renate had sequestered herself "incommunicado" in her last creative resurgence, painting wall-sized canvases of *trompe l'oeil* nature scenes. I was on my own, and when Philip asked to share my room until his commissions came in, I ignored the commune rule that overnight guests not stay longer than two weeks.

At the commune's Sunday night meeting, Don, refusing to look at me, said, "Bob, as president of the house, has something to tell you."

Bob looked at me kindly through his colorless eyelashes and said, almost apologetically, "We have voted, and it was decided that if Philip does not leave immediately, you have to move out."

I failed to mourn the loss of my commune family—probably because Philip provided me with so much mood-lifting weed. Using a ritual that Philip had learned from the Beatles' own swami to find a rental, I drew in lipstick on my commune bedroom window a child's stick figure picture of a house with wavy lines behind it. Sure enough, in the next day's *LA Times* classifieds, we found a beach house for rent that we could just afford.

With its steeple roof, it looked like my drawing. Originally built as a real estate office, it had no heat or insulation, and its whitewashed walls resembled a movie set, the paint peeling as if an art director's crew had aged it. Tall, unscreened Dutch windows opened onto the Pacific Ocean, which was so near it appeared we were at sea.

I fall in love with houses the way I fall in love with men, at first sight, and Philip and I rented the beach house before anyone else could. We furnished it with a king-sized waterbed, dangled crystals on threads from the window frames, and from the rafters we hung a clear round fishbowl in which swam a brilliant blue betta that my cat Jadu watched circle all day. Philip bought me a Victorian claw-footed tub and placed it under a window. It was hooked up to the kitchen faucet by a removable hose and emptied onto our patio downstairs, which was always buffeted by waves.

So began our life of play magic, getting high, bikini beach days in our ocean backyard, making love in our heated waterbed, and taking moonbaths together in the tub with the Dutch windows flung open onto the sea, unfiltered moonlight falling on our slender, wet bodies.

I was ecstatic. I was going to be like Anaïs—in tune with the rhythms of nature and my inner rhythms, as she was when she'd lived on her houseboat on the Seine. I was going to have it all: Philip to love me, a house on the water, shelves full of books, artistic friends, the fun of filmmaking, a life of laughter and play.

One afternoon, Anaïs phoned.

"Oh, I'm so glad I reached you. I was so worried!" she cried. "I called the commune, and they said you weren't there anymore."

"Didn't they give you my new phone number?"

"No. Rupert finally got the idea to try information."

"I'm fine. I'm great. I didn't know you were back yet. Can I come tomorrow?"

∞

The next day at her front door, Anaïs sang, "Tristine, you have to visit Bali! Every person you meet there is an artist! A whole country of artists!"

Rupert stood at her side, beaming his Hollywood smile. He put down their tiny poodle Piccolo, who'd been squirming in his arms, and handed me his snapshots from Bali, pointing out his favorite—of Anaïs in a swimsuit, up to her calves in the calm surf.

"Look at what a great figure Anaïs still has," he boasted. "Like a girl." She was then sixty-nine.

My jaw dropped at how lithe and youthful and happy she looked. It was just the reaction Rupert was looking for. Satisfied, he left to take Piccolo to the park.

I was bursting to tell Anaïs that I'd found my own Rupert and fallen in love, but she lilted, "Before we have our talk, let me show you the diaries I brought back from Japan."

She had them spread out on the lid of the grand piano and gracefully unfolded each accordion diary for me, one with images of dragonflies on its cover, another with delicate flowers, another in which she'd begun to write, black with a dashing orange stripe. I compared her delicate handwriting and neat margins with the uneven scribbling in my own journals. My writing was irregular and runaway, and my books were big, heavy things that would endure all my ramblings.

When Anaïs closed the accordion diary and glided toward the sliding glass doors, I erupted with my news about living with Philip at the beach house, the words gushing up like soda from a shaken bottle.

I begged Anaïs, "Will you and Rupert come to dinner at the beach house to meet Philip? He's a great cook."

"Of course." She smiled. "I can't wait to meet him. I know Rupert and I will love him if you do."

My heart leapt in gratitude. I threw my arms around her, thanking her, the two of us standing at the unopened sliding glass door, the sun streaming in on the cold, clear day.

"I fell in love, too," she said, "with the rock and sand gardens in Japan. Rupert took me to Ryoanji, and the garden was so tranquil I wished I could bring it home." She pointed down to a white rectangle at our feet. "So Rupert made me a miniature sand garden here."

Rupert had removed some of the floor bricks to create the sand-filled hollow at our feet. Next to the rectangle of white sand lay some small rocks and a miniature rake.

Anaïs kneeled Japanese-style, resting lightly on her ankles. I tried to imitate her, but my knees tottered on the way down. I attempted to balance on my heels, but they dug into my behind uncomfortably, so I sprawled, supporting myself on one arm.

Still poised on her ankles, Anaïs leaned forward to pick up the miniature rake. She began to pull it slowly, carefully through the sand, creating a pattern of parallel rolling waves. I had the impulse to grab the rake from her hand, the movement looked so pleasurable.

She said, her voice undulating like the waves drawn in the sand, "It's like a diary, seeing the pattern my hand makes. A form of meditation. It changes every day: sometimes a mandala, sometimes straight lines."

She pulled the small rake so slowly that we became aware of every grain falling into place.

"Rupert and I came back early because I had to have some medical tests." She put the rake down and, with a flat palm, annihilated the perfect pattern she'd made. I almost cried out, *Don't!*

I asked, "Is everything okay?"

"They removed a tumor."

I felt the sliding door and walls of the house about to collapse, glass shattering on the brick surrounding us. "No!"

She put her hand to my face. "Don't worry, Tristine. There are doctors now who can cure cancer just with your mind and your will."

Cancer. Everyone I'd ever known who'd had cancer had died from it.

She continued gently. "My healer Dr. Brugh Joy says I'm an excellent candidate to make the cancer cells go away with my ability to visualize. I've had so much practice in my novel writing."

"But you will do the other, you know, medical stuff? Chemotherapy?" I wasn't sure I'd pronounced the word correctly.

"My visualizing will work." She held my gaze with her aqua eyes. "I don't want this to ruin your happiness. I'm not letting it ruin mine. We are here together right now, looking out at the pool and the lake, contemplating the sand garden." She began moving the rake again in a delicate zigzag. "Our love for each other is here now, and our love for our men."

We sat in silence, the sunlight through the sliding doors making everything sharp. I could hear a high piercing ring that cut through all the beauty. I was in love and loved. I was bursting with happiness. I had Anaïs's friendship. And she was dying. It was all dying.

I phoned Renate when I got home. Though she had been present during Anaïs's surgery at Cedars-Sinai, Renate hadn't said a word about it to me. She made no apology.

"You seemed so preoccupied with your love affair." Even now she seemed reluctant to share the details.

"What can I do?"

"You have to stay positive. She staved it off for twenty years; she can do it again. Anaïs has the power within herself to transform the illusion of physical illness. You'll see."

And because mind magic had worked to get Philip and me the beach house, and because Anaïs had so successfully manifested her desires in the past, I did believe she would heal herself.

∽

It took me until I was twenty-eight to finish all the course work and pass the PhD written and oral exams. By then Philip's hip menswear sales were going so well that while waiting to hear back on the university teaching positions I'd interviewed for at the MLA convention, I took a break from earning my own way. Within the year I would have to accept a job that required I move out of state, and I wanted to enjoy my time at the beach house with Philip. I believed I'd found the best of Anaïs's two worlds in Philip. As Hugo once was, Philip was a good breadwinner, and like Rupert, he supported my artistic ambitions without having such aspirations himself. I smiled, recalling what Anaïs had said when I'd once asked why she'd chosen Rupert.

"Why do you ask?" Her tone a warning not to say anything negative about him.

"I don't know. You're so extraordinary, and he—" I caught myself. "You're an artist, and he isn't."

With her soft, guttural laugh she'd told me, "I learned a long time ago, Tristine, that there can only be one star in a relationship, and I decided it should be me."

It was surprising, though, how quickly I got bored being the star of the relationship, unlike Anaïs. I loved Philip's gentleness, his slow hand, the opium-dream length of his kisses, the assured gong of orgasm with him, but our lovemaking simply couldn't compare to the inferno I'd known with Neal. With Philip's new age otherworldliness and all the pot he smoked, our lovemaking was ethereal and dreamlike, but not mythic. More worrisome, Philip wanted to get married—in part because it would help with his immigration status, but also because he wanted to start a family, which I didn't.

To my surprise, with his paying all the rent and freeing up my time, I seemed to have lost my willpower. Even though I wasn't teaching and was home all day, I couldn't get anywhere on my PhD dissertation.

I sat at my desk in a corner of the one-room house every day and was lucky if I squeezed out half a page. The sea and sky were gray and flat, the low-hanging haze stuck like a sigh in my chest. I was writing about other women's lives. I wasn't living my life as Anaïs had done, and I wouldn't really be free to live until I finished the damned dissertation, and by that time Anaïs might be dead.

I pushed away the negative thought, believing it could harm her. Maybe the problem, I considered, was that I needed a room of my own. Anaïs had a writing room of her own, even if it was the size of a closet. I asked Philip if we could put up some walls to create a private office for me. He had another idea. He bought me a big blue tent and pitched it so that it covered most of the downstairs deck.

It was a romantic space, inviting fantasies of Arabian nights—its blue walls rippling in the breeze, the surf crashing on boulders a few yards away—but it proved unsuitable for writing. I sat huddled in the damp cold, using a Coleman lantern for light. Huge waves would swamp the tent when storms hit. When the sun dried the canvas walls I'd sweep out the sand, a Sisyphean task.

I did find a use for the tent, though, with some of the women who had been in my consciousness-raising group. We'd accomplished our action of establishing a Women's Studies program, but our work of consciousness wasn't over because there were areas where we were still internally oppressed. I invited six friends to meet in the tent to explore that most primitive, forbidden, and inaccessible part of ourselves: our sexuality. What we liked. What we didn't. What we needed courage to change.

When I told Anaïs, she begged me to tape-record the sessions for her. So on the first night, gathered on large pillows in a circle, the surf pounding the rocks nearby, I asked my women friends for permission to start a tape recorder.

"Why?" Clara demanded, flipping back a ringlet of copper hair. I should have remembered how much Clara disliked Anaïs.

"Because she has cancer and can't join us," I said, "and this is something she's always cared about."

When we voted, the majority ruled that I could start the recorder, on the condition that, as in our consciousness group, nothing any of us said would be repeated outside those canvas walls—with the one exception that Anaïs could listen to the tapes.

Clara objected, "You're all crazy. You don't know what she's going to do with those tapes." Persuaded by Clara's caution but moved by Anaïs's illness, the group decided that Anaïs should have a limited window to listen to the tapes, and then I had to retrieve and destroy them. Even so, Clara insisted that when she was speaking the recorder be off.

So began the tent tapes. We explored our sexual experiences and feelings, and put them into words for the first time with the same radical honesty we had brought to the consciousness-raising group. We used the same format as in the early days of the group, each woman speaking in turn on the night's chosen theme, forming a circle around the Coleman lantern.

The theme of our first night was first arousal. What were the earliest erogenous zones we were aware of? Mine were related to tickling. At what age did we discover masturbation? One woman never had! How did we pleasure ourselves? A teddy bear, the edge of the bed.

To everyone's surprise, our memories of first arousal had little to do with men—or women, for that matter. Horses, dogs, cats, and cartoon characters were more primary. One woman made us laugh by saying she first masturbated to the vision of turds falling into a toilet, and another described how she got off to the imagined advances of an ugly boy with pimples whom she hated. Another remembered her fantasy of a girl with a broken arm, which later morphed into men missing an arm, a leg, an eye. The dirties, the nasties, the ugly, for some reason, were prevalent in their earliest fantasies. Only mine were stereotypically romantic, a knight on a white horse in the forest. Even in my conveyor belt fantasies, I got rescued by a heroic boy.

Over the following weeks, we explored what pleased us in the lantern light, what we endured, as well as our fantasies during intercourse. One woman imagined while having sex that she would be caught and punished for it. Another confessed she found the physical act of intercourse so funny that she giggled during it, which made her boyfriend furious. To my surprise and chagrin, I was the only one who didn't have fantasies during sex about anything or anyone other than the man I was with. The other women's reports were filled with a mad and colorful array of characters and creatures, and I was awed by the amazing variety within just our small group.

Unlike our larger consciousness-raising group, in which there had been several lesbians, all the women here preferred guys. Nevertheless, I found myself listening carefully to hear if Clara had ever fantasized about women, as I had been having fantasies about her. She dismissed the question offhandedly, denying any interest. The narrow door through which I might have known Sapphic love closed that evening, sealing off a realm of pleasures.

When Anaïs wanted something, she was anything but passive, and I had never experienced her lobbying me so intently as she did for those tent tapes. Upon her return from a European trip, she immediately phoned me to bring over the tapes. Our group had spoken with such unexpected openness that I regretted having convinced them to share the tapes with her. If we'd taken a vote again, I would have sided with Clara. She was right; we didn't know what Anaïs would do with the tapes. Anaïs had recently asked me if I, or my students, had any erotic stories to sell; she said she was in touch again with "the Collector" for whom she and Henry Miller and other struggling Village artists had written pornography.

Despite my misgivings, I delivered the recorded tapes with the reminder that in two weeks I had to pick them up and destroy them.

I didn't hear from Anaïs for several weeks, and then she phoned me. "Tristine! I need your help."

"Is it about the tapes?"

"No, they're wonderful. It's that Henry Miller sent over this filmmaker Bob Snyder who did a documentary on Henry and wants to make one on me." She explained that Snyder wanted to start with a scene of her teaching, and she needed some extras. "Could you get some of your students to be extras?"

"I'm not teaching this semester."

"Well, just bring some friends. No one will know."

Since we were having the last meeting in the women's tent that night, I asked the group if they wanted to go to Anaïs's house to be her pretend students for the shoot. With the exception of Clara, they all wanted to. Clara demanded to know if I'd destroyed the tapes yet, and when I said they were still in Anaïs's possession, she warned, "She's going to figure out from the voices who's who. So much for confidentiality."

None of us had thought about that. We all decided not to tape our last session for Anaïs. Everyone demanded that before the film shoot, I get back the tapes I'd given her.

I made arrangements with Anaïs to pick up the tapes from her house twice, and twice she cancelled on me but promised she would have them ready the day of the film shoot.

However, when I arrived at the Silver Lake house with my friends and asked Anaïs for the tapes, she pleaded, "Can't it please wait until next week?" Then there was so much hustle and confusion with camera set-ups and lighting that everyone forgot about them.

Bob Snyder instructed the extras, including me, to sit at Anaïs's feet so that she could be filmed dropping pearls of wisdom to us. Ordinarily I would have been excited to see a movie being made, even this little documentary with its fake scene of Anaïs teaching, but I felt disconnected. I couldn't take my mind off the phone conversation I'd had that morning with the chair of the English department at Indiana University. He'd called to find out if I'd decided to accept his offer of a tenure-track position.

I'd prevaricated because, even after months of internal debate, I was still unable to decide whether to accept the offer. On the one hand, it would mean I'd have to leave everything I loved in my life: Anaïs and Renate, living with Philip at the beach house, my sisterhood of women friends. On the other hand, I knew I should grab a three-year, guaranteed tenure-track job at a major university in a market where suddenly there were no jobs to be had. Those of us on the cusp of the Boomer bubble had run like lemmings when told there was a need for more college professors, but no one had figured out that by the time we'd gotten our PhDs, the bubble would have burst. My fellow grad students were hissing at my rare good fortune to have any offers, even if they all had been in less than desirable locations.

After the filming, when my friends gathered around Anaïs, I slipped out alone to the backyard. Standing by the hedge where the hillside dropped, I could see house lights begin to twinkle on the slopes below. They spread like the Milky Way down to the lake's shimmering surface. I felt Anaïs approach and slip her arm around my waist.

"What's wrong, Tristine?"

I told her about my inability to decide whether to take the Indiana job.

"Oh, I thought you had already decided to turn it down."

"No; I don't want to leave you and I don't want to leave Philip, but Indiana is letting me create my own Women's Lit classes, and if I turn it down I'll be selling out the Women's Movement, and all the women before me who fought for my opportunity, and my students who see me as an example. So I changed my mind. Then I changed it again. Over and over. It's making me crazy. Either way I choose, it feels like I'm cleaving off half of myself."

"Why doesn't Philip come with you?" she asked.

"I knew that would be your suggestion. I knew you'd say, 'Find a creative solution,' so I begged him to come with me, but he said there was no market for mod men's fashion in Indiana."

In fact, Philip's response had shocked me. Sweet, passive Philip had said, unequivocally, "No." He wouldn't move to Indiana; he wouldn't leave his work. I knew we would not survive long-distance. And even if after three years I were lucky enough to find a job back in California (which had been Renate's recommendation), I didn't believe Philip would wait. I'd begged him, "Tell me not to go. Just tell me to stay with you."

"I can't do that," he'd said gently. He sat on the waterbed that rocked under his weight. He dropped his head, and his hands disappeared into his blond shag.

"Why not?" I sniffled.

"Because later you would blame me."

I probably would.

There were other problems in my relationship with Philip that I would have liked to present to Anaïs as she and I stood with our arms around each other's waists, looking at the stars now twinkling above the hillside lights. But I realized it was all too complex, and my thoughts too jumbled, for her to deal with in the middle of a movie being shot about her. So I tried to keep my question simple: Should I give up the job offer and stay with Philip, who was unwilling to come with me? Or should I go so I could respect myself and likely lose him entirely?

In the past, whenever I'd presented Anaïs with one of my emotional puzzles, she'd close her eyes as if about to plunge underwater. After several moments with her lids shut, she'd emerge with a brilliant insight that would solve the problem. It might be a revelation about one's underlying motivations that, once recognized, brought clarity; or she might offer a metaphor that contained a nugget of wisdom.

But Anaïs didn't close her eyes and consider. She pivoted me, her arm around my waist, so that instead of looking out at the gleaming reservoir, we faced her brightly lit house.

Together we watched a tableau through the glass doors as my friends socialized animatedly.

Anaïs murmured in sympathy, "Can't you ask the university for more time?"

"I did. The chair said yes and offered me more money because he thought I was being a tough negotiator."

Her half laugh came from low in her throat, but she tried to be encouraging. "The Kinsey Institute is there, you know."

I snapped, "That has nothing to do with what I'd be doing there! I'm not a sexologist." Immediately, I regretted my tone.

"Of course not." She sighed. "I just thought because you did that fascinating research with the women in your tent . . ."

"I have to get those tapes back."

"I told you, I'll return them!"

Retreating in the face of her displeasure, I tried to pull her attention back to my problem. "Renate says whatever choice I make will be the right one, but I know whatever choice I make will be the wrong one."

She turned to me, her aquamarine eyes holding mine. "The problem isn't your ambivalence, Tristine. It's that you freeze instead of flowing forward." She raised her right arm like a ballerina and let it glide sideways, suggesting a smoothly flowing river.

"But how do I flow forward when I have to choose one path and I can't?" I could hear panic in my voice.

She offered an enigmatic smile. "I followed both paths until the way became clear."

She had managed to flow forward on two paths—to live in two places at once, to be the wife of two men at once—for seventeen years.

But I couldn't do that. Come January, I either went to Indiana by myself or stayed in Los Angeles with Philip.

I noticed how tired Anaïs looked under her makeup and wondered if her cancer had really retreated.

Her penciled-on eyebrows lifted in alarm. "Excuse me. I have to take care of something. Bob is trying to put Rupert in the film."

We watched the director's young assistant position fill lights around Rupert, who was sitting in a chair while Snyder held a meter next to his face.

"Anaïs, he's just using Rupert as a stand-in for your shot."

"No, I know what I'm talking about." She squeezed my hand with her cold fingers before she rushed inside.

I wanted her to stay. I needed her to reassure me that she was curing the cancer. That if I did decide to go to Indiana, she would be fine when I got back. I started toward the house, circling around the pool, stepping carefully because there was no light on that side of the yard.

I glanced up and saw Anaïs leading Snyder out through the glass doors onto the flagstone patio. I stopped in my tracks, not wanting to interrupt, unable to tell if they'd noticed me.

"Bob, we talked about this." Anaïs's voice wavered with anxiety. "Rupert is not to be in the film."

"Be reasonable!" Snyder made no attempt to keep his voice down. "Your audience will want to see your handsome husband. Rupert is very photogenic, you know." Snyder pressed his stubby fingers together in supplication.

"Yes, I know. But we agreed that Rupert would not appear."

Anaïs didn't want Rupert in the film, of course, because Hugo would inevitably see it. But Rupert had been introduced as her husband to the director, as was customary in the LA arts circle we ran in. She could hardly explain that she had another husband in New York from whom she kept Rupert a secret. Snyder was a "small time" documentary filmmaker and "not very high class," as Anaïs had described him to me. He could not be trusted.

"I need to remind you, Bob," Anaïs said, "that you agreed this film would be about my professional life, not my personal life."

"Are you trying to tell me how to shoot my movie? We need a balance, a balance. I'm the filmmaker here. I know."

She didn't take the bait. She lowered her voice. "The audience of my work knows me only as Anaïs Nin, my professional name, which is also my maiden name. It would be too confusing to bring in Rupert Pole as my husband."

"Oh, that's no problem." Snyder sounded relieved. "All the young women are keeping their maiden names now. It just shows how ahead of the times you are. All we have to do is have you identify Rupert as your husband in the voiceover."

Right, I thought. Have Anaïs announce on film, for Hugo to hear, "This is my husband Rupert Pole." I was shocked when Snyder then spoke as if he were some important Hollywood director and she were just his actress:

"Let me remind you, Anaïs. The contract states that I have final cut."

"But I have creative control," she objected.

"That's not in the contract."

She stepped back, fuming. "You tricked me. I said I wanted creative control."

"You signed the contract."

She calmed herself, lowering her head like a sorrowful Madonna. She said sweetly, sadly, "I'm sorry, Bob, I know you are the director and that you tricked me into giving you final cut, but we have to do this my way or there can be no film."

"Are you threatening me?" he snarled, but sounded scared.

"Not at all. You have the contract on your side. Unfortunately, you will not have a film to cut."

"What do you mean? I already have film in the can."

"You mean the scene we just shot with the students? Let's see what kind of film you can make out of that. I will no longer appear in the film."

She began walking away from Snyder, toward me. He yelled after her, "I'm calling Henry Miller!"

Anaïs turned back. "Why would you call Henry?"

"He got me into this. He told me plenty about you!"

Henry knew about Hugo and Rupert; what if he'd told Snyder? What if it had been Snyder's conniving plan all along to get Anaïs's double life on film?

She remained composed, however. "Henry lies," she said. "You had better tell me what he said so that I can correct it."

"When we're alone." Snyder flung an arm toward me, now in his line of sight.

"There's nothing you could possibly say to me that Tristine cannot hear." She acknowledged my presence with a nod. "Unless, of course, you are worried about being sued for slander."

"Never mind."

"Perhaps *I* should call Henry. We are very close. Perhaps he will have second thoughts about letting you finish your film on him."

"He wouldn't do that. We're friends."

Anaïs said, "I assure you my friendship with Henry is longer and more intimate."

Snyder looked like a confused bull in the ring, his neck weakened after the banderillos have planted their barbed sticks. He steamed in place, not daring to say another word.

She turned her back on him and joined me. He pivoted the opposite direction and stormed into the house. He tugged on Rupert's arm until Rupert rose from the chair and, looking confused, disappeared again into Anaïs's study.

"Clear the set!" Snyder snapped, and his assistant started to shoo out my friends, who told me later they'd felt rudely dismissed.

I put my hands on Anaïs's shoulders and kissed her on both cheeks. I hadn't grown any taller since the first time we'd embraced, but she felt smaller and frailer. "Don't let Snyder bully you," I said.

She smiled. "Don't worry, I know how to handle Bob Snyder."

And she did. He'd managed to catch Rupert on film walking through the scene we'd shot that day, but in the final cut, Rupert is identified only as Anaïs's escort.

∞

Anaïs and Rupert came to dinner at the beach house the following week. She'd promised to deliver the tapes to me then but said she'd forgotten them. A week later, I drove to her house, unannounced, so she couldn't give me any more excuses. When I reached the end of the long, narrow driveway, I saw Rupert bringing out the trash.

"Oh, Tristine, you should have phoned," he boomed. "Anaïs is out of town. She's accepting another honorary doctorate."

"I believe she left some audio tapes for me to pick up."

"Oh, those tapes you made with the women in your tent? We listened to those together." He grinned lewdly. "They were very stimulating."

I felt a surge of anger. "Those were private! She wasn't supposed to share them!"

Rupert just continued standing there with a stupid, satisfied look on his face.

"Do you know where the tapes are?" I walked toward the back door that led directly into the kitchen, but he blocked me with his thick frame. "I need to get them back," I insisted.

"I think Anaïs would like to keep them."

"She can't keep them! I told her that."

"Well, you'll have to talk to her. She'll be back next week." He escaped inside the kitchen door and locked it against me. I was furious and slammed my car door shut, intending to storm away, but I had to inch my car back out that narrow driveway.

*How could she?* I fumed while speeding home on the Santa Monica Freeway. She had used our earnest and sensitive self-explorations as pornography for Rupert. I had told her the tent tapes were only for her ears; I'd told her about the women's confidentiality, and that a special exception had been made for her. I had assumed she was part of our sisterhood. I knew she was a liar, but I'd thought that was only to men. I thought she understood; you might lie to a man but you would never betray a sister.

How wrong I had been, I berated myself. Why would I have ever trusted Anaïs with the confidences of my friends? I knew how she was, adamant about others keeping her secrets, but careless in exposing the intimacies of others. Luise Rainer, the actress Anaïs had compared me to when we met, and the writer Leslie Blanch had both accused her of publishing private details about their marriages revealed in confidence. Anaïs had betrayed those friendships in the *Diaries*, so what made me think she wouldn't betray me and the friends I'd convinced to trust her? Clara was right. Anaïs wasn't a feminist; she was a male-identified woman. She was of another generation, had never been in a consciousness-raising group, had gone from her mother's house surrounded by her protective brothers to become Hugo's bride at twenty, and had never lived without at least one husband at her side. Oh, she'd understood sisterhood well enough to benefit from our promotion of her as a woman writer, but she didn't have a clue about the supportive trust that grew between women.

When I phoned Anaïs the following week, I complimented her on receiving another honorary doctorate, but could not hold back my disappointment in her. "I told you those tapes were only for you! What am I going to tell the women who trusted me?"

"Don't tell them anything," she replied lightly.

"I want to come to your house tomorrow to pick them up."

"Why do you need them? Are you going to publish them?" Anaïs asked.

"No! I'm going to destroy them."

"Oh, don't do that. I'll take care of them. They shouldn't be destroyed."

"Are *you* going to publish them?" I asked her.

"Who told you that?"

"No one. You're the one who said you were looking for erotic stories to buy." I stopped short, knowing that when she was guilty she would just lie more. "Please let me pick them up."

"I don't know where they are," she said. "They got misplaced."

"Oh, don't do this," I moaned.

"What do you mean?" There was a clear warning in her voice. I had stepped over the line.

I was silent, afraid of what I might say.

"Just tell those women," she said in her most soothing voice, "that I returned them to you, and you destroyed them. They don't need to know anything else."

"What will you do with them?" I asked. "Are you going to give them to that porn collector?"

"I don't know what you're so worried about," she said, dismissing my concern. "Rupert and I could hardly hear the voices over the sound of the waves."

I was so upset by the conversation that I immediately phoned Renate.

"Those women trusted me, Renate," I groaned. "If I lie and say what Anaïs told me to tell them, and then one of them discovers the tapes in that collector's hands, or at the Kinsey Institute, or published somewhere, I couldn't hold my head up!"

"Don't be ridiculous," Renate chided. "Those tapes aren't going anywhere. Anaïs just wants to keep them. If they worked to arouse Rupert once, they'll probably work again. It's not so easy anymore, you know."

"What do you mean? He's still crazy about her. They're always spooning in front of everyone."

Renate's great sympathy for Anaïs came through in her saddened voice. "She sees the way he gawks at all the young women who come there to pay her their obeisance."

"That's the other thing. She treats those come-lately 'Ninnies' the same as me."

"That is not true, Tristine," Renate objected. "Now you are being unfair."

"She praises them, encourages their writing, calls them her daughters . . ."

"Stop! That's just Anaïs wanting to hold onto every morsel of her celebrity. She knows it won't last forever. It's already fading. What time is it?"

"Four twenty-five."

"I hate to interrupt this fascinating conversation, but John Houseman gave me two tickets to see Nureyev tonight at the Dorothy Chandler."

I couldn't tell if she was inviting me, so I didn't say anything.

"Why don't you meet me at the restaurant? They validate the parking."

I hesitated, but Renate clinched the deal. "Don't you want to see that perfect male body in a leotard spinning and leaping across the stage?"

∞

The restaurant turned out to be so expensive that we just ordered vodka gimlets. I shared with Renate Anaïs's advice when she and Rupert had last come to dinner, that I should stay in LA with Philip and pursue my interest in screenwriting.

"Hmm. I'm not surprised Anaïs told you to stay with Philip instead of going for the lectureship. I completely disagree with her, but she believes a woman can't be happy without a man."

"I've never heard her say that."

"Haven't you heard her repeat, 'A woman alone is not a beautiful thing'? What do you think that means? I've told her not to say it. The feminists don't like it."

"I don't think she really is a feminist."

"Probably not. I am though. It's our one bone of contention; she disapproves of my solitude. Otherwise, we are completely copacetic."

The alcohol seemed to have gone to Renate's head. She was suddenly capricious and more voluble than usual. "You know why Anaïs and I are so alike, don't you?" She gave me a thin-lipped smile. "I mean besides our both being European transplants and culture hounds."

She was playing one-upsman. She liked to remind me that she had known Anaïs longer and was her closest friend.

"Because you're the same age?"

"No, actually Anaïs is eighteen years older than I."

I was surprised. They looked the same age; I'd assumed they were. But maybe it was true what Anaïs had said, that Renate's bitterness toward men had aged her.

Renate used her cloth napkin to pat her lips, leaving a lipstick stain. She said, "Did Anaïs tell you that she and I were both in incestuous relationships?"

At first I thought Renate was speaking metaphorically as we often did, but she continued, "My uncle molested me, and Anaïs had an incestuous affair with her father."

"I don't believe you."

The alcohol had changed Renate's personality. Her usually precise enunciation was slurry in a few places. "You think I don't know my uncle molested me? He lived with us. Ha! And all the while Freud was living next door, and my uncle was his patient. The great *doctor* probably knew what was going on and did nothing. I'm sure my uncle's case is documented if you don't believe me."

"No, I don't believe you about Anaïs and her father. He abandoned her; that's all."

"He abandoned her when she was a child. Hers wasn't childhood incest like mine. When Anaïs was in her late twenties, your age, and already married to Hugo, she met her father again and seduced him."

How dare Renate play with me this way! She was drunk, and I didn't feel safe around her.

I'd put her in her place. "Anaïs and I talk about our fathers all the time, and she's never said anything like that."

"No? I'm surprised."

"It's impossible," I insisted. "She wrote about a flirtation with her father when she was in her late twenties in her published *Diary*. The most they did was flatter each other and admire each other's narrow feet, if that's what you're calling incest. She says she wanted to entice him into loving her, but as a daughter!"

"Well that's not what happened. She seduced him."

"You're wrong," I said. "Anaïs is the most joyful person I know. If she'd seduced her father the guilt would have driven her insane. That's what *Oedipus* is about."

"Don't you know Freud has been discredited?"

"I'm not just talking about Freud. The incest taboo is a lot older than Freud."

"If you mean *Oedipus Rex*, it's a play about a myth." Renate handed a passing waiter her gimlet glass with a nod that she would like another. "You of all people know that Anaïs specializes in breaking taboos. You've even helped her."

"Bigamy is different from incest!" I protested.

"Really? How so?"

I was sure they were different but I couldn't find the words to explain. The nausea churning in my stomach was making it hard for me to speak at all.

Renate shrugged. "It's not such a big deal."

"It's the biggest deal!"

"Tristine! I never imagined you were so conventional."

Conventional? What Renate was talking about was beyond the pale. The room was beginning to turn around me; the waiter and coffee station on my right were sliding counterclockwise to my left.

"It was two consenting adults," Renate said. "It wasn't like me with my uncle. I was a child. But Anaïs planned it."

"Stop it, Renate! She would never do that!"

"She seduced her father to hurt him the way he'd hurt her mother, by making him fall in love with her and then abandoning him."

That had the jolt of credibility. I could imagine wanting to make my father experience my mother's pain to even the score. But not that way.

"Personally I think she did it as a surrealist act," Renate continued, apparently enjoying herself. "Breton and Artaud and that gang, they were all trying to outdo each other: who could push the boundaries the furthest, break the most taboos. Anaïs one-upped them!"

That explanation, too, hit with a *whack*.

"Anyway," Renate said, "she only had intercourse with her father a few times and she was the one who ended it."

I felt clammy. I was going to throw up. I was too dizzy to make it to the ladies' room. I wanted to lie down on the cool marble floor so I would not fall. I tried to breathe.

"Have a sip of water," Renate said.

Through the unworldly atmosphere, my hand reached out and accepted the glass from hers. "Stop talking about it," I pleaded.

"I'm sorry." Renate looked concerned for me. "I didn't mean to upset you. Let's just get a check and go see the ballet."

"You go. I have to go home. I don't feel well."

"Suit yourself," Renate said, "but I think you're making a big deal over nothing."

Driving home, I staved off my nausea by thinking about the town of Bloomington, Indiana I had visited when interviewing for teaching positions. Going to that Midwestern college town could be a new beginning; a clean, blank slate. No Anaïs with her duplicity, no Renate with her never-mentioned dead son, no Philip with his perpetual pot smoking, no more guilt-inducing Christmases in my mother's decaying house.

That night I tossed on the sloshing waterbed as Philip slept. I was plagued by images of Anaïs costumed as the moon-goddess Astarte with her head in a birdcage, her sequined nakedness flashing light; Renate dressed in black like Morticia; Curtis Harrington impersonating a debased Roman slave; all of them actors in a demonic orgiastic ritual. I recognized the images from Kenneth Anger's *Inauguration of the Pleasure Dome*, which I'd seen when it screened at UCLA. Its frenzied finale had been disturbingly arousing, edited in fast cuts with multiple superimpositions of fire and occult symbols.

I crawled out of bed, trying not to rock Philip awake. I opened the Dutch windows and let the damp ocean air blow on me, watching the moon move behind a mist of clouds. I thought about Renate's past association with black magic. She'd told me she had been close friends with Marjorie Cameron, a self-proclaimed black witch, and

that Cameron had been a follower of Aleister Crowley, who'd practiced sexual magic.

I inhaled deeply in an attempt to restore my reason. Even if Renate
and Anaïs had play-acted with people who practiced the occult, that
didn't mean Anaïs had intentionally seduced her father. The father
who, I recalled with a chill, had himself been fascinated with the
occult. I recollected the dark surrealism of Anaïs's poetic novel *House
of Incest*. Anaïs claimed it was about narcissism, being able to love in
another only that which mirrors one's self. But could it also be that,
like her other so-called fiction, *House of Incest* was really a distillation of her life, and its imagery of Lot with his hand on his daughter's
breast the horrific truth about her father and herself?

My mind was now piecing together shards of memory and fear,
and something Anaïs herself had once told me: that as a child, the only
time she got attention from her father was when she was naked in the
tub and he would burst into the bathroom, the flash of his camera
blinding her. Was that early invasion of her privacy why she could so
blithely violate the boundaries of others? Anaïs sexualized everything,
every relationship, even our daughter/mother bond—encouraging me
repeatedly to swim naked in her pool though I always refused, voy-
euristically directing my sexual liaisons, using the tent tapes as pornography. Why was I so sure she would stop at daughter-father incest?

I had found a mirror to myself in Anaïs, but now that mirror was
showing the image of a monster, and I wanted to shatter it. I was so
angry at her, angry that I could no longer defend her as a feminist,
angry that I'd let her use me for so many years because I'd idolized
her, angry that when I needed her wise clairvoyance, I couldn't trust
her advice because I'd come to see her as a terrible guide. What kind
of guide could she be if she was so perverse as to have seduced her
father? An urge to expel Anaïs and her whole outré world rose in me
like molten lava.

I went back to bed, still queasy, and wished that I had a solid mattress under me instead of the undulating waterbed.

∞

Two months later, I flew to Indiana in my flimsy winter coat. I arrived right after a storm had completely covered everything with snow: a blank, white slate.

# CHAPTER 29

# Bloomington, Indiana, 1974

## TRISTINE

I'D THOUGHT THAT BY MOVING to Indiana I would escape the dark surrealism that had tinged Los Angeles since the bizarre Manson murders, yet I found it waiting for me in America's heartland, lurking like the phosphorescent mushrooms in the dank Hoosier woods.

Indiana turned out to be like one of my recurrent childhood nightmares: of walking along cautiously, but falling nevertheless into a hole that pulls me into another dimension—mysterious, terrifying, where all that exists are the rock walls sliding by and the sensation of plunging into darkness without end.

Things did not start out so badly. I rented a house with some photography students who blew up their grainy black-and-white images of fallow fields and lonely churches and plastered them on billboards set along the country roads. Though I ignored the rabid English department politics, I enjoyed my role as an avant-garde feminist lecturer from California, hired because I could teach both the traditional canon and the hot new field of women's studies.

Then, over summer break, the only good friend I'd made on the IU faculty blew his brains out in a soybean field. Soon after, a group of coeds from my spring semester's Twentieth-Century Women's Lit class declared that they, too, had been seduced by the romance of suicide thanks to having read Sylvia Plath's *Ariel* in my class; though I resolved never to teach Plath again, her black gloves beckoned me as well.

The bottom didn't fall out, though, until Clara phoned to report back to me on Philip's sustained silence. When I'd left him after summer vacation, we were on good terms. My understanding was that he was still my boyfriend, who would be waiting when I flew back at Christmas. But Clara reported that Philip had moved out of the beach house, given notice to the landlord, and taken an apartment with a new girlfriend to whom he was engaged, all without mentioning a word about it to me. And one other piece of news: I'd left my cat Jadu in Philip's care, and Jadu was dead, either eaten by coyotes or hit by a car on Pacific Coast Highway.

The hidden explosive device—buried when my father left—was triggered by Philip's betrayal and detonated. Eight years before, when Neal had left me, I'd been surprised that all existence was not wiped out. Anaïs and Rupert and Renate had encircled and protected me from impact. This time, though, I was entirely alone.

With detached interest, I watched myself become a perpetual motion machine that did nothing but shake and leak tears. It didn't eat, didn't sleep, and had no stop switch, although it somehow turned itself off for the hours I taught in the classroom. Anaïs had been right; she was the only one who had understood that although taking the job was the honorable and feminist thing to do, my emotions and nerves could not follow suit. I'd let happen what Anaïs had warned me about in the beginning: I had failed to protect myself from re-injury by a man.

I hid in my upstairs bedroom, watching the endless, frigid rain roll down my windowpane and splash in the courtyard below. When the phone rang and Anaïs said hello, it was a voice from another life.

"Tristine, are you alright? I got worried that I haven't heard from you. How is it there?"

"Not so good."

Gently she asked, "What's the most immediate problem?"

"I have a blister on my foot that's infected."

"Have you been to the doctor?"

"I don't really have one here."

In no time I was telling her about Philip having abandoned me and the airless, black depression I'd fallen into.

"Come home immediately, Tristine. You need the support of your women friends."

"I can't bail on this job. I'd never get another."

"Why not?"

"I'd have a permanent black mark on my name for breaking my contract. Chairs of English departments talk to the chairs of other English departments."

"I see," she said calmly. "Alright, don't do anything until you hear back from me. Just try to eat and sleep—and go to a doctor, any doctor. Remember, I love you."

The next day I received a forwarded letter from the UCLA School of Theater, Film, and Television accepting me into their graduate film program. The letter was baffling because, while I'd thought about going, I'd never applied to film school. Admission to UCLA's grad film program in 1974, as now, was a coup and required an application with sample film work and recommendations, none of which I had and none of which I'd submitted. Yet when I phoned, the film department secretary assured me that I was expected to show up to register for classes the following week.

When Anaïs called a few days later, I asked her, "Did you get me admitted to UCLA Film School?"

"No, I don't know anything about that." She sounded confused. "I'm calling to tell you about a teaching job waiting for you here in Los Angeles if you will accept it."

She had cooked up a faculty position with International College in Westwood, a British-style tutorial program started by some maverick UCLA administrators where, for a lot of money, students could get an advanced degree studying one-on-one with Marshall McLuhan, Buckminster Fuller, Judy Chicago, Ravi Shankar, Yehudi Menuhin, Lawrence Durrell, Kenneth Rexroth, Gary Snyder, or Anaïs Nin. So many students had signed on to study with Anaïs that she was able to tell the college she wanted me to co-teach with her. She would be the big name that pulled in the students and she'd meet with them at her house once a month, while I would do the bread-and-butter work of teaching them weekly.

"Do you think it's unfair that I'd be taking half the money and only doing a quarter of the work?" Anaïs asked me, concerned.

"No!" It would be more than I was making at IU for a fraction of the time. I could pay the rent on the beach house by myself and have enough free time to go to film school and become a filmmaker. I didn't understand how UCLA Film School had intuited my dream, but at this point I was willing to give myself over to fate, since all my intellectual effort to make a rational, politically correct career decision had landed me alone and miserable.

The prospect of film school and the teaching job Anaïs had created for me were handholds to a new beginning. But I knew I lacked the will to start over in LA. I couldn't face the shame of having been dumped by Philip and of my dumping my respectable academic career for the roulette wheel of filmmaking. Besides, I was so run down with weeping and malnutrition that I didn't have the strength to terminate my teaching contract and get back to the beach house before it was rented to someone else. The lights had all gone out in me.

It took all the energy I could muster to follow Anaïs's instruction to see a doctor. When he examined my infected foot he scared me by saying that if I'd waited much longer, he'd have had to amputate. How could I have ignored a blister that bad? Between sobs I told him how I'd been jilted by my boyfriend and no longer wanted to live.

He said, "If you don't get it together in a week, I'm putting you in the hospital."

"You mean to amputate my foot?!"

"No, a mental hospital."

I laughed, then realized he was deadly serious. When I left his office, I thought, *Thank you, you just made my decision a lot easier.* No way was I going to be locked up in a mental hospital in the middle of fucking nowhere!

I ran home hobbling on that blistered foot, called the chair who had hired me and told him my mother had had a heart attack (which was true, though she'd recovered), and I needed to go home. When he kindly offered to find someone to take over my classes for the semester, I immediately booked a red-eye flight to LAX, threw some things into my suitcase, and phoned one of my devoted students to drive me to the Indianapolis Airport.

While waiting for my student to arrive, I caught a glimpse of my gaunt, sallow reflection in the corroded bathroom mirror. There was no way that stricken face could return to Los Angeles and succeed at anything. Yet if I stayed in Bloomington I knew I would end up in that mental hospital.

I studied my mouth in the mirror. It was not just sad, it seemed narrower, and . . . bitter. I looked ten years older. I recalled what Anaïs had said about bitterness aging you, but how could I get rid of it? My heart was permanently broken and my psyche shattered.

I needed a new dream. One so buoyant that it could float like a hot air balloon and pull me out of the depths. As a child I'd imagined pretty clothes, a crown on my head, or a chocolate candy tree to keep myself from despair. I'd visualized myself as a famous movie star whom everyone wanted to touch, so I wouldn't care that no one touched me. I'd promised myself I would become a famous writer with her picture in a magazine, so it would no longer hurt that I was all but invisible. Later I'd imagined myself as a distinguished professor of literature so that people would have to respect me.

But having failed at those dreams, it was harder now to put my faith in a ginned-up fantasy to comfort myself. Now I knew the charlatan's gears behind my compensatory trick. But I did it anyway. I looked at my tear-ravaged face in the mirror and told myself: *You will go to film school and become the most renowned woman film director in the world. You will no longer be the fragile woman who was dumped and fell apart. You will be powerful and admired and you will direct movies that will win Academy Awards. No one will know that you fell off the wall and shattered. No one will be able to see the million cracks. It will not matter that you were admitted to film school without qualifying. No one will guess that you no longer care and have no hope, because you will act so driven that you will fool even yourself.*

# CHAPTER 30

# Malibu, California, 1974-75

## TRISTINE

I WAS ABANDONED AND ABANDONED again, and then I abandoned myself. I abandoned my hard-won career, and once I'd returned to LA, I abandoned my body to one man after another, just for the thrill.

When my plane landed at 5 a.m. at LAX, I hit the ground running on adrenalin. Arriving by taxi at the beach house at dawn, I cleaned the house, re-arranged the remaining furniture, napped for an hour on the cold waterbed, and showed up at UCLA in time to register for a full load of film production classes. Now I had to keep running hard and fast enough to keep the wolf of depression from catching my heels.

My mother could not have been pleased with my surprise visit after I told her that being an English prof hadn't worked out and I'd enrolled in film school. But she allowed herself no sign of disappointment, sautéed me a plate of mushrooms—my favorite dish—and offered me furniture from her endless stash to replace what Philip had taken from the beach house.

Likewise, my women friends came to my rescue. One held and rocked me for hours as I wept, another updated my wardrobe from her own closet, another helped me edit my assigned episode of *Gunsmoke* into a feminist satire so I wouldn't miss my deadline, and when I wailed about losing Philip, Renate mocked his Cockney accent and shagged hair to make me laugh. For her part, Anaïs spent hours patiently explaining to me her understanding of the cyclical low point of the dark night of the soul and how to trust the slow, inner process of healing.

She also picked up my ash-hot movie dream and ran with it like Renate's former all-star husband toward the goal post. Her eyes glittering, she confided to me, "If I were a young woman today, I would choose filmmaking," and she determined that I should become the female Fellini. She recommended films I should see, starting with her favorite, Ingmar Bergman's *Persona*; on my behalf, she tackled her friends who had anything to do with the movies. She scored us dinner and lunch invitations into the homes of directors, actresses, and producers she knew. They were elegant, elderly people, mostly European expats, who would have been pleased to help me were they still active in the business.

Anaïs was more successful looking out for me financially while I sustained the expense of film school. She promoted me as a freelance writer to supplement the teaching job she'd gotten me, telling magazine editors who wanted her for articles and reviews that they should hire me instead.

Like the prodigal son, I received more attentiveness than before I'd left. Anaïs and Renate were determined to save me, probably to make up for having failed to save Peter. No young woman could have asked for more devoted mentors when most in need. Anaïs coached me in positive thinking: "You get to choose your reality. You choose your thoughts." And Renate advised, "The cure to paranoia is to give events the most positive interpretation possible," giving an example: "You are so lucky to be rid of Philip. The gods were doing you a favor."

Both Anaïs and Renate tried to teach me about the release of forgiveness, but I preferred the energy of my fame-and-fortune revenge fantasies. Sabina was back, and she provided me with an eventful sex life to make up for my absent love life. She seduced younger guys in film school as well as older guys already on the fringes of the film business.

I was living the life Anaïs had invented by editing Hugo out of her Paris *Diaries*: I was a financially independent young woman with her own romantic house, where I invited lovers for the excitement each could bring, for as long as they pleased me. When dawn's pink light tinted the ocean, I would kiss my lovers farewell so I could enjoy my beach house alone and begin a new day of making movies. When the English department chair in Indiana phoned and, to my surprise, said they were holding my lectureship for me, I had no ambivalence telling him I would not be coming back.

As for Renate's awful revelation that Anaïs, when she was my age, had slept with her father, I dismissed it as Renate's temporary insanity brought on by hard liquor. Renate never mentioned the topic again, and I certainly would never ask Anaïs about it. Why would I think she would tell me the truth, anyway? I doubted there was anyone Anaïs told the truth to all of the time, though I'd also come to believe that she usually lied for the best of reasons, to help those she loved to love themselves.

She was again my savior and inspiration, my morning and evening star. I'd become so accustomed to her solicitous care of me, that I'd all but forgotten Renate's proviso: "Apprentices do services for their mentor."

The day before our last International College class of the semester, Anaïs phoned. "Would you stay for a chat, Tristine, after the students leave?"

When I arrived at Anaïs's house with the students, I was disturbed to see an off-kilter brunette wig hanging like drooping beagle ears on the sides of her small face. Though the question of her cancer always hovered, like a Halloween bat on a string, we darted around it. There was no denying now though that the chemotherapy was weakening her.

Despite the fact that her visualizations had not made the cancer go away, she still held faith that, combined with chemo, the imaging would work. I, too, believed she was curing herself because she appeared so happy, more sparkling, lighter than I'd ever seen her. My heart might be so broken it would never heal, but she modeled for me the courage of gaiety in the face of a cancer that threatened to destroy all the happiness for which she'd worked so long.

She told the students, who were confused by seeing her with hair a different color each month, "As long as I have to receive chemo, Rupert and I are having fun with it. One week he gets to make love to a blond, the next to a redhead, this week to a brunette!" Her laughter chimed.

The end of our class was announced, as usual, by Rupert clanking pots and pans in the kitchen. All the lingering students finally out the door, Anaïs rushed to the bathroom to re-adjust her wig, and Rupert slipped on Piccolo's collar for a walk, while I put on the kettle and assembled cups and Lipton tea bags.

"I finally found out how I got admitted to film school without applying," I said when Anaïs rejoined me. "When I was a grad student, I filed a half-page petition to take a film class but found out I couldn't take a class in another department without dropping out of the English PhD program. So I withdrew the petition, but the cancellation form evidently got lost and the petition went through. The film department chair called the English department chair for a recommendation and got such a good one that he admitted me to the film program on the spot!"

"Synchronicity!" Anaïs declared, knowing I understood exactly what she meant: through such meaningful accidents, life winks that you are on your path.

"That brings me to the reason I asked you to stay today," Anaïs began as we settled by the fireplace. "I know your dream now is to make movies, and what I am going to propose could delay that dream for a few years, so I want you to think about this carefully."

"Okay."

"I've been meeting with lawyers and making arrangements for my literary estate."

I didn't like the sound of "literary estate." It was the plan for when she would be dead.

"They told me I should select an authorized biographer," she continued. "Would you be my authorized biographer?"

Suddenly I was filled with confusion. The tide of indecision, in which I'd floundered before going to Indiana, rushed back in to swamp me. I had visualized finishing film school and getting into the movie business during the time she wanted me to spend writing about her life. At one time her proposal would have thrilled me, and I still coveted the hours alone with her that it would require, but I well knew what "authorized biography" meant. It meant leaving out her secrets and constructing a fictional version of her life to protect Hugo and Rupert. It meant telling her lies for her, which of course I'd already done, but doing so in print under my name. It meant crafting thousands of sentences that would hide the truth about her *mariage a trois*. It meant getting a biography published, but one that would be a ruse posing as scholarly research, a book that could discredit me for the rest of my life.

"You don't need a biography," I said. "Your diaries are your autobiography. It would be redundant."

"Yes, I know. But there are rumblings about people and publishers interested in having a biography written on me. We don't want some unsympathetic stranger snooping around in my life, do we? This would deter them."

"I see." I could feel my forehead furrow and consciously tried to smooth it. If I wrote her biography I would be entirely identified with Anaïs for the next three years at least, probably my whole life. I already grated at being seen as just an extension of her. Often my association with her was the only thing people found interesting about me. Her shadow was so large, and the contours of mine were so similar, that I feared my identity would always be subsumed under hers.

But how could I say no to Anaïs when she had created the teaching job that was supporting me, had fulfilled her role as my mentor in countless ways, had reached out to rescue me from despair in Indiana and tucked me under her downy wing? I knew how indebted I was to her and that it was my turn to repay her for my apprenticeship. If I was anything, I was a good soldier. The loyal one. The one who goes down with the ship. How could I say no to Anaïs?

"Why don't you think about it and let me know." She smiled.

The following week she phoned early, before I'd had my coffee. Tensing my shoulders as though expecting a guillotine's blade, I waited for her to ask my decision about writing her biography.

Her request was more urgent, though. In a strange, hoarse whisper she said she'd been flying back from a speaking engagement in northern California, when her abdominal pain became excruciating. "I have to go back in the hospital today, and I was supposed to appear Saturday at Royce Hall for that UCLA Fine Arts Speakers event."

"They can reschedule it," I said.

"No, it's sold out. They say it's too late to cancel. I want you to go in my place."

"I couldn't," I gasped. How could I do that with a few days' notice? How could I take her place in any case? "People just want you."

"You won't have to do it alone. I asked Jamie Herlihy, too, and he said yes immediately." I heard the implied reprimand. She urged, "You can just read the paper you wrote about *Diary II*."

The idea of standing at a podium and reading a long paper of literary criticism to 2,000 Anaïs Nin fans who'd come for her feted charisma truly seemed like a bad idea. "Your audience will walk out. They'll demand their money back."

"Jamie will just talk informally, so it won't all be your reading," Anaïs implored.

Unlike me, Jamie Herlihy was a literary star in his own right. He had written *All Fall Down* and *Midnight Cowboy*. His wit and Irish theatricality could hold an audience, while for me, a nobody, to read a long academic paper, when people had paid their money to see Anaïs . . . They would be outraged.

I said, "Renate should do it instead of me. It would be magical for people to see a living, breathing character from one of your novels." Anaïs didn't respond; I could hear muted coughing. I went on, "I could introduce Renate. Tell the audience how you wrote about her crazy adventures in Mexico and Malibu in *Collages*. Then I could read from *Collages*, and Renate would walk onto the stage. The real-life character! It would be surreal!"

Another muted coughing fit.

I added, "I bet Renate would love to do it!"

Finally, Anaïs recovered enough to say, "It's the wrong audience for Renate. Besides she's moving this weekend, so she can't.

"Please do this for me, Tristine," Anaïs pleaded. "I don't have the strength to call anyone else." Her voice was fading. I could hear the pain in it. A wave of fear unsteadied me as I realized she was going into the hospital again; she'd be hooked up to those ochre feeding-tubes again. I'd have to visit her there again, and that meant she wasn't getting better. She was getting worse.

"I'll do anything for you," I said, surrendering.

∞

Jamie Herlihy and I clung to each other in the greenroom. Our escort had just told us that Royce Hall was at capacity—they were turning away people, and the fire marshal had shut the doors.

"I'll be fine once I'm out there," Jamie said nervously.

"I won't," I said. "They're going to be bored out of their minds by my paper." I had the chills I was so scared.

"Just improvise. That's what I'm going to do. I'll discover what I'm going to say once I'm up there."

"I can't do that. I wish I could."

"Don't worry. I'll warm them up for you!" he called as our escort led him down a long hall with dim floor lights on either side, a gangplank to doom I would soon have to walk.

Twenty minutes later, I could hear bursts of laughter and applause from where I waited behind the stage. Anaïs's audience loved Jamie's ad-libbing, but they would not love my reading to them. Panic gnats threw themselves in concert against my temples. I didn't feel steady on my feet.

I needed to calm my panic or I would not be able to stand in front of that audience. It would be better to endure their anger and boos than to ruin the evening by failing to perform at all. I had been an actress, I reminded myself. I had been the lead in my high school plays. I didn't have stage fright then. What was different now?

Then I was playing a character, disappearing into another's personality. Now I had no character to hide within.

Out of desperation, I hit on a trick I that I've used many times since to deal with my stage fright. I make believe that I'm someone else going up on stage. I have been, at different times, Tom Wolfe, Hillary Clinton, and, once, the Holy Ghost. I decide that I won't go up there and that this more capable being will go in my body, and he or she will do the talking. That night, I decided since the audience wanted Anaïs Nin, I would let Anaïs go on stage in my body.

I assumed her graceful, erect posture as I climbed the fearsome steps to the podium. I set down my paper, paused and smiled as she would have, endowing love and understanding to the audience. I was grateful for the glaring lights that made the crowd a black empty space.

"I apologize that unlike Jamie Herlihy, I cannot entertain you. I'm here because Anaïs is in the hospital, and she asked me at the last minute to read an essay I wrote about *Diary II*."

There was dull silence.

I looked down at the papers in my shaking hands. Was the light bright enough to read? Barely. "I really do apologize that this literary criticism will be boring to many of you," I said with Anaïs's little laugh. "But this is what she asked of us, so please bear with me." I spoke a little about the importance of Anaïs's *Diary* and what she'd shared with me about her editing process, that each volume had been edited for its central theme.

Dead silence.

I explained that the topic of my paper was the theme of *Diary II*, Anaïs's theory of subjective time as equivalent to relativity. I thought I heard a few groans. I knew the topic was as abstract, as intangible as the black nothingness out there, but all I could do was go forward. I began to read, concentrating on what I was saying. Looking out into the void, I used my dramatic training to emphasize what little conflict there was in my paper: Anaïs's arguments with Henry Miller, her belief in the value of the diary's immediacy versus his belief in the distillation of memory required for literature. As I read, I heard Anaïs's voice coming through me, not her accent, but her rising and falling cadence, and since I quoted from her *Diary* extensively, her words mixed with mine. I poured all my love for her into reading her words.

At one point, when reading a passage of hers about the power of the present moment, I paused for emphasis and held the pause. The present moment. The only sound was the rhythmic breathing in the darkened auditorium, in and out, the beating wings of a great seabird, carrying us together to Anaïs's hospital bed.

When it was over and the audience had applauded, I felt light as paper, weightless as a ghost. Hugging Jamie good-bye, I collected my purse and jacket from the greenroom. I couldn't wait to be in my car on my way home, glad that it was over, ecstatic with relief that the audience hadn't booed me, that their ardor for Anaïs was so great that they would have sat through anything for her.

I felt my sleeve being pulled as I was almost out the door. I turned around to see the young woman escort who had led me with her flashlight down the dark tunnel to the stage. "Don't go yet. There's someone who wants to talk to you."

"I didn't invite anyone."

"The audience. They're asking for you."

She forcefully guided me to another door and opened it. There was a line of women, and when they saw me they smiled uncertainly, a hopeful, crazed look in their eyes. They were there for a piece of Anaïs.

I felt safe as long as the women were ordered in a line, but as soon as I started to talk with the first one, the rest broke out of formation, surrounding me, crowding me, suffocating me. I couldn't see a way out. I was frightened and tried to move through them, but they wouldn't let me. I could see they had brought gifts for Anaïs, handmade scarves, paintings, flowers and handcrafted books. Their tender, unripe faces were full of rapture like those of my students the night Anaïs visited the commune.

"You look so much like her!" a woman with a crooked smile cried, and others agreed.

"You have to settle an argument." A stout woman bustled forward with her middle-aged friend. "You really are Anaïs's daughter, aren't you?"

An innocent looking girl pushed a hand-beaded purse into my hands. "I made it for her. I want you to have it." Tears filled her eyes.

"I'll give it to Anaïs," I promised.

"I want you to keep it," she said and, trembling, came close for a hug.

Jamie eyed me suspiciously. I knew he was seeing me as the ambitious understudy eager to usurp her mentor's place, a ruthless

Eve Harrington in *All About Eve*. But he was mistaken. I didn't want Anaïs's place. I didn't want the purse beaded for her. I didn't want the gifts or the sweet-smelling bouquets thrust into my arms. I didn't want the suffocating hugs. I didn't want Anaïs's borrowed fame. To my amazement, I no longer wanted fame at all. Being surrounded by these excited, delusional people frightened me.

They showed me that people want to be fooled, and that it was easy to fool them. All I'd done was imagine myself as Anaïs, and people, needing her to be there, believed in the lie. It left me feeling inflated, pumped with helium, but also cynical. I'd satisfied the dream I'd held for so long of becoming Anaïs, if only for one night, but when it happened, it felt creepy—like being a body snatcher.

∞

Only three days later Anaïs, back from the hospital, phoned to find out how the event had gone. I still felt drained, as if my trick of becoming her in the auditorium and the rush of her fans had been a seizure that had left me limp, hollow, my ears ringing.

"How did it go?"

"Alright. They didn't boo."

"What else?

"I have a bunch of gifts to bring you. How did you get out of the hospital so soon?"

"What do you mean?" She sounded affronted.

"I mean all the other times you had to stay longer."

"Oh, they just had to fatten me up this time."

"Couldn't they have waited until after your appearance?"

"No, they thought I was that weak."

"Oh. I'm sorry. People really missed seeing you."

She said the purpose of her call was to invite me and Jamie to come tell her about the event, and she wanted both of us to stay after to meditate for her cure with the "white light people."

"What do they charge for that?" I asked skeptically.

"Nothing. They want to help. It's just white light, Tristine."

∞

There was total gridlock on the freeway and I arrived almost two hours late. The house was dark except for lit tea candles everywhere, and the white light people, teenagers in diaphanous robes, were ready to begin. Anaïs's eyes were shut so I put down the gifts and tried to creep unnoticed to an empty chair next to Jamie. The young men with scraggly beards and girls with long braids made a semi-circle around Anaïs, who sat up straight in a kitchen chair. The meditation, which one of the young men guided us through, was to feel the white light penetrating Anaïs's body, healing all her cells from the top of her head to her toes. I threw myself into it. With the effort of moving boulders, I concentrated on that white light dissolving her cancer cells.

My eyes were closed, but when I heard weeping, I opened them.

Anaïs was coiled into herself. "I turned against God." She struggled to speak between sobs. "Because of my father."

She looked like a trembling, terrified child instead of the woman I knew. The white light kids huddled together in consternation while Rupert rushed to her side and held her as she continued to sob uncontrollably. Jamie and I exchanged an alarmed look.

As I sat there not knowing what to do, Renate's revelation of Anaïs's adult incest with her father broke through my willed amnesia. I had convinced myself that it had just been Renate's drunkenness, but Anaïs's desperate cry and her emotional collapse in front of my eyes gave it credence. Was I witnessing the Oedipal curse that Anaïs had escaped until then? I recalled the terror and awe at the end of Sophocles's tragedy, where King Oedipus is cursed for his violation of the ultimate taboo—along with all his supporters.

Indeed, seeing Anaïs quaking with despair cursed me as well. It made me question her whole philosophy of self-healing through creativity. Anaïs had assured me, and proclaimed publicly, that diary writing and psychoanalysis had healed her from the wound of her father's abandonment. She credited her analysis with Dr. Bogner for enabling her to move beyond her obsession with her father and write about other subjects. She'd even claimed to have forgiven her father!

I had trusted that if I followed faithfully in Anaïs's footsteps, I would eventually outpace the effects of father abandonment: the crippling insecurity, the need for approval in a man's world, the abiding fear of loss, the attacks of anxiety and hyper-vigilance. I had believed myself blessed in one way: my intimacy with Anaïs, the person who shared my particular wound and had healed herself. She had gone on from an unhappy childhood like mine to a big life, savoring love, adventure, literary success, travel, and friendships. In maturity, she seemed to dwell not only on stage, but in life, in her wise and centered persona of Djuna. Her achievement of happiness had given me hope.

Now it appeared that I had been deluded. For here was Anaïs near the end of her life, hunched in a fetal position, sobbing about her father, the wound he'd inflicted still not healed, and she had let a bunch of pimply faced, eighteen-year-old white light zealots do it to her. If this could happen to Anaïs, after all the maturity she'd worked for, after her thousands of hours of psychoanalysis, after her tens of thousands of journal pages, what hope was there for me?

The leader of the white light group timidly leaned down to Rupert, who was holding Anaïs in his arms, her head buried in his chest, her hunched shoulders shaking as if palsied. "We'd like to try something we think might help."

Desperate, Rupert readily agreed, and the timorous young man told Anaïs to breathe with him as he counted. "Breathe in. One omm, Two omm . . ." Jamie and I saw Rupert nod that we could leave, and we tiptoed out.

The next day when I told Renate about Anaïs's tearful collapse she said, "Anaïs neglected her spiritual life all those years, and now when she needs it, it isn't there."

It sounded harsh, but I knew Renate was saying it as a warning to me.

∞

Several weeks later, Anaïs phoned sounding much better. "I didn't get a chance to speak with you the other evening, you got here so late. Jamie and I talked for two hours before you arrived."

Damn, I'd been hoping that she hadn't noticed how late I'd been.

She continued, "Come tomorrow while Rupert is out so we can have a visit just the two of us. We need to talk about my authorized biography."

Oh no! I'd thought that freighted idea was dead. Now I really knew I couldn't write it. With the fraudulence I'd felt while pretending to be Anaïs at Royce Hall, and having witnessed her spiritual despair, I wanted to be done with her lies. I'd seen the guilt her falsehoods had caused her, and I didn't want that in my life. I'd lost faith in her myth of "living the dream."

I wasn't alone. The Women's Movement had become more tough-minded and now found Anaïs to be an embarrassment whose soft "difference feminism" identified women stereotypically with emotions and intuition. I, too, felt myself pushing away from her. I tried to suppress a recurrent thought: the sooner she was gone, the sooner I would be free of her and her outdated philosophies. Options other than writing her biography were pulling on me, not ones I necessarily had the wherewithal to follow, but I knew if I agreed to write her faux biography, it would curtail any other options. My apprenticeship now felt like servitude, and I was eager for it to end.

When I arrived, Anaïs appeared remarkably recovered from her hysterical collapse, her eyes bright aqua stones. We settled on the built-in couch, and Anaïs for some reason began, "We never talked about those horoscopes you had drawn of the two of us."

Why was she bringing those up now when I'd given them to her the previous Christmas? Not knowing what to get her, I'd been talked into a commission by an astrologer who wanted to do an analysis of Anaïs's horoscope overlaid with mine, our "paired charts." I didn't believe in astrology, but I'd given Anaïs the beautifully hand-painted charts and analysis because I thought she did. She was always talking about being "under the sign of Pisces." She'd never thanked me for the Christmas gift, which baffled me because ordinarily she had exquisite manners.

Nor was she thanking me now. "I really do not believe in astrology."

"I thought you did. Both you and Henry Miller wrote about that astrologer Moricand you were friends with in Paris."

"Oh, him. I thought he was interesting for a while, but I learned a chart is no better than the person who makes it. It just tells you about the mind of the astrologer, and I prefer my own imagination."

"But don't you think the analysis of our charts was uncanny? She said we aligned like two adjoining pieces of a puzzle. She said my life's work would be as a popularizer of your work."

"Exactly! She wrote that everything you accomplish will come from your association with me!" Anaïs sounded angrier than I had ever heard her. "You aren't just my satellite!"

I was surprised. I'd assumed Anaïs would be pleased about the astrologer's emphasis on my devotion to her and her work. Was she now saying that I should not be too identified with her? Maybe this was an opening.

"But, you know, I'll be completely identified with you if I do your biography," I began.

"Oh, that's what I wanted to tell you," she interrupted. "I asked Evelyn Hinz to do it, and she said yes."

Evelyn Hinz? Anaïs had made a point of introducing me to Evelyn, an academic who'd recently visited Los Angeles from Ottawa, or was it Manitoba? Somewhere in Canada. At Anaïs's request, I'd driven Evelyn from a downtown hotel to Anaïs's house and dropped her off. Now I knew why and I felt used. I was startled by my sudden resentment and jealousy of Evelyn.

My alarm must have been apparent because Anaïs went on to explain. "Evelyn is working for tenure at the University of Manitoba. She can get grants to keep her going. They are giving her a sabbatical to write."

A moment earlier all I'd wanted was to get out of writing the biography; now I was offended that Anaïs had asked someone else, someone with the security of a tenure-track position and paid sabbaticals, which I'd given up. Someone who wouldn't be burdened by having to obscure the truth, because she didn't know the truth.

Anaïs was expert at reading me. She said, "You shouldn't be writing my biography, Tristine. It would take up all your time. You have your own work to do. Movies to make. Your own books to write."

At the moment I didn't want to do any of those things. "You have more faith in me than I have in myself," I grumbled.

"That's because you have yet to become your own person." She fixed me with her sea green eyes. "I can see the growth happening, though. You are stronger than you used to be. You are so much further along than I was at your age." I was pleased that she thought I'd grown stronger, but she added, "You are still afraid of your power, though. That's why you feel you need to wear a mask."

"I don't wear a mask," I protested.

"Not with me, but around other people. Jamie Herlihy says you are trying to appear as something that you're not. He's very perceptive about people."

Jamie Herlihy! He'd seen me wearing Anaïs's persona in Royce Hall and must have told her I was trying to usurp her. That was why she had changed her mind and chosen Evelyn.

I said, "You know that I admire you and I want to be like you—"

"Oh, I don't know why anyone would want that!" Her hand brushed away the thought as if it were smoke. "No, Jamie thinks you overcompensate; that you try to act sophisticated and Hollywood so you appear superficial, and that's not who you really are. I used to do that, too. I wore hats and flamboyant outfits, because I didn't feel interesting enough in myself."

"Maybe Jamie's right," I admitted to Anaïs. "Maybe I do want to seem Hollywood and glamorous because I'm afraid of being boring." I hoped that copping to it would stop what felt like her attack on me.

My admission did seem to disarm her. Her pitch lowered to her wise Djuna voice, soothing and gentle. "It's because you grew up in the Valley with such a limited life."

Even though I was upset, I was struck by her insight.

"But that is past now," she crooned. "Now you have interesting friends and work. You have a wonderful house at the beach. The research you have done on women's diaries is very important. I believe in your writing. I've shown you in every way that I want your friendship. Why do you think that is?"

"Because I'm devoted to you?"

"No, Tristine! I think you are a sensitive, intelligent, and talented person, and I'm telling you *not* to be devoted to me. To be my friend but to be devoted to your own growth. You know that in all the years we have known each other, you have never let me read your diary. Why is that?"

I told her the truth. That I was too embarrassed by the writing.

"Do you write about sex? You know how much I liked those tapes you made with your women friends."

Yes, I knew. I thought about reminding her that she'd never returned the tapes but realized that would only raise her hackles again. Yet I could hardly trust her with my diaries. I answered her truthfully and strategically: "Sometimes I write about sex, but that's not why I'm embarrassed. It's because my thoughts are all over the place and so much of my diary is just moaning and griping about my life. Believe me, my diaries aren't like yours. They're no fun to read, even for me."

"Tristine! You know my diaries are rewritten. You can't compare! Why don't you let me read just one volume?"

"My handwriting is so sloppy you'd never be able to make it out."

"Oh yes, after a few pages, I'll be able to."

I recognized she was not going to back down and conceded. "Maybe I could type out a volume like you used to." At least then I could cut out the most chaotic parts and the sexual descriptions she'd likely share with Rupert.

"Do what you wish." She sounded exhausted. "But don't wait long."

She didn't object when I offered to go.

My feelings were a jumble as I drove home—anger at Jamie Herlihy for telling Anaïs that I wore a mask; hurt that Anaïs had believed him; resentment that she'd led me on about writing her bio and then chosen Evelyn; but, at the same time, relief that I hadn't had to say no, which would have proven me an ingrate. I didn't envy Evelyn's task of wrestling with Anaïs's half-truths, yet I was jealous and resentful.

By the time I parked on Pacific Coast Highway and entered my house, there was a prickly worm in my gut trying to make its way out. I picked up my current diary, a heavy volume with wood covers. I released my resentment toward Anaïs, line after line, page after page. I wrote as fast as I could, not caring if it made sense, not caring if it was unfair, just purging it, and when it was all out, I slammed the journal shut.

After a quick dinner I sat at the table, gazing at the dark sea and abalone sky, and picked up the journal again. On a new page I wrote, *Why do I resent Evelyn for authoring Anaïs's bio, when I don't want to write it?*

*Because Evelyn is going to get a book published.*

I stared at the unexpected answer. This was like playing Magic 8 Ball; I could put in a question and get a response out of the void.

I wrote, I *thought I wanted to make movies. Isn't that what I want?*

Again, an unexpected answer came: *You do, but you don't have the money you need for film and processing, and no one is going to give it to you.*

I continued to write to myself, sometimes in dialog, sometimes free writing, confronting myself with the hard reality standing in the way of my dream of becoming a film director. Even if I could somehow borrow thousands of dollars to make a film that would win competitions, it was no guarantee it would get me an entry-level job in the film business, let alone convince somebody to give me millions of dollars to direct a feature. I had thought that since I'd found academia almost too easy, it meant that with effort I would succeed in the movie business. But I soon learned I wasn't the only one in film school to have promised myself I'd be someone if I became a director. Kids with big inheritances wore T-shirts that read, "All I Want to Do Is Direct," and they had the capital behind them to pay for production costs and designer jeans while they rode the expensive Hollywood merry-go-round, grasping for the gold ring.

I had no idea whose voice was confronting me with these unfair realities, but I could tell it wasn't some mystical message from another realm. It was too practical for that. It reminded me that, besides Anaïs's authorized biography, I'd had another opportunity to have a book published and even get an advance. An enterprising LA publisher had heard about my research on diary writing and asked me to write a how-to/self-help book on the subject. I'd discounted his offer as beneath me. I'd never even read a self-help or a how-to book except for *How to Win Friends and Influence People*, which I'd found in my father's left-behind library when I was thirteen. Yet the practical voice in my diary encouraged me to reconsider the publisher's offer.

Exhausted by hours of writing, I fell asleep with some relief but still no clarity. I awoke with one clear thought: I'd be a fool to have served Anaïs all these years and not accept what she could offer that no one else could—enlightened feedback on my diary writing, especially if I was considering writing a book on the subject. That morning I began to type out an old volume of my diary for Anaïs to read, editing as I went, cutting out the most cathartic and salacious parts.

A week later, I drove my typed pages out to Silver Lake. Before leaving them in the mailbox at the end of the long driveway, I printed on the envelope in black marker: *For Anaïs's eyes ONLY!*

I was alarmed when Rupert phoned a few days later. Had he violated that envelope despite my clear prohibition? That would be the limit! How could I go on with people who lacked basic decency?

"Anaïs is feeling very weak today," Rupert said, "but she has something she wants to tell you."

What could be so urgent, I wondered, if she was too weak to dial herself? Perhaps she couldn't wait to let me know the quality and exceptionality of my diary writing! Perhaps she realized she'd been foolish in her choice of Evelyn to write her bio and wanted to apologize to me.

After some muffled sounds, Rupert added, "Anaïs has been doing research on the persona for you."

What? That was Jamie Herlihy's criticism of me, that I wore a persona, a mask, that I was superficial. Anaïs had called just to harp on that again?

When she came on the line, her voice was so faint I could barely make out the words. "I remembered that Jung writes about the persona," she said, "so I went back and found in my diary what I wanted to tell you. Now that it's published with an index"—her dry laugh cracked—"I can find things in it."

She paused for such a long time that I worried something had happened to her.

Then from the receiver I heard the whisper of an aged, shrunken Sybil delivering a riddle as from an ampulla: "The mask should be held eighteen inches in front of the face."

I visualized a Venetian festival mask on a stick, cardboard thin. She was saying that because I didn't hold my mask far enough away, I didn't know the difference between myself and a persona, and that's why I was such a superficial phony.

I expected she would elaborate, but Rupert must have taken the receiver from her. "Did you understand that? A mask eighteen inches in front of the face."

"Yes, thank you," I said, feeling annoyed at his repeating her words. And that was it; he hung up. I was devastated. Not only had Anaïs not apologized to me, she'd stuck the knife in deeper.

A week later, Anaïs called again without Rupert's intervention. Her voice, though still faint, was back to its musical lilt.

"How are you?" she asked.

I exhaled with relief. I could tell by her tone that this time she was calling to soothe my feelings.

"I'm okay," I answered. "How are you?"

"Oh, I have good days and bad days."

I waited for her apology.

Instead she said, "I wanted to get back to you right away. I read your diary."

I stopped breathing. *Be calm,* I told myself. *She'll give you her compliments first.* The way she always did with the students.

She began, "Everything is there, other people, places, descriptions . . . but you are not there."

"But the whole thing is my point of view."

"Yes, but your feelings are absent, so the writing is superficial."

Superficial, that word again. How could my diaries be superficial? That was the worst thing you could say about somebody's diary, and she'd hardly said anything good. I bet she hadn't even read more than a page. She was still looking to justify Jamie's criticism of me.

She continued, "You need to ask yourself when you are writing, 'What did I feel?' You report what someone said but not how you reacted to it. And your intellect is a tyrant, a kind of madman that takes over."

How dare she! My intellect was the only thing about myself of which I was proud. She saw my trained intellect as a tyrant because she had no respect for rationality. She hadn't been through grad school! I rebutted, "I thought there was an excess of feeling. That's why I never let you read them before."

"Anxiety, exaggeration, and over-dramatization are not the same thing as real feelings, Tristine."

I quickly got off the phone for fear of saying what was on the tip of my tongue: *How would you know a superficial phony, Anaïs? You live your life as a lie. You're just repeating what Jamie said about me because you're still mad that your fans adored me in place of you at your tribute and that I didn't jump at the chance to write your phony bio. All you care about is your image, not about me, and despite how many times you say you aren't a narcissist because you gave your typewriter to Henry Miller, you* are *a narcissist! Just like my father. Just like your father who you slept with! And Renate says you did it to prove you were the most daring surrealist. Talk about a mad intellect!*

My ego lacerated, I crawled into a sea cave of isolation to moan. Once there, I used my diary, as I always had, to exaggerate, overdramatize my·feelings and sublimate them into intellectual abstractions. Only after what Anaïs had said, I couldn't help seeing what I was doing. So I tried Anaïs's advice to dive more deeply, just to see what would happen, writing on the page, *What do I really feel?*

It was humiliating to find the tantrums of an angry, resentful child—my "Ugly Trissy." I also found a punishing, exacting male voice that I named my "Internal Critic." I wanted to expel them both, but instead I began to converse with these previously unrecognized parts of my personality.

During this period of wounded introspection, I had nightmares that jolted me from sleep and sliced back in when I dozed off again.

Tidal waves crashed over my house. A violent man pounded on my front door, his fist smashing through splintered wood into my face. A repulsive, furry, one-eyed creature stared up at me imploringly from its pool of afterbirth.

The more I recorded dreams in my diary, the more I received, in clusters and cycles now, a hurricane of dreams. I was underwater with them; it took half the day just to write them down. In reward for paying attention, though, I began to have transcendent dreams. In one, I tossed in turbulent waves clinging to a raft below my house. From an open Dutch window, a serene "guru woman" watched me floundering below. In the morning I recognized that I was both figures and this began a series of dreams in which the same serene woman appeared as a priestess wearing a Grecian gown like Anaïs's favorite white muumuu, although she didn't look like Anaïs and didn't have her French accent. She wasn't Anaïs. She was a part of me, out of my unconscious. She was mine: the wise, essential self that Anaïs had characterized as Djuna and promised I would one day discover.

I had reached ground zero, but I had done what Jung warns those who would dive into the unconscious never to do: descend without a tether back into the real world. Not having his ties of home and family, I'd isolated myself and refused to come up for air.

I was determined to solve Anaïs's riddle before I quit.

*The mask should be held eighteen inches in front of the face.*

Anaïs did not say I should not have a mask. She'd said to hold it far enough away not to confuse it with my essential self.

I had confused a lot of masks with myself. I'd worn the persona of an uncomplicated coed at USC, of the seductress Sabina to hide my fear of men, of a staunch leftist-feminist to stand up to my father, and the bright makeup of a happy-go-lucky party girl in film school to cover the cracks of my shattered trust.

Anaïs certainly had worn masks, too—dazzling creations, their beauty attracting her followers and their artificiality repelling her detractors. She'd switched them with her acrobat's dexterity: the polished persona of an international banker's wife, the mask of a surrealist artist, the seductress she'd named Sabina, her impersonation of a forest ranger's wife, and the literary persona of a free, independent woman, created by eliminating any husbands from her public image.

No, Anaïs could hardly tell me to give up my masks when she'd so effectively flicked hers like flamenco fans. Maybe she was saying that personas, while seductive and useful, are not the dancer, and like the dancer's fan, they can be discarded, replaced, or retrieved when the music changes. Perhaps I could lay aside my current persona of a glamorous, up-and-coming filmmaker to adopt the prematurely mature persona of a wise, how-to-write-a-diary author, and afterward lay it down and pick up my hip filmmaker persona again.

CHAPTER 31

# Los Angeles, California, 1976

## TRISTINE

RENATE'S PHONE CALL WAS A barbed hook that pulled me up from my submersion. "When was the last time you saw Anaïs?"

With a stab of guilt, I realized that while nursing my bitterness and looking inward, I'd avoided Anaïs for over five months.

"You better go right away," Renate said sternly. "She's in the hospital." And she added bitterly, "You'll have to call Rupert to get permission. He's now her gatekeeper. He's barred me from the hospital."

"Why?"

"He never liked Anaïs spending time with me."

To my relief, Rupert seemed pleased to hear from me. He arranged for me to visit Anaïs at the hospital on an evening when he would be delayed because he was meeting with Digby Diehl of the *LA Times*. He asked that I keep her company until 6 p.m., when he should be back at the hospital.

Anaïs was alone when I arrived, propped against a pillow, writing in a small journal with her winged glasses on. She looked tiny in the

metal hospital bed. She wore a lacy negligee and a pink terrycloth turban that matched the color of her rouged cheeks.

To my surprise the room was bare of flowers or gifts. When word
had gone out the previous year that Anaïs needed a transfusion, young
women had circled the block at the Women's Building downtown to
give blood. Yet she appeared to have been forgotten now.

She glanced up and removed her glasses. Her heavily outlined eyes,
once jewel bright, had faded to dull gunmetal. "Come in, Tristine."

She leaned forward, an invitation to kiss her shrunken cheeks.
Above her head hung a translucent bag containing yellowish liquid.
When I leaned in to kiss her, I saw that the evil-looking tubing was
attached to a needle embedded in her bruised hand and I felt queasy.
Losing my balance, I fell towards the bed, her startled eyes flashing into
mine. I threw out a hand to catch myself on the edge of her mattress.

She winced. As I pulled myself upright I cried, "I'm so sorry! I hurt
you!"

She dismissed my concern with a wave of that poor hand, the tubing following like puppet strings. "I'm fine," she assured me with a
weak smile. "Pull up a chair."

I started to lug over a heavy steel chair, the only one in the room;
but it made such an ugly screech scraping the floor, I just perched my
bottom on its edge. I placed my large purse on my knees and dug in it
for the little toy bird I'd brought. Mother, who to her credit was never
jealous of my devotion to Anaïs, had found the little stuffed bird in one
of her boxes of junk. It had looked festive at Mother's house with its real
red feathers decorated with tiny pearls and mirrors, so I'd brought it to
the hospital instead of flowers. As Anaïs took it from my hand, though,
I thought what a puny gift it was, really just a Christmas decoration.

Trying to enhance it, I said, "I brought him to sing to you. But
you'll have to imagine his song."

Anaïs cupped the bird in her palms tenderly as if he were breathing. "I love him!" she cried, and made the same fuss over that token

gift as she'd made over my armful of Ginkgo leaves the first time we met.

I found myself whispering as to a child, "His feet have wire in them so we can put him wherever you want."

"Attach him to the bed post!" she exclaimed, pointing to the foot of the hospital bed. "He'll sing to me first thing when I wake up."

Her big smile in her shrunken face fell then, and her voice took on the sad strains of a violin in minor key. "I miss the finches in the morning at home."

"Renate told me you've been here almost a month this time," I said. "I'm sorry I haven't come before now. I didn't know you were in the hospital." I stopped, realizing from her astute look that it was futile to make excuses. I wanted to tell her that I was past the childish resentment that had made me stay away, yet I didn't want to bring it up.

But she did. "Tristine, did I hurt you when I criticized your diary?"

"Yes, but you were right."

"I didn't mean to hurt you. The drugs I take for pain make it hard for me to think sometimes. And I assumed you were strong enough for criticism now. You have grown so much."

"I'm not as strong as you think."

"Please forgive me. I felt there were things you needed to hear and I was afraid I might not have time to tell you."

"No, I should have—"

She waved her bandaged hand, wiping away the offense of my absence. "Thank you for coming while I'm in this awful place. I lose track of time here."

And with that, she cleared the distrust between us. We were again the best of friends, blood sisters, naughty ingénues in a tête-à-tête. She insisted on being brought up to date on my life. I told her about the dream work I'd been doing and about the contract I'd signed to write the how-to book on diary writing.

"That's wonderful! Get it done in a jiffy!" She raised her unbandaged hand from the bed and tried to snap her fingers, but could not make the sound. "Show me your book proposal so I can write you a preface. But don't wait too long."

She meant *don't wait until I'm gone*, and this time I knew it was real. The knowledge that she would not be in the world opened as an infinite void before me.

I focused on her black-penciled eyes, the outlining thick and uneven, a child's frightened eyes looking out from an attempt at grown-up makeup. Her voice became small. "They're going to do tests tomorrow. I'm afraid this time."

It broke my heart to see her so shrunken and fearful. She was begging me for reassurance. More than anything I wanted to give it to her, something to make up for my neglect over the past months. I would have said anything to comfort her, to give her a moment of peace, of relief; just that morning, on the phone, Renate had suggested a way.

"You know what Anaïs wants, don't you?"

Renate had asked rhetorically, though I felt obliged to answer: "No."

"She never really cared about money. She doesn't want fame. She wants glory."

"And how is glory different from fame?"

"Fame is in your lifetime and disappears. Anaïs has had that. What she wants, what she has always wanted, is glory—to be remembered forever with admiration."

So when Anaïs turned her head to me on the starched pillow and pleaded, "I'm afraid I'm dying," I promised, "You cannot die, because you will always be remembered."

I saw the corners of her thin lips curl slightly upward, so I continued, "Young women will read you for centuries to come. Over and over again, they'll discover their sexuality through you. You are time-less because you have given voice to the eternal woman."

Seeing a glint in her eyes, I went on, not caring that I was repeating myself, not caring that I was gushing, trying to express my passion to her with my hyperbolic declarations of her undying glory, standing like an acolyte, hands at my sides, crying out what was in my heart. "Through you, women will find their inner life. Coming of age will not have to be so lonely for girls anymore. You will have daughters of daughters, who will find the second birth by reading your diaries."

She struggled to raise herself in the bed. "Prop up my pillow, please. I'm enjoying your company. I've been spending too much time with the wrong people."

By "the wrong people" she must have meant Evelyn Hinz and those hippie white light people. I was glad she saw she should be spending time with me instead, but that meant I had to keep coming up with things to inspire her. I wanted to exclaim my love for her, to cry out that I could not bear to lose her, but I was afraid it would quicken her fear that she was dying.

I ventured, "I've been thinking about this card deck of women authors I had as a girl. There were cards for Louisa May Alcott and Harriet Beecher Stowe and Edith Wharton. Now they're going to have to add your picture, and even girls of seven will know who you are."

"What do girls do with the cards?"

"You're supposed to play a game like Fish, but we made them trading cards and begged or poached our favorite authors from each other."

"Did they have George Sand in the deck?"

"I don't think so. Maybe it was just American women. But you're an American author."

"You see me as an American author, *Tchrristine*?" Her French accent was so pronounced that for a moment I doubted myself.

But I answered, "Absolutely! You're as all-American as F. Scott Fitzgerald!"

As I said it, I realized how much like Fitzgerald's mythic character of Jay Gatsby Anaïs was. She had Gatsby's charm and generosity and his romantic readiness to stake all for the dream.

She was looking much better. Her eyes would never again be turquoise, but the sea's depth had returned to them.

"Could you hand me that mirror?" she asked me. "And my makeup bag?"

Somehow I managed to remove them without toppling her makeshift pyramid of books, mail, and notepads on the nightstand. She applied a coat of pink lipstick, just a shade deeper than her turban, and pancaked her face. "Rupert will be here soon." She gave me her freshened smile. "Now what was that about your women authors deck?"

"You'll have your own card! You'll be like the queen of spades!"

"Except I'd have to be the queen of hearts!" She grinned, her gums showing more than usual. It made her look like a nine-year-old who hadn't grown into her teeth yet. For a moment time shifted and we were both little girls playing with our deck of women authors, revering them, and imagining what it would be like to be one of them.

She said, "I do hope they add George Sand to the deck. I've always wanted to be in her company, you know."

Her words echoed what she'd told our first class of International College students, when she still looked healthy, before the chemo had drained her. She'd been discussing with the students the obstacles Aurore Dupin had faced as a woman writer in the nineteenth century, why she'd assumed the male pseudonym of George Sand and worn britches. Anaïs described how Sand had outraged the public by openly taking lovers such as composer Frédéric Chopin, and, more discreetly (it was rumored), her friend Marie Dorval.

"It would have been wonderful to live in Sand's time," Anaïs had exclaimed, "when friends had to travel long distances by carriage to visit, so would stay at each other's houses for weeks on end, putting on plays and entertainment. There was time and opportunity for real intimacy between friends then."

I'd wanted to ask her what she meant by real intimacy between friends. I needed to know if she had ever loved a woman like George Sand with Marie Dorval. My wound from Philip's betrayal was still so fresh, and my distrust of men so jagged, that I had been wondering if I should change my sexuality to loving women. Anaïs was my model in so many ways, and if she'd known a woman's love, I believed she could show me the way.

When we'd ushered the last of the students out and I stood alone with Anaïs in the entry hall, I found the courage to say, "Anaïs, have you ever had an affair with a woman?"

Her Mona Lisa smile contradicted her answer. "No." I didn't know whether to believe her, given her proclivity for deception.

She'd looked in my eyes and said gently, "Why do you ask?"

"I want to know everything about you. I was sure from reading the Paris diaries, that you and June—"

She was slowly shaking her head no.

"No? But the way you wrote—"

"I wanted that with June, but she denied me," she said plaintively.

I still didn't know whether to believe her. In her published diaries it certainly had sounded as if she and June Miller were in a passionate sexual relationship, but perhaps her love for June had been as my love for Clara: undeclared, unconsummated, and even more intense for that.

Standing in the hallway, Anaïs put her hands on my shoulders and brought her face close to mine. I thought she was going to kiss me on the mouth and I didn't know what to do. It felt aberrant because she was so much older than I, but I loved her too much to pull away.

She didn't kiss me. She whispered, "In my next life, I will love women."

I heard my own husky voice: "There will be a place in my house for you."

I was glad that, for once, without thinking, I'd found the right words. I'd found a way to tell Anaïs I loved her, even if inexactly as in a foreign language. The words of erotic desire could only approximate my passion for her, which was so much larger and more enduring.

In the two years between that intimate conversation at her house and my visit to the hospital, I'd learned that switching one's sexuality was not really a matter of choice. Yet that day in her hospital room, I realized also that no relationship I'd ever had with a man was as intense as my ardor for Anaïs.

Feeling shy suddenly, I told her, "You know, you're the star pioneer of the book I'm doing on diary writing. That astrologer had it right, Anaïs. Everything I do, everything I accomplish, came from you. I am continuing your work, only in my own way."

Anaïs gave me her glorious smile of approval. She said, "You are my best daughter."

Without modesty, I crowed, "I think so, too!"

"But I don't see how you can say I write anything like Fitzgerald."

"Not stylistically, but you both believe in the American dream, that we have the right to re-invent ourselves—"

Just then the hospital room door opened. I turned, thinking it was Rupert.

But the tall, stooped figure in the doorway, leaning on an ebony cane—was Hugo!

My eyes swung back to Anaïs, who was so panicked that she tried to climb out of her hospital bed but was pinned there by the stretched tubing.

She scolded Hugo, "I told you not to come!"

The disappointment on his long hound's face was hard to witness.

"Anaïs," he pleaded, "why do you refuse to see me? I know how ill you are."

"How do you know?" She focused past him and I did, too, knowing that Rupert could arrive any minute.

"I spoke with your doctor," Hugo said gently.

"You didn't have my permission!" she cried.

"Anaïs, I'm your husband." He had tears in his eyes. "Do you want me to leave?" he offered pitifully.

"No, not after you've come all this way." She sighed. "I didn't want you to see me looking like this." She touched spindly fingers to her pink turban.

"You are as beautiful to me now as the day you were my bride," he said.

I interrupted, "I'll guard the door so you two can have some privacy." I hoped Anaïs would understand that I'd be on the lookout for Rupert.

She said, "Hugo, you remember Tristine."

I tried to sound welcoming—"It's nice to see you"—but added, amazed at the ease of my invention, "The doctor said that Anaïs is not to have long visits."

"Right," he said distractedly, clearly eager for me to leave.

As he watched me back out the door, behind him Anaïs mouthed, *Stop Rupert!*

∞

I sat on a chair just outside Anaïs's door trying to quiet the blasting alarms in my head. Anaïs had kept Hugo and Rupert apart for thirty years, and any minute now they were going to converge when she was too weak to deal with it. The only hope was to get Hugo to leave before Rupert arrived. As if I could delay Rupert by imagining it, I saw him sitting in gridlock on Sunset Boulevard and driving in circles, unable to find a parking place.

When I checked my watch for the tenth time, Hugo had been in the room with Anaïs for over fifteen minutes. I decided I should go in to interrupt them, but just then I heard fast footsteps approaching. I looked up to see Rupert sprinting down the industrial green corridor!

He looked flushed. I ran up to him. "You're early."

"We just drank champagne at the meeting. We don't have to look for donors because Joan Palevsky is writing a check for the whole $250,000 for Anaïs's diaries!" He pushed past me. "I have to tell Anaïs."

I stepped in front of him. "You have to wait. She's getting a procedure."

"I'm going in!" Stubborn as always. As he pushed past, he issued an order: "You can leave now."

"But she asked me to say goodbye before—"

"I'm telling you to leave!"

I was so upset at his rudeness that I fled down the hospital corridor.

# CHAPTER 32

# Silver Lake, California, 1976–77

## TRISTINE

As I drove to visit Anaïs, now home after two weeks in the hospital, I dreaded learning what had happened when Rupert discovered Hugo at her bedside. Just when she and I had come so close! I'd run like a rabbit, frightened by Rupert's bark instead of helping her. She'd been relying on me to save the day and in the end I'd failed her.

She answered the door in an empress muumuu with a smock tied over it, looking much better, her color back. She apologized that she had to sort through some files while we visited. "I'm organizing my papers for UCLA."

I fetched a chair from the kitchen and set it outside her office door.

Having seen her condition in the hospital, I was surprised by her strength as she lowered herself to her knees to remove the lid from a cardboard file box. I offered to get down on the floor to help her, but she refused and then ignored me as she examined the contents of a file.

Finally I said, "Rupert told me at the hospital about Joan Palevsky's donation to buy your diaries."

She didn't respond, seemingly absorbed in deciphering a file name. Was this going to be it? I would squirm and talk, and she, doing busy-work, would act as if she had not heard me? I declared, "I tried to stop Rupert, Anaïs!"

"Dear Tristine." She looked up at me affectionately. Was she giving me the extra sweet treatment before cutting me out of her life, as I'd seen her do with people who had not been sufficiently faithful? Or was she really forgiving me because, after my declarations at the hospital, she loved me now as my mother did, unconditionally?

I ventured, "What happened when Rupert discovered Hugo at your bedside?"

"I will tell you. Only first, let me tell you about my visit with Hugo, before Rupert barged in."

∞

# ANAÏS

Hugo leaned his cane against her nightstand. That motion was enough to topple Anaïs's glasses from the pyramid of mail and books. Looking down at the floor, he assured her that her glasses hadn't broken and lowered himself, clasping the bars of her hospital bed, to retrieve them. Winded from his effort, he braced himself against the bed frame as he handed the glasses up to her.

She managed to balance them again on the makeshift pyramid as Hugo, still kneeling and holding onto a metal bar on the bed, gazed up and declared his love for her, begging her to come home with him. She looked down on him beneficently, realizing that he could not walk out on her now—he couldn't seem even to get back on his feet. Nor could he play on her guilt, because she was the one close to death who needed sympathy. It was the perfect time to confess to him.

She said, "Hugo, darling, we have always had a sophisticated marriage, one based on love and respect. Several times I've tried to tell you that there was another man in my life, but you didn't want to hear it."

"I don't want to hear it now," he grumbled, looking down at the linoleum floor, evidently resigned to remaining on his knees.

"But you have to listen now, because this other man, his name is Rupert Pole, was not just an affair. I married him."

Hugo looked confused, as when he would wander into the kitchen, open a cabinet door, and be unable to recall why he was there. After a long delay, he said, "You couldn't marry him. You're married to me."

"Because I love you so much, I could never leave you and never divorce you. So I did something worse, something illegal."

She watched her words tear off the blinders he'd worn through their marriage. His face slowly fell and his voice capitulated. "I know lawyers who can take care of messes like that."

"I have a lawyer. A woman lawyer. It's taken care of. But I'm dying and I have to clear things up with you."

This man had suffered so many shattering blows, she thought with compassion. The loss of his income and pension, his health, his pride in accepting an allowance from her. Now this, his memory of their happy marriage. "You were everything to me: father, husband, friend, and lover," she assured him, "and it will always be so. I will make sure that after my death you will continue to receive your income and that your medical care will be covered by my estate."

"You're not going to die! I'll get you the best doctors at Sloan Kettering. You can't stay in the hands of these bushwhack, West Coast doctors!"

"This is where I want to be. I want to die in the house Rupert built for me here. Until then, I want to swim in my pool and feel the California light."

He was weeping.

"Please don't cry, Hugo. Please forgive me. My healer, Dr. Brugh Joy, believes it is my guilt for loving more than one man and my deceptions that caused my cancer."

He looked up. "No!"

"You can help save my life, dearest, but only by absolving me. The situation I created was unusual, but please try to see it within the realm of the human and thus forgivable. Please forgive me, and be my savior one more time."

"Yes, yes, I forgive you! There is nothing to forgive. I always knew I only had a part of you. You were a creature of flight and had to fulfill your nature."

*What a beautiful thing for him to say*, she thought, and then he admitted, "I knew that to hold onto you, I had to let you go, or I would lose you completely." He looked up from where he still knelt on the floor. "Thank you for staying my wife."

"Even if not yours alone?"

"Yes." He started to weep again.

"Stop, Hugo, darling. I can't bear to see you cry. Look in my eyes as we used to do for hours when we were first in love."

He raised his faded gray eyes to her obediently. She leaned down toward him to touch the side of his face. "Do you remember when I told you I had found the secret to happiness?"

He wiped his eyes, trying for stoicism, for manliness. "I'm sorry, I don't, Anaïs."

"My trick of displacement?"

"Please don't tease my bad memory. I've just received a shock."

"I've been using my displacement trick here in the hospital. Instead of writing in my diary about my pain, I write about music. I imagine death as a rising symphonic crescendo. My secret to happiness is that I give myself completely to the joyous moments when they come. And when it comes to the catastrophes, I use my imagination to displace myself." She stroked his cheek. "You're an artist, my talented Ian Hugo. You can transcend this pain with your imagination. Just think of me as on another journey." He kissed her fingers as they brushed his mouth, and she bent down closer to him. "As for the joyous moments, dearest, we savored them together, and I am so happy it was with you. You have been my true husband for fifty years. Nothing and no one can take that away from us."

He was gazing at her now in wonder, as in their courtship days and early marriage.

"Please, Hugo, get off the floor. There's a chair you can sit on."

He grabbed for his cane but could not manage to get off his knees even when he pushed himself against the bed. He flailed, losing his balance, and caught himself on the bars of the hospital bed with both hands, his ebony cane falling to the floor.

Once he realized he hadn't broken anything he laughed, chagrined, and Anaïs laughed with him to ease his embarrassment. "Oh, we are a pair, aren't we? One on crutches and the other in a hospital bed!"

When their laughter finally subsided, Anaïs, wiping tears from the corners of her eyes, said, "Stay there. I think I like you kneeling." She touched his face again. "Now, please, listen to me carefully. This is important. Rupert is young, sixteen years younger than I am. He is physically able to lift me and prepare the foods I have to eat. He can take care of me. Would you deprive me of that comfort? That is why I have to stay with Rupert."

It wasn't the only reason, of course. Sex had given her a connection with Rupert that she'd never shared with Hugo, but she had been so candid, finally, that this omission to save what remained of Hugo's ego was inconsequential.

Struggling for dignity, Hugo said, "I can't go against your wishes, but at least let me come visit you regularly now that I know the truth."

"No, it's too expensive, and it will be too hard on your health. There should be only one invalid at a time."

"But I can't go on being banished like this," he begged. "I'll die of worry."

"I'll speak to Rupert. I'll ask him to let you phone," she promised.

But, of course, first she had to tell Rupert he was not her only husband.

Rupert was in no state to listen to anything when he barged into her room.

Hugo grabbed for his cane and successfully rose from his knees as Anaïs officially introduced them. "This is my husband Rupert Pole. Hugo Guiler."

Instead of putting out a hand to shake Hugo's, Rupert bellowed, "What's he doing here? I thought we agreed all visitors would go through me!"

"I was as surprised to see Hugo as you are," Anaïs said calmly, and begged Hugo to leave the room. "You understand, Hugo, dear," she said, "so I can have the same talk with Rupert."

Leaning heavily on his cane, a fragile old man, Hugo shut the hospital room door behind him.

Anaïs said to Rupert, "Sit down please, darling. We need to talk."

The heavy metal chair screeched as Rupert pulled it to her bedside and sat.

"What's going on?" he demanded. "Why is Hugo here? Does it have to do with all that estate-planning? That has got to stop, too!" She just watched him indulgently until he realized he was sounding like a bully. Abashed, he mellowed his tone and told her, "I have good news. We have a donation for the entire cost of UCLA acquiring your diaries."

Anaïs was overcome with relief. The money would help take care of Rupert and Hugo after she was gone! It would afford Hugo a full-time nurse when the time came and fund a literary trust to pay Rupert to keep her name alive. Ten years before, she'd re-written her *Diary* to cater to the times, a desperate gamble. It had paid off in a trifecta, with book royalties, fame, and now this bequest for her two men.

"Rupert, you are going to have to look out for Hugo when I'm gone. You have to promise me."

"I promise, but we won't talk about you being gone." His anger had dispersed. It was a storm she had learned to let pass, knowing that when it did, his essential goodness would shine again. He gently lifted her bruised hand with the needle in it and kissed the damp palm. "You are going to get well."

"You and I both know that isn't true."

"No, I don't know that isn't true!"

"I believe you do know because otherwise you would not be eyeing my successor."

The veins reddened on his nose. "What do you mean? There could never be a successor to you."

"I mean your new girlfriend." She was referring to the Japanese literature student who had come to pay respects to her and had caught Rupert's eye.

He overreacted and countered, "Anaïs, this is crazy! How much of that Darvon did they give you today?"

She tried to stay in her wise, serene Djuna voice. "Rupert, I thank you for trying to protect me from the truth, as I always tried to protect you, but I want to tell you that it is alright." She struggled to resist her tears at the thought that she would be gone and another woman would love him, would swim in her pool with him, would receive his caresses. She snuffled. "I approve of your choice. She is lovely. She is exactly the woman I would have chosen for you."

"Anaïs! What is this about?"

"I never divorced Hugo."

"What do you mean? That IRS stuff again?"

"I want you to forgive me as Hugo did when I told him that I married you while I was still married to him."

She waited for his rage to erupt, but her words had not yet hit their mark. "Are you talking about when we got remarried in Mexico? You've lost me."

"I have learned that some women," she said in her most soothing voice, "at least myself, can love two men at the same time, though in different ways. And I believe it is true for a man, for you right now. I don't doubt for a moment that you love me with your entire being, darling, and that does not preclude you from desiring someone young and healthy."

"Stop it! I'm sorry I even looked at her!"

"Rupert, you will need a woman when I'm gone. I would prefer that you have someone to love and take care of you."

Now he had tears in his eyes, but she continued, "I tell you this because I am releasing you and forgiving you, and it is what I am begging from you in return. To forgive me for not being able to let go entirely of Hugo. As you know, he saved me and my family from poverty, and out of gratitude I could never injure him, and so I never asked him for a divorce."

"But you told me you were divorced. I . . ."

She knew he was waiting for her to make some excuse, to retract her words. She'd always saved him by coming up with something, so that he could continue to believe in her. But this time she just gazed at him sorrowfully. He pulled back, realizing what she had managed to keep at bay all these years, the magnitude of her deception.

She did not backtrack. She continued forward, fueled by the unfamiliar wildness of truth telling. "I could not deny myself the opportunity to love you and be your wife, so I became a bigamist. All the back and forth to New York? That was why. I had, I have, two husbands."

Though his jaw was still clenched, he looked defeated.

"When I die, you and Hugo will both be beneficiaries of my estate." She had his full attention now. "But for the all-important job of executor, I have chosen the man who understands and loves me the most, the one to whom I am most deeply bonded, the one who is my true love. You, Rupert."

"I love you so much, Anaïs!" he cried.

"So please tell me that you forgive me. Set me free from guilt as I have freed you."

"I do."

"Please say the words, 'I absolve you.'"

"I absolve you, Anaïs," he repeated with all his actor's intensity.

# TRISTINE

"Tristine! I'm free! I told them both the *trrut*. Everything," she exalted, a youthful lilt in her voice as she placed a hand on the edge of her desk to help her rise from kneeling. Once upright, she raised both arms in triumph. "And they both forgave me!"

*What else could they do*, I thought. *Camille on her death bed.*

"No more guilt, no more hiding," she sang, as if to make sure I understood the importance of her release after all her years on the trapeze. She had swung between those two men in terror of falling off, of one of them letting go of her, of inflicting pain on one of them, and now she rejoiced: "I'm really free!"

I grinned back at her, ecstatic to see her so happy.

"Rupert really has accepted the situation." She pulled open a drawer in the corner file cabinet. "Hugo phoned here last Sunday, and Rupert greeted him as if they were old friends. Then Rupert handed me the phone and took Piccolo for a walk."

"That's wonderful," I exulted with her, though I had an unexpected aftertaste of envy. "So now Evelyn Hinz gets to write the truth in your authorized biography, now that your story has a happy ending."

"Tristine!" She broke into a pink-gummed whinny. "You really have gone Hollywood!"

Knowing she was teasing, I came back, "Just because Hollywood knows people love a happy ending doesn't make it wrong. They taught us in film school that the audience will forgive you almost anything if you give them a happy ending."

"Perhaps, but even with a happy ending, Hugo and Rupert would be seen as cuckolds." I thought from the way she said "cuckolds," making it sound in her high notes like a cuckoo calling, that she might not really consider that a major hindrance, but then she repeated the old warning: "My trapeze has to remain a secret, even after I'm gone. You can't tell anyone until—"

"I know, Rupert dies."

"Yes," she said hesitatingly. "Until the last one dies. Which will probably be Rupert because he's younger."

"Rupert doesn't really have a girlfriend, does he?"

"Oh, yes he does, and I've seen how they look at each other," she said evenly, but then her eyes welled as she clutched my hand. "I know Rupert cannot be without a woman, and I don't want him to be alone in this house when I'm gone, but Tristine!" Her tears overflowed. "I am suffering so from jealousy."

I was furious with Rupert. How could he be so careless as to let Anaïs know that he had found someone already? Why couldn't he have waited? Why couldn't he, at least, have been vigilant in hiding it, as she had been for him? I wanted her to be joyful again, as she had been only moments before, but her tears were smearing the ink on the manuscript in her hands.

Not knowing how to comfort her, I restated what she had once said to me: "If you love someone, you will be jealous. If you weren't jealous, it would mean that you don't really love Rupert, and you do."

She clung to my words. "Dear Tristine, how did you get so wise?"

"From you."

She gave me a grateful smile and pulled a tissue from a box by her typewriter. Drying her tears, she changed the subject, practicing her trick of displacement. "You know that little red bird you gave me at the hospital? You inspired me! I asked Rupert to tape-record the finches in the yard. He went out at dawn to capture their song so I could replay it at the hospital while looking at your sweet bird on my bedpost!"

She then dashed around her office, placing files into storage boxes like a girl assembling her trousseau. She seemed so fully recovered that I dared to hope that Dr. Brugh Joy was right: guilt had caused her cancer, so released from her guilt she would be cured.

This is where I wanted her story to end, with her elation and freedom. With our friendship reconciled and my love proclaimed. She had flown higher than any woman, taken more emotional risks, and at the eleventh hour, pulled off a last triumphal arabesque. In the end, she'd told the truth to both husbands, and they loved her so much, they both forgave her to save her life.

When I think about Anaïs and Hugo and Rupert, I don't see how it could have been any other way. Both men kept themselves from knowing about Anaïs's double life because they wanted to be with her. They both realized that having half of Anaïs Nin was better than all of any other woman.

When Anaïs would say to me, "I am a woman ahead of my time, and that has been my greatest tragedy," she was usually referring to her writing. But certainly she was ahead of her time in creating her own designer relationship, as well. Today women marry women, men marry men; no one thinks it odd when a woman marries a man sixteen years her junior. Interracial relationships are unremarkable, polyamory is a lifestyle option, and open marriages have their own online dating sites. Today, when over half of marriages end in divorce, people wonder if one form of relationship can fit all. Today I have girlfriends who've chosen never to marry and don't regret it, others who have decided that what they really like is several lovers at the same time, and others who have chosen celibacy. Today, scientists speculate that some people, like some field mice, may have a "monogamy gene" while others lack it.

Today, I suspect that Anaïs and Hugo and Rupert might have discreetly maintained their *mariage a trois* without all the lies and guilt from which she felt so joyously freed that afternoon.

∞

The story did not conclude with my Hollywood ending, though. Months later, Anaïs was back in the hospital and this time it wasn't to fatten her up. It was to eviscerate her.

"They removed everything, even her intestines," Renate told me. "It's too late. The cancer is everywhere."

I visited Anaïs at home after she was released, as soon as Rupert would allow. On an overcast morning, he let me in, instructing me to wait in the foyer. A priest, so young he still had acne, scurried by me to the front door. He had the blank, traumatized look of someone who has just seen through a portal into Hell.

A weight plunged through me. Was I too late? Had the priest been there to give Anaïs last rites? As the weight fell, it snagged on a barb and pulled on my gullet hard. I thought I had put aside my judgments of Anaïs, but her calling for a priest felt like a final betrayal. Through all the years I'd known her, Anaïs had adamantly set herself against the Catholicism of her girlhood and called herself a pagan. Yet it had to have been Anaïs herself who'd instructed Rupert to request Extreme Unction. Rupert was, if anything, anti-papist.

I remembered then that Anaïs had befriended the pop artist nun Sister Corita, who had belonged to the Immaculate Heart order of my high school. My resentment dissolved as I recognized I'd likely call for the last sacrament at the end, too. It was, after all, an irresistible deal, a get-out-of-Hell-free card. No matter how many sins you had committed in your lifetime, the Catholic sacrament would wipe your soul clean as a just-baptized baby's.

What I'd resented moments before now swayed me. If Anaïs could revert to her Catholicism, why couldn't I do likewise? I prayed: *Holy Mary, Mother of God, please let Anaïs still be alive and let me be the one to receive her last words.*

I heard slidings and brushings from behind the hospital screen set up in front of the bedroom area and the faint sound of whimpering. She was still alive!

As a uniformed nurse retracted the screen, Rupert led me to a narrow hospital bed that had been set up next to the queen bed with its soiled lavender backrests. Rupert and the nurse disappeared into the kitchen, leaving me alone with Anaïs. I thought it was incredibly generous of him to give me these last precious moments with her.

Her lids were half open, her face colorless, her skin stuck like damp silk to her skull. But she was breathing.

I leaned down to kiss her and was taken aback by the stench around her. I avoided inhaling as I whispered, "I saw a priest leaving."

"I agreed to let a priest come," she said in a hoarse, barely audible voice.

I said, "I always thought the Catholic Church had an advantage in having the sacraments, especially the last one."

She didn't say anything. She looked in pain. She tried to shift her body and the stench became worse. Rattled, I carried on, "I always thought Extreme Unction was the best sacrament. You get to have oil rubbed on your face, and, without having to do anything, all your sins are removed."

I looked for oil on her forehead, but not seeing any, assumed the nurse had wiped it off.

Suddenly agitated, Anaïs tried to raise herself. In a voice surprisingly strong, she cried, "Extreme Unction? That's for when one is dying!" She glared at me. "You think I'm dying?"

Oh my God! How could I have been such an idiot? She wasn't dying yet at all. I had imagined she was dying, which made it look as if I couldn't wait for her to go! Now she knew what I'd tried so hard to hide: that I was eager for her to be gone so I could find out who I was—without her.

I wanted to disappear through the floor. I stammered, "I just saw that priest, and—"

"I gave him my confession! Usually Father Lucas comes but he couldn't today so they sent a substitute."

I tried to backtrack. "No, I know you aren't dying. I was just saying how Extreme Unction is my favorite sacrament. Confession is good, too. What did he give you for a penance?"

"Nothing."

"Nothing? That's amazing! I used to get ten Hail Marys and ten Our Fathers just for disrespecting my mother." This was not going well. Anaïs had swooned back onto her pillow. She was now so still that I wondered if she really had died, and my negativity had been responsible. Wait, what had she said just before expiring? "Nothing." That was quotable.

But no, her lips were moving! I held my breath and bent my ear close. I heard her faint, plaintive cry, "I've started to wear my father's ring. Why do you suppose I'm wearing my father's ring?"

I looked at her skeletal hands. There were no rings. I wondered if the painkillers she was taking had made her delusional.

"I don't see a ring," I told her.

"I put it on this morning. It's too big. It falls off." She giggled like a little girl.

"Is it a wedding band?" I whispered.

"That's what I'm asking," she cried impatiently. "Why am I wearing my father's wedding ring?" She groaned, then cried out in pain, "Rupert! Help! It burns! Like a hot poker! It burns!"

Rupert came rushing back with the nurse. Anaïs pleaded to them with a child's helpless panic, "The bag broke again."

Rupert shooed me back into the entry hall, and the nurse replaced the screen. I wanted to leave, but Rupert, desperation in his bloodshot eyes, begged me to wait. "It will only take fifteen minutes. Please don't go."

I stood again in the entry hall, shifting my weight from side to side, berating myself. Stupid! Why did I blabber on about Extreme Unction? My shame was displaced, though, by my rising anger. How could Rupert, and how could her doctors, have made her go on like this, in piercing pain, surrounded by her own stench? In our last phone conversation, Renate, who had mended fences with Rupert, had insisted that it wasn't just Rupert and the doctors; Anaïs herself refused to let go. Renate had warned me not to visit anymore.

I checked my watch impatiently; it had been more than twenty minutes. I promised myself that if Rupert ever thought to bring me a chair, I was going to say I had an appointment and leave.

With nothing else to do, I worried Anaïs's question: *"Why am I wearing my father's wedding ring?"*

I'd expected that Anaïs would show me how to die gracefully, with acceptance and wisdom, as she had shown me how to live. Instead, she seemed to be disintegrating like Dorian Gray from an ever-youthful beauty into a terrifying specter. Her ghastly physical decay was accompanied by a psychological deterioration that made me think Freud had been right about Oedipal guilt. What else could her hallucination of her father's wedding ring mean other than guilt for replacing her mother in his bed? What could her delusion of wearing her father's ring and reaching, like Faust in the end, for the sacraments mean except that she believed her demon father had come to claim her, as Beelzebub had come for Faust? I was hyperventilating with fear of being swept into the vortex of her damnation.

*Stop it!* I admonished myself. I was doing what I always did, interpreting my experience through some literary reference instead of knowing it directly. I was exaggerating and distancing my feelings as Anaïs had said I did in my diary.

I no longer wanted to know myself secondhand. I wanted to know myself directly from my immediate experience and from within. So I asked myself one of the questions I'd been writing in my diary: *What is the reality of this present moment?*

The reality was that Anaïs's body and mind were being consumed by cancer and that there was nothing that she or I or anyone could do about it and that in itself was terrifying. She wasn't Dorian Gray, or Faust, or Oedipus. She was Anaïs, frightened and dying (though perhaps not as quickly as I'd imagined), and she needed my comfort as her friend.

When Rupert finally returned and brought me again to her bedside, he positioned a chair for me next to her. In addition to having been cleaned up, her sunken cheeks had been rouged. Fortunately, she seemed to have forgotten my woeful *faux pas* of mentioning Extreme Unction, as well as her delusion of wearing her father's ring.

"Oh, Tristine! I have to tell you!" she chirped. "Last night I dreamt that Rupert and I were making love in the pool, and this morning I told him my dream. You know, before we met Rupert couldn't recall his dreams, but now we tell them to each other every morning. When I told him the lovemaking dream, he said, 'Oh, but Anaïs, that was no dream!'"

I smiled as if this were a new, delightful story—even though I'd heard it from both Anaïs and Rupert several times before. Nonetheless, it was the confirmation of the credo she wanted to leave me with: *Life sets traps for you, and it is your job to escape, even if only by way of the dream.*

∞

Eventually, Rupert closed the gate to all visits, commandeering what was left of Anaïs. Having had to share her for so many years with Hugo, it seemed he was getting even by keeping the last of her to himself.

Truth be told, I was grateful that Rupert made it so difficult to visit, as I was grateful to Anaïs for giving me her myth of enduring romance through which to imagine her ending. I told myself that Rupert was taking loving care of her. I told myself that she and I had said good-bye as much as we'd be able. I rationalized that working to meet the deadline on my book was more of a tribute to her than waiting in the foyer until Rupert allowed me to see her in her pain and humiliation.

The truth was I couldn't bear to see her.

So I threw myself feverishly into work and even more into play. I went to parties, attended film screenings, flirted with guys I had no memory of the next day, and started an affair with a horror film director I met in New York. I tried to forget about Anaïs's suffering and the ghosts that lurked over her deathbed.

Rupert still allowed me phone calls with her. I had first to leave a message on the answering machine, now always on. Returning my call, Rupert would invariably begin with a report on her condition as if it were the weather: "This is one of Anaïs's bad days." Or, as he announced, prefacing what turned out to be my last conversation with her, "This is one of Anaïs's good days. She would like to speak with you."

I'd been struck by an unnamed fear that had prevented me from finishing the last chapters of my book, and impulsively I'd phoned Anaïs and left a message.

Her hoarse whisper didn't sound like her. "Rupert told me you had a question."

Now that I had precious minutes to speak with her, I didn't want to spend them on something as trivial as a writer's block. "I wanted to know how you are."

"Not so well," she rasped. "How is your writing going?"

The more I avoided explaining the reason I'd called, the more she pressed, so finally I described to her the apprehension that had caused the block. "It's a fear of retaliation against women who reach too far, fly too high," I said. "Like the backlash against George Sand, or Gore Vidal's hostility towards you. I think we have to dim ourselves, so others don't get threatened and do it to us."

"No! That is the wrong way to think about it! Don't put yourself down. That's the voice of guilt telling you to dim yourself." She sounded like the lucid, nurturing mentor she'd once been, but that was followed by her convulsive cough. I could hear a struggle as Rupert tried to take the phone from her, but before relinquishing the receiver she managed, "I found that when I shone my brightest, I helped others the most. Stay elevated, Tristine!"

∞

Renate and I chortled over the obits. *The New York Times* reported that diarist Anaïs Nin was survived by her husband Hugo Guiler, while the *Los Angeles Times* named Rupert Pole as her surviving spouse. What irony: her secret had been made public in the newspapers, yet I was still sworn to keep it until both her husbands had died, which could be—and turned out to be—another thirty years.

APPRENTICED TO VENUS

CHAPTER 33

# Malibu, California, 1977

## TRISTINE

I SWAM, STROKE AFTER FRANTIC stroke, my eyes burning from the salt-water, reaching, thrusting into the void where she was now, all that she was now. Anaïs was in her element in this vast expanse of water; I wanted to be there—with her one last time.

After Rupert had phoned to say he'd scattered her ashes near my house from the helicopter that morning, I'd stopped editing my book galleys and waited for the release of tears. But none came, as none had come when he'd informed me of her death. All I felt was a numb ache, and now here I was in a crazy, quixotic gesture, swimming out to her to say goodbye.

When I was so far out that it seemed I was halfway between the shore and the horizon, I stopped and bobbed in the undulating waves, treading water. When a swell raised me I could see my house in the distance, small as the stick figure picture of it I'd drawn on the commune window. When I sank in a trough, I saw nothing but constantly shifting light and dark patches of blue. Anaïs and I were just specks of carbon in this great expanse of water. This was what I'd wanted all along: to merge, to be with her, to be her.

I had wanted to be Anaïs but could not. We had affinities, yes; both hypersensitive, dramatic, tending toward narcissism, wounded by our fathers. Because of those affinities I had used her to define myself, had measured myself in relation to her accomplishments and come up short. I would never be as beautiful, as graceful, as self-disciplined, as focused as she, nor as good a dissembler. Though she'd tried to tutor me, I would never learn to play the geisha with men. That difference alone meant I'd never enjoy a madcap, artistic life like hers, free from earning a living, free of draining responsibilities.

Our differences went back to how we'd responded to our fathers' abandonment at eleven. She'd expressed her grief directly, passionately, begging her father to stay, crying inconsolably for years. I had responded to my father's abandonment, as to the news of her death, with alarm and anger but no tears. Anaïs lied to others, especially men, but her acceptance of her feelings made her truthful with herself. I had lied to myself in denying my feelings, hollering, "Good riddance!" when my father absconded. My smartass personality protected me then, but left me blindsided when Philip deserted me.

The timber that still rammed my gut whenever I thought of Philip abruptly made me aware of my body, fatigued from treading water. I turned on my back and squeezed my eyelids to shut out the sun. Its light blazed brightly against my lids, like fire burning through film, like awareness burning through the dark. Anaïs had felt her feelings directly when she was eleven, but when I'd reread her accounts of her reunion with her father when she was twenty-nine, there was something off-key, an indirectness, a distance, the hypnotic poetry of trauma. In her published writings, Anaïs had presented herself as in control of her adult reunion with her father, but when I read more closely I saw that it was her father who had seduced her.

He invited her to spend a week with him at a Mediterranean hotel and the first evening engaged her in seductive conversations about their twinship, the same eyes, hands, feet, the same Don Juanism. He pulled her into his mad Nietzschean fantasy that as artists they were above the rules that govern other people. It was he, the parent, who refused his role as protector; it was he who was the perpetrator.

Yet it was she who took on responsibility, telling Renate that she had seduced him. Why? Because, as I now recognized in myself, bravado was more tolerable than the helplessness of grief. It had to have been especially so for an adult, married woman, whose need for her father's love was so great that she'd been unable to deny him anything. She'd covered her shame with Sabina's audacious cape—the persona of seductress far preferable to the role of devastated victim.

Following her feelings had led Anaïs to the trauma of adult incest, whereas denying my feelings had separated and estranged me from myself and from men. We each paid, in different ways, for our fathers' abandonment. She was my reverse reflection, the puzzle of a mirror reflected in a mirror, reflected in a mirror—the narcissist's funhouse. As she had sought twinship with her father, I had sought twinship with her, sought a glorified version of myself in her, and therefore could not abide our differences. I had lauded her bigamy because it partook of the bravado I admired in myself, whereas I demonized her incest, because I could not find myself in it. Nor could I forgive her insane act of incest until, in writing this book, I could forgive my own psychological breakdown in Indiana. I could not forgive her being such a flawed mentor until I could forgive myself for losing myself in her. I could not forgive her helplessness at the end—spoon-fed, carried from bed to chair, terrified by old ghosts—until I forgave myself for turning from her then.

A swell hit my face. The waves had become turbulent, and I wished the pain from their slap would overcome that of my remorse. I had lost precious time with her because of my resentments, my judgments, my fear. The water in my smarting eyes was indistinguishable from that of the briny ocean, but the clutch of my stomach and my jagged gasps for air told me that grief had found me. I heaved in waves of it, mourning for a world without her, for an era now gone forever. Never again would she enter a room and make me feel so not alone. Never again would I rush to her house to be met at the door by the marvelous.

When at last the fist jerking on my ribs released, I floated, drifted; for how long, impossible to tell. No distance now between thought and feeling, no dissonance between my desire to be Anaïs and her desire for me to be me. No struggle now, just the motion of the sea, rocking like a woman keening, swinging like an infant in her mother's arms.

In idolizing Anaïs and seeking her reflective gaze of approval, I had allowed her to use me for her own ends. She took far more than my innocence. Yet I sensed that what I'd lost was less valuable than what I'd received: a mentor who shared my particular wound and inspired me to heal it through writing, a guide to owning my sexuality, an inspiration to value my creativity and inner journey, the model of a woman who could soak up so much joy. Thanks to her I didn't give up hope for both devotion and passion in love. She taught me to embrace good times wholeheartedly when they come and to transcend life's tragedies through the imagination, as she'd imagined herself in a symphony when dying. She gave me a hand up onto my life's work, understanding that we are heroines who author our own stories; elect how we see them, choose what they mean, and choose again. Much of who I am came from Anaïs and has served me well.

For the wonder of Anaïs was not that she had sunk so low as to commit adult incest; the wonder was how she'd matured since that freakish episode, how she'd expanded into a plenitude of self, accepting the errors and blindnesses as necessary, working diligently on herself, developing and growing to become a wise and compassionate woman who reached out to heal other broken souls. The wonder was that Anaïs, a deeply flawed person—a narcissist, a bigamist, a liar, and a deviant—was so lovable. The wonder was that from such a defective source shone so much light before her diminishment.

The sun was fading, and as I returned to treading water, I became alarmed by my chill and exhaustion. Foolishly, Don Quixote chasing a metaphor, I'd swum too far in my grand gesture to say good-bye. I was not a strong swimmer, and nobody knew I was out there. Frantically, I swam in a crawl directly towards shore, but soon was spent. The immensity of the ocean roiled beneath me and tugged.

In the distance, I could see the lighted windows of my house and wished I were there instead of in the cold, nacreous water. I remembered my dream where my guru woman stood at the Dutch window, calmly watching me tossed in the waves below. In the dream, I was in those waves but I was also my guiding presence, haloed at the window. Using the glow of those windows as my beacon now, I side-paddled in a switchback, pulled by the beckoning light, following the dream.

When I reached the breakers, the moon had risen and the sun was stretched into an ovoid, resisting its eclipse. I gave myself to the crashing surf, elevated on a high wave, rising like flying, cresting in an explosion of foam and bubbles, gliding onto the grit of sand.

As I climbed the old stairs on the side of the house, shivering, covered with goose bumps, my legs shaking, I felt the exhilaration of freedom. She was gone, and I had said good-bye.

After a warm shower, wrapped in my robe, I opened the Dutch windows to the night and listened to the crashing waves below. Not far from the moon, I saw dazzling Venus, brilliant as a fiery diamond, and thought of Anaïs elevated on her giddy trapeze from spouse to spouse.

Observing Venus that evening as I would for decades to come, I recognized that despite my scrutiny of Anaïs's every word and deed, her mystery could be grasped only on her own terms of metaphor and myth. For in that realm it so happens that once in a hundred years or so, as often as Venus makes her transit across the sun or certain rare fire flowers bloom, the goddess of love descends to inhabit the body of a girl who will become a beautiful woman. The mettle of the young woman's character will not matter; the more malleable, the better for Venus's ends. Nor need she be faithful except to her own wild essence, like a fox or a heron. Perhaps, as Anaïs, the goddess also chose to become a writer, a diarist, to remind all women that beneath Earth's girdles and jackets lies our limitless capacity for lust and love.

# Acknowledgments

I WISH TO THANK MY agent Stephany Evans for her steadfast belief in this book, and my editor Chelsey Emmelhainz, who got what I was trying to achieve and whose clear vision and careful editing focused the text.

A special thanks to two friends, novelist James Rogers and my former screenwriting agent Nancy Nigrosh, for reading and re-reading the manuscript, refueling me with their recommendations and enthusiasm, to Molly Friedrich for her generosity in giving me notes, and to those writer friends who read early versions and made suggestions, Diana Raab, Steven Reigns, Marijane Datson, Brad Schreiber, and Chip Jacobs.

Thanks also to my young readers, Kateland Carr and Elena del Real, for sharing where the book resonated, to Michael D. Roback, MD, for advice and rollicking editing discussions, and to Nancy Bein, John Upton, Donald Freed, Jamie Rainer, and members of the Immaculate Heart Community for caring encouragement. I am grateful to Dean Echenberg, MD, and to Vancouver photographer Derek

Lepper for digging in old files and sending images of me in the Malibu house from the early 1970s.

I wish personally to thank Anaïs Nin's excellent biographers, Deirdre Baer and Noel Riley Finch, in appreciation of their research and works upon which I relied, and to all those Nin friends and scholars who have shared with me their knowledge, including Paul Herron.

There are two men, now deceased, who I must also thank: Nin's editor John Ferrone, who read the manuscript at its inception and, even in his illness, gave me notes, and Rupert Pole, who gave me written permission to read Anaïs's handwritten diaries and letters at UCLA Special Collections and to tell his complicated love story with her.